THE LNWR PRECURSOR FAMILY

David & Charles Locomotive Monographs

General Editor:
O. S. NOCK, B.Sc., C.Eng., M.I.C.E., M.I.Mech.E., M.I.Loco.E.

Published titles

The Midland Compounds, by O. S. Nock

The Stirling Singles of the Great Northern Railway, by Kenneth H. Leech and Maurice Boddy

The LNWR Precursor Family, by O. S. Nock

In preparation

Stars, Castles & Kings, Part 1, by A. F. Cook

Caledonian Dunalastairs, by O. S. Nock

Stroudley's Locomotives, by O. S. Nock

Stars, Castles & Kings, Part 2, by A. F. Cook

Gresley's Pacifics, by O. S. Nock

The five thousandth engine built at Crewe; the George the Fifth Class 4-4-0 'Coronation' built in June 1911 and named in honour of the coronation of King George the Fifth

DAVID & CHARLES LOCOMOTIVE MONOGRAPHS

THE LNWR PRECURSOR FAMILY

THE PRECURSORS, EXPERIMENTS, GEORGES, PRINCES
OF THE LONDON & NORTH WESTERN RAILWAY

O. S. NOCK, B.Sc., C.Eng., M.I.C.E., M.I.Mech.E., M.I.Loco.E.

DAVID & CHARLES : NEWTON ABBOT : DEVON

ISBN: 978-1-4463-0587-4

First Published in 1966 by
David & Charles (Publishers) Ltd.
Newton Abbot, Devon

CONTENTS

PREFACE

WHEN this volume was first announced the title was given as 'The Joy Valve Gear Express Passenger Engines of the L.N.W.R.' But that all-embracing title would have included all the Webb compounds, and this was certainly not the intention. This book is concerned with the family of inside-cylinder 4—4—0 and 4—6—0 locomotives that commenced with the *Precursor* of March 1904. It was a remarkable family, 571 strong, fascinating in its vicissitudes of fortune, in the extreme diversity of the names of individual engines, and perhaps a perfect epitome of the hold the steam locomotive can have upon the affections of men. Locomotives, and particularly express passenger locomotives, are generally supposed to be feminine in gender. If this is so the Crewe engines were certainly not the 'glamour-girls' of the age. Among the gorgeous blues, greens and reds of pre-grouping days they went about their work in black. It was, nevertheless, no ordinary black, and when properly got up had a wonderful deep shine that earned the nickname of 'blackberry black'. The lining-out was quiet, and dignified, and the management of the 'Premier Line', which had Britannia as the centre-piece of its crest, evidently thought it quite unnecessary to put the railway initials on engines or tenders. If one looked closely, the initials could be found, quite small, on the nameplates.

The story of L.N.W.R. locomotive prowess from the building of the *Precursor* in 1904 to the year 1916 shows an almost meteoric rise to pre-eminence among the railways of Britain. For although the Great Western and some others had larger and nominally more powerful locomotives, in sheer haulage effort on the road the North Western would have taken some surpassing. How that remarkable family of engines fared after the grouping of the railways is a story of intense interest, intermingled with the clash of strong personalities and all the spice of keen partisanship.

This book embodies the results of many years of close study of London & North Western affairs, and the help of many men in a diversity of walks in life. My previous book, *The Premier Line*, brought a wealth of correspondence and further facts, and since its publication many friends who were originally Crewe men have contributed to the pool of information on which I have now been able to draw. Among these I must mention particularly R. A. Riddles, formerly Member of the Railway Executive for Mechanical and Electrical Engineering; Lt.-Col. K. Cantlie, E. V. M. Powell and D. H. Stuart. To the last-mentioned I am particularly indebted for help in preparing the case histories included in the Appendix. To G. Dudley Whitworth I am no less indebted for checking this voluminous data.

From Mr. A. E. Robson, the present Chief Mechanical and Electrical Engineer, London Midland Region, I have received much help in the form of working drawings of all the locomotives concerned, from which the drawings in the text have been prepared, and also the loan of private reports of the dynamometer car trials carried out in the early years of the L.M.S.R. I am also particularly indebted to Mr. C. Williams, of Crewe, for help over individual engines. It is remarkable to recall that Mr. Williams published his first list of L.N.W.R. locomotives, the named ones, as long ago as 1910, and the complete register of *all* locomotives in service on the line, in 1912. This was the first work of its kind, and a monumental task. It was no less monumental in its meticulous accuracy, and it is good to know that its author is still happily with us.

I have made extensive reference to the files of *The Locomotive*, *The Railway Magazine*, *The L.N.W.R. Magazine*, and to the Journal of the Stephenson Locomotive Society, and I am grateful to Mr. B. W. C. Cooke, editor of *The Railway*

Magazine, for his permission to use a number of train running logs that have appeared in the 'British Locomotive Practice and Performance' articles. My thanks are also due to the Council of the Institution of Locomotive Engineers for permission to reproduce the drawings of the Dendy Marshall arrangement of cylinders. In connection with the illustrations I am particularly indebted to Mr. R. W. Crawshaw, Public Relations and Publicity Officer, London Midland Region, for many interesting photographs.

O. S. NOCK

Silver Cedars, High Bannerdown, Bath
November 1965

CHAPTER 1

THE PRELUDE

THERE is nothing more tragic than to witness those cases where a very great man, with advancing years, suffers a decline in status and in the confidence in which he is held by his employers. Such a case was that of Francis W. Webb, Chief Mechanical Engineer of the L.N.W.R. from the year 1871. He rose to the zenith of his career under that tremendous personality, Richard Moon, Chairman of the L.N.W.R. from 1861 to 1891. Moon, one of the greatest men who ever passed across the stage of British railway history, regarded as herculean the task of managing Crewe works and, having chosen men of the calibre, first of John Ramsbottom and then Webb, he gave them both an absolutely free hand. Both were outstanding organisers. Both were superb production engineers, and under Webb Crewe developed into one of the finest and most efficient engineering manufactories to be found anywhere in the world.

The chain of command, from the works manager down to the sectional chargehands, was clear and straightforward; everyone knew exactly what he was supposed to do, and although a large number of quantity-production methods were introduced, and standardised practices were in use for almost every aspect of locomotive construction and repair, the utmost store was nevertheless set upon the quality of individual workmanship. The department was organised to the last degree for maintaining the 3,000 locomotives needed to handle the traffic of 'The Premier Line' of Great Britain, while the works was fed by an excellent drawing-office staff, who were accustomed to producing new designs at very short notice sometimes. For Webb, in addition to his qualities as a 'works man', was also a prolific inventor, and it was in this respect that his reputation eventually foundered—to such an extent that in popular regard he has come to be remembered far more by the failure of his later locomotives than by his thirty years of wise and

progressive administration of the locomotive department in general, and of Crewe Works in particular.

There is no need to dwell upon the failure of his compound express locomotives, except to stress the overall position as it existed at the turn of the century. Although the 4-cylinder compound 4—4—0s of the 'Jubilee' and 'Alfred the Great' classes were designed by Webb to haul heavy trains of 300 to 350 tons, they were not reliable at the speeds demanded by the express passenger services of the period, and in October 1901 the General Manager's office issued a circular stipulating that all trains loaded to an equivalent of 17 six-wheeled coaches, or more, were to be double-headed, irrespective of gradient, schedule, or class of locomotive available. It was a drastic decree; but while it represented a condemnation of Webb's locomotives the system of reckoning train loads in 'coaches', rather than actual tonnages, was open to many anomalies. 'Equal to 17' in six-wheelers represented about 230 tons; but if instead one had a train composed entirely of 12-wheeled bogie dining or sleeping cars, each of which would be reckoned as '2', eight of these vehicles, 'equal to 16', would weigh something like 320 tons!

But by one means or another Webb's retirement was hastened, and in the early months of 1903 he was succeeded by George Whale, who had been Running Superintendent, and who naturally had a very clear idea of what was needed to run the traffic. Whale was not a scientific man—an inventor or a mechanical designer—but a first-class practical railwayman whose entire life had been spent in the service of the L.N.W.R. His mandate was clear enough: to get larger and more reliable express passenger locomotives on the road as quickly as possible, to eliminate the vast amount of double-heading all over the system that was necessitated by the 'equal to 17' rule. I should explain further that, at the beginning of the twentieth century, loads of 200 tons or more would have been considered heavy on many railways, but not so on the L.N.W.R. North Western trains were among the heaviest and best-filled of any in the country, and the 'equal to 17' rule was a source of acute embarrassment.

To carry out his mandate Whale had two first-class attributes at his elbow: an excellent design staff, headed by J. N. Jackson, the Chief Locomotive Draughtsman, and the inimitable leading draughtsman, Tommy Sackfield; and the magnificent organisation and resources of Crewe Works. So far as a new design of locomotive was concerned there had been enough of innovation and experiment in the later Webb days. What was needed was a locomotive of solid reliability that would be simple to handle, cheap and quick to build. Whale, as a running man, would be under no delusions as to which were the most reliable engines in the existing locomotive stud, while Jackson and his men would be equally appreciative of the design details that gave the least trouble and expense from the viewpoint of maintenance and repair costs. One thing was certain: compounds were out! Despite the brilliant success of de Glehn and du Bousquet in France, and despite the excellent results being

obtained from the Smith-Johnson 4—4—0s on the Midland, at Crewe the sentiments were 'never again'. In running the trains Whale had had his fill of compounds, and in planning the new locomotives he turned to the splendidly reliable simples which were still the hard core of the North Western motive power stud.

Two types were outstanding, the 2—4—0 'Jumbos', of both 6 ft. 9 in. and 6 ft. 3 in. varieties, and the 0—6—0 18 in. goods—more popularly known as the 'Cauliflowers'. Although similar in general appearance and in their standards of overall performance, the two classes differed fundamentally in their machinery. The 'Jumbos' had the Allan straight-link motion, while the 'Cauliflowers' had Joy's radial valve-gear. Webb was the first locomotive engineer to take up the Joy gear, after it had been fitted experimentally to an old Bury 0—4—0 of the Furness Railway. From all accounts, the feature that most appealed to Webb was that no eccentrics were needed. That gave him more room between the frames to get in larger bearings for the driving axles. The first of the '18-inch' goods 0—6—0s, engine No. 2365, was exhibited during the Summer Meeting of the Institution of Mechanical Engineers at Barrow, in 1880, and at Webb's instigation Joy had been invited to read a paper on

Francis W. Webb, Chief Mechanical Engineer, 1871 to 1903

David Joy, designer of the Joy radial valve gear

The first 'Precursor': Webb's 5 ft. 6 in. 2-4-0 of 1874

One of the most famous of the 'Precedents': No. 955 'Charles Dickens'

One of the '18 inch' goods 0-6-0s: the 'Cauliflowers'. First main line engines to have Joy valve gear

13

his new valve gear at that meeting. The advantages derived from a valve motion made up of an oscillating horizontal and rotational component can best be described in Joy's own words:

'When the two are acting in the same direction the movement of the valve is very rapid, and this occurs at lead and for the opening of the port. Then follows a time when the two movements are opposed, resulting in a slow action, almost a "dwell" holding the port steadily full open; when again, by a combination of the movements, the port is quickly closed.'

The absence of eccentrics certainly allowed Webb to put in very generous bearing surfaces on the driving axle, and in later engines of the numerous '18-inch' goods class Webb introduced a central bearing in addition to the main bearings in the frames. The provision of such ample bearings enabled the locomotives to be worked hard for indefinite periods without any fear of overheating, and this central bearing was also used on the Webb 4-cylinder compound 4—4—0s, in which all four cylinders drove on to the leading coupled axle.

This axle was thus heavily stressed, and the extra bearing in the centre was naturally advantageous. These compound engines also had the Joy valve gear. In certain circumstances the provision of three bearings for a single driving axle might be considered a point of doubtful advantage, as it introduced additional problems of lining up, and maintenance. But with the standards of workmanship prevailing at Crewe it was just one of those things to be taken in the stride; and by the turn of the century it was an established feature of construction.

Webb's 2—4—0 passenger and 0—6—0 express goods classes had the same boiler, and an extremely good one it was. It was small by the standards prevailing in the last two years of the nineteenth century, but it was an exceedingly free steamer, and could scarcely have been simpler to fire. On the more important duties, North Western engines of those days were mostly supplied with good quality Welsh coal, and the deep, narrow fireboxes of 'Jumbos' and 'Cauliflowers' were ideally suited to burning this fuel built thickly on the grate. The

LONDON AND NORTH WESTERN RAILWAY.

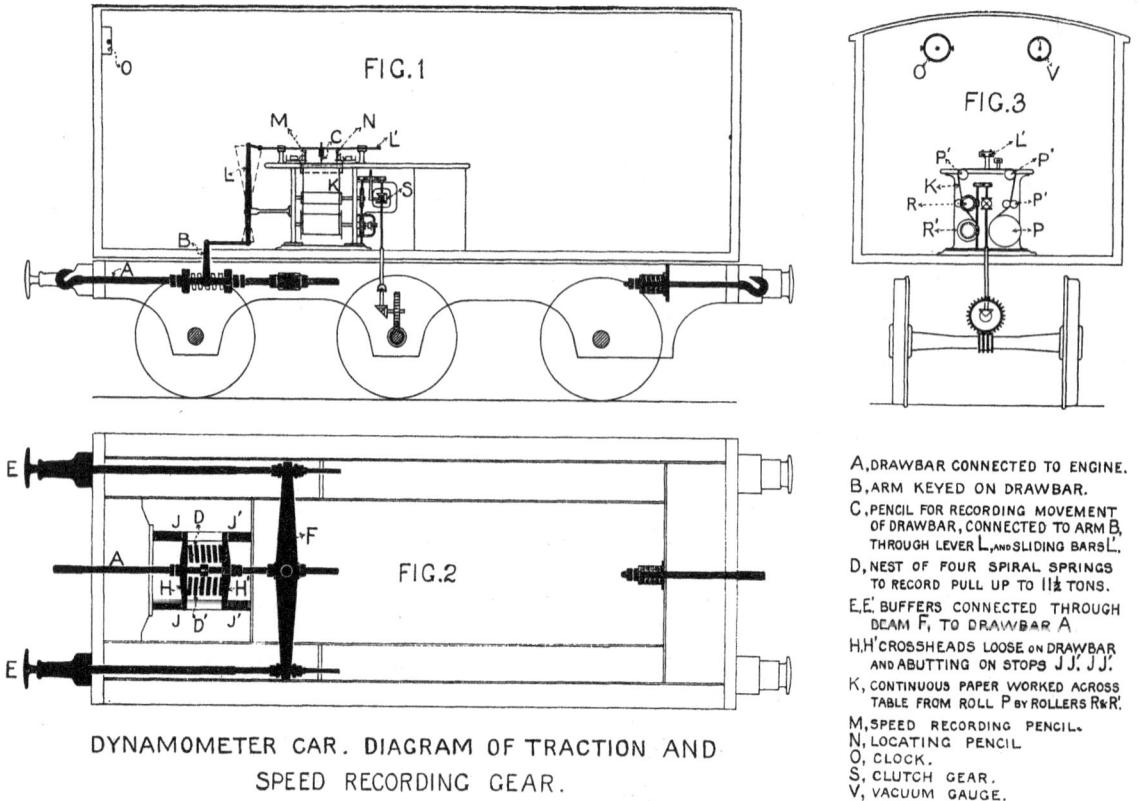

A, DRAWBAR CONNECTED TO ENGINE.
B, ARM KEYED ON DRAWBAR.
C, PENCIL FOR RECORDING MOVEMENT OF DRAWBAR, CONNECTED TO ARM B, THROUGH LEVER L, AND SLIDING BARS L.
D, NEST OF FOUR SPIRAL SPRINGS TO RECORD PULL UP TO 11½ TONS.
E, E, BUFFERS CONNECTED THROUGH BEAM F, TO DRAWBAR A
H, H' CROSSHEADS LOOSE ON DRAWBAR AND ABUTTING ON STOPS J J', J J'.
K, CONTINUOUS PAPER WORKED ACROSS TABLE FROM ROLL P BY ROLLERS R & R'.
M, SPEED RECORDING PENCIL.
N, LOCATING PENCIL
O, CLOCK.
S, CLUTCH GEAR.
V, VACUUM GAUGE.

DYNAMOMETER CAR. DIAGRAM OF TRACTION AND SPEED RECORDING GEAR.

depth of the box below the fire-door enabled the fireman to place the coal precisely where it was needed with the minimum of difficulty. Contemporary observers have left the impression that the 'Jumbos' in particular when worked hard were very heavy coal burners, basing their deductions upon the frequency with which cinders rained upon the carriage roofs. But as will be explained later in discussing details of George Whale's locomotives, this was not due to fire-throwing at all, but to frequent use of the Webb ash-ejector.

From what I have written so far, upon the leading features of the Webb 2—4—0 and 0—6—0 simple locomotives, one can readily discern the concept of the new Whale express passenger engine design of 1903. Although no documentary evidence exists by way of confirmation, one can clearly imagine the broad specification given to Jackson and Sackfield: 'Give me a 4—4—0 with 19 in. by 26 in. cylinders that will steam as freely as a "Jumbo": Joy valve gear, with three bearings on the driving axle; and for goodness sake be quick about it, because I want 100 of them in traffic within two years!' Thus, in a few words, can be described the genesis of the 'Precursors' which, in retrospect, can be seen as the phenomenon of the 1900-1910 decade in British locomotive engineering.

In appearance and finish they continued wholly in the traditions of the L.N.W.R. They may have been painted black, but the finish given to it was superb. No money was wasted on creature comforts for the enginemen. In those days any such 'development' would have been despised! But the black paint on boilers, splashers, cab sides and tenders was given a gloss so that a North Western engine stood out among a group of more gaily painted contemporaries, as at Carlisle, or York. It was like some immaculately groomed black Rolls-Royce standing among brilliantly-finished lesser breeds. There was, of course, nothing of the Rolls-Royce about the goings and comings of North Western express engines, and yet they could equally not be stigmatised as 'Tin-Lizzies'. They were, rather, the Land Rovers of the locomotive world: a superb 'engine', that would roar and rattle its way to journey's end on time—'come Hell, come high water'. And with that wonderful deep shine of the black went those very plain, but individualistic, nameplates. It was typical of North Western pride in the job that they were so burnished that they looked like gold! It had always been so on the 'Jumbos' and the compounds; it was no less so when the new 'Precursors' began to take the road from March 1904 onwards.

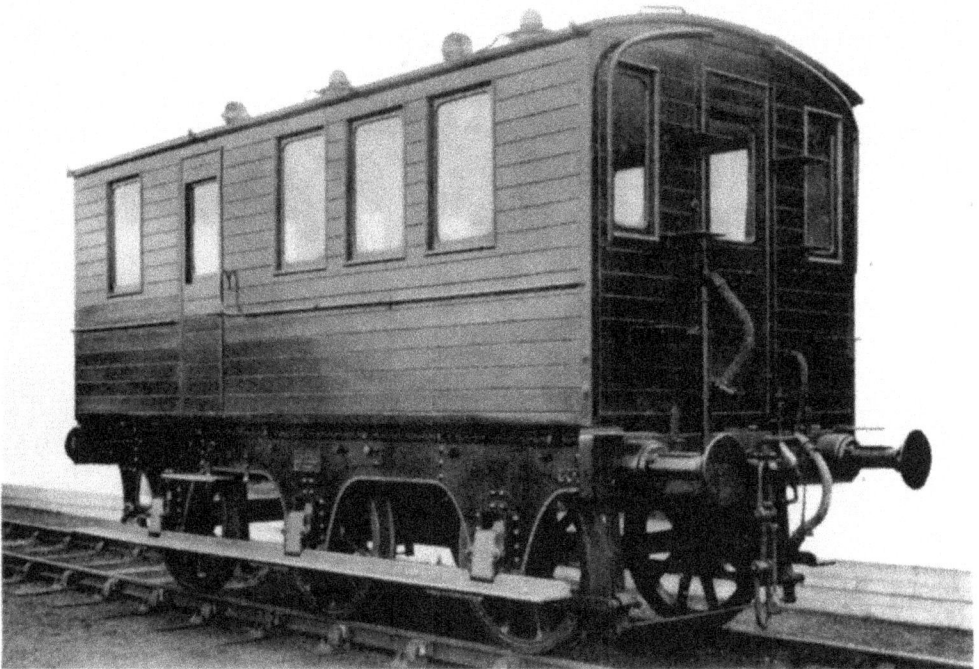

The first L.N.W.R. dynamometer car, built 1894

15

CHAPTER 2

THE 'PRECURSORS'

WHALE'S appointment as Chief Mechanical Engineer dated from a board meeting on April 2 1903, and he took over from Webb at the end of May in that year. In little more than nine months from that time the first of the new engines was completed at Crewe, the 4—4—0 No. 513 *Precursor*, bearing the date March 1904. With the vast resources at his disposal, this period of nine months would not have been unduly short if nothing more than an experimental prototype was involved; if it had been built by what are sometimes called 'knife and fork' methods, leaving the outlay on tools for quantity production until the prototype had been proved by extended trials. But the *Precursor* was in every way a 'production job'. Nevertheless, deep though the confidence of the higher management lay in Mr Whale, there had been so many disappointments in recent years in North Western express passenger motive power that there was naturally a certain time-lag between

the completion successively of the first small batches, to observe whether fulfilment was in accordance with promise. Five engines of the new design were turned out in March-April 1904, and another five in June. But their performance during the heavy summer traffic of 1904 settled all doubts, and in the early autumn of 1904 Whale was instructed to build another hundred of them as quickly as he could. Those hundred engines were turned out in 76 weeks!

Although the *Precursor* was indeed the precursor of an entirely new era at Crewe, she could nevertheless be described as a thoroughly standard North Western job. There was nothing novel or untried in her basic design, or in any of the fittings. The boiler was a much larger version of the 'Jumbo-Cauliflower' design, and the cylinder and valve arrangements were virtually those of the 'Cauliflowers'. At the same time one rather curious feature of Webb's boiler design was immediately discarded.

The Whale 'Precursor'; built Crewe, March 1904

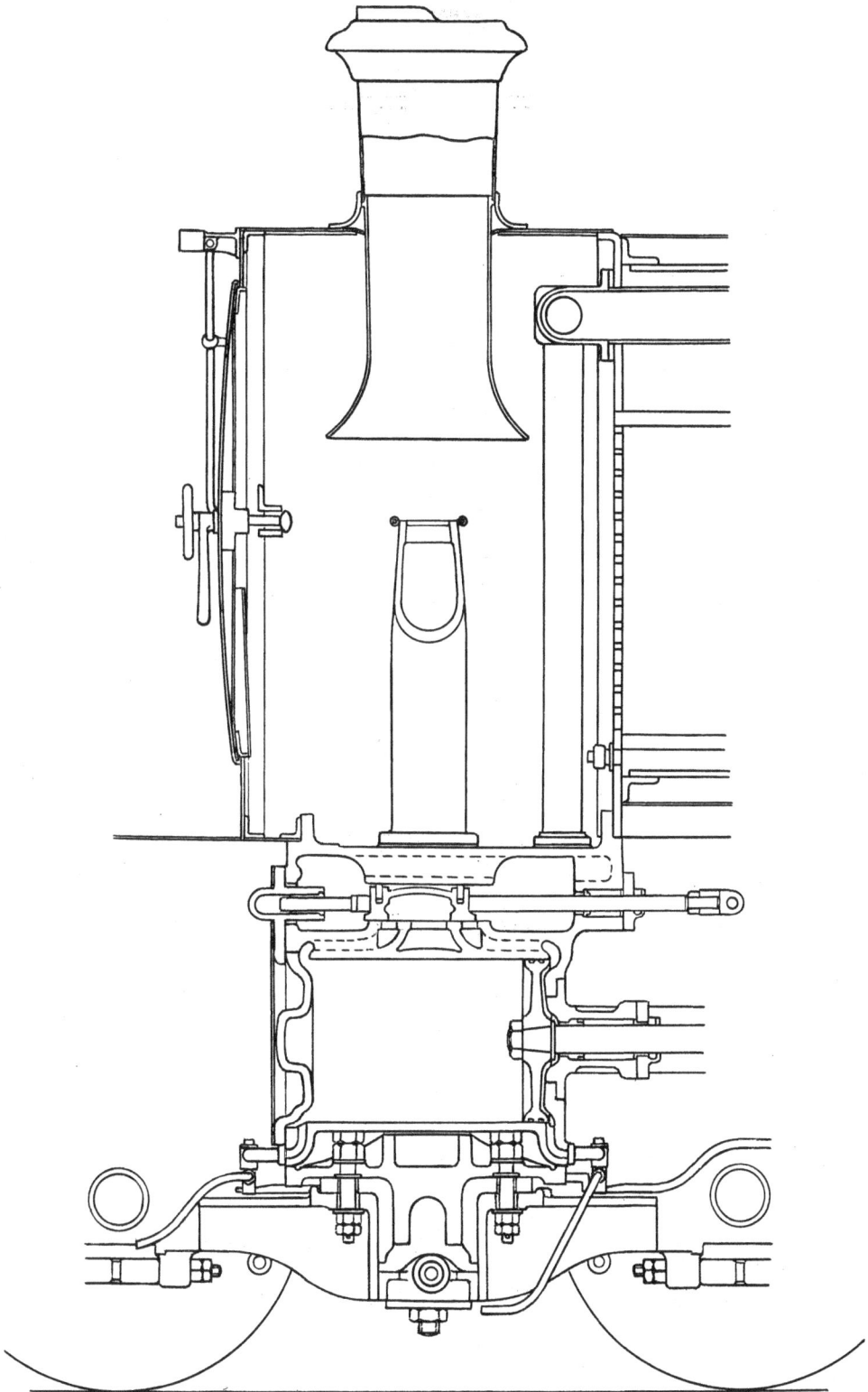

'Precursor' class locomotive: longitudinal section of smokebox and cylinder

B

On all engines from about 1880 onwards he had provided a 'water grate' *under* the firebox. There was no foundation ring to the firebox, and the side and end water spaces were continued downwards to connect with a full-width water space which extended horizontally beneath the grate bars. The ashes were removed from the grate through a hole in the bottom. It was claimed that this feature improved the circulation of water and promoted more rapid steaming. This did not work out in practice, as cold water remained at the bottom under the ashpan, and after a long run in winter-time the water bottoms were frequently coated with ice, derived from spray from the water troughs.

In 1906 G. J. Churchward of the Great Western Railway read his celebrated paper 'Large Locomotive Boilers' to a meeting of the Institution of Mechanical Engineers. The paper was most comprehensively illustrated with all shapes and sizes of boilers, and included many 'fancy' designs. In the original paper the North Western was represented by that of the 'Alfred the Great' compound, duly equipped with water bottom, and this certainly looked a trifle odd compared with the boilers of some vast American types, with the newest Great Western experimental designs, and with those of the then-new 'Atlantics' of Great Northern & North Eastern design. During the discussion C. J. Bowen-Cooke was called upon to speak. He was then Running Superintendent of the Southern Division of the L.N.W.R., with his headquarters at Rugby, and he was able to bring things up to date so far as Crewe was concerned by describing the 'Precursor' boiler. He told the meeting how the abolishing of compounding had enabled them to reduce boiler pressures from 200 to 175 lb. per sq. in., and went on to say that 'simple engines had been adopted, having large boilers, constructed on well-known, plain and straightforward lines, with a rather old-fashioned but most efficient type of deep firebox'.

Apart from the ease of firing, there is another point about deep fireboxes that is perhaps not so greatly appreciated, and that is the depth of fire actually in contact with the water space. Much of the trouble with leaking stays can arise from abrupt changes in temperature, and a great deal of Churchward's highly scientific development work on the Great Western, which led to the perfecting of his particular form of taper boiler, was centred upon the avoidance of local 'hot spots', which could give rise to unequal expansion, and consequent leakage, at tubes and stays. Experience had shown that far less trouble in this respect occurred with deep fireboxes and thick fires, than with the newer types with shallow grates that had to be worked with thin fires. Moreover, the 'Precursor' firebox was something with which the men were immediately familiar. Though larger, it was proportioned exactly the same as that of a 'Jumbo', or a 'Cauliflower', and it could be fired in just the same way.

The boiler itself was admirably proportioned to sustain a high rate of evaporation; the tubes were $1\frac{7}{8}$ in. outside diameter, with a distance of 12 ft. $2\frac{1}{4}$ in. between the tube plates. Originally, the tube heating surface was no less than 1,848.4 sq. ft., but at a later date the upper rows of tubes were omitted, together with two vertical rows of five on each side, and this reduced the heating surface slightly to 1,728.5 sq. ft. The grate area was 22.4 sq. ft., but the very deep firebox provided a firebox heating surface of no less than 161.3 sq. ft. Thus, originally, the *Precursor* had no less than 2,009.7 sq. ft. of heating surface. The original general arrangement drawing, signed by Whale and initialled by both Jackson and Sackfield, shows a working pressure of 185 lb. per sq. in. at the safety valve, and this figure is also quoted on a drawing of the 19-inch 4—6—0 goods which was published in *The Locomotive Magazine*. But in actual practice the valves were set to blow off at 175 lb. per sq. in., and this latter figure was always quoted in all

A 'Precursor' near the top of Camden bank, awakening the echoes

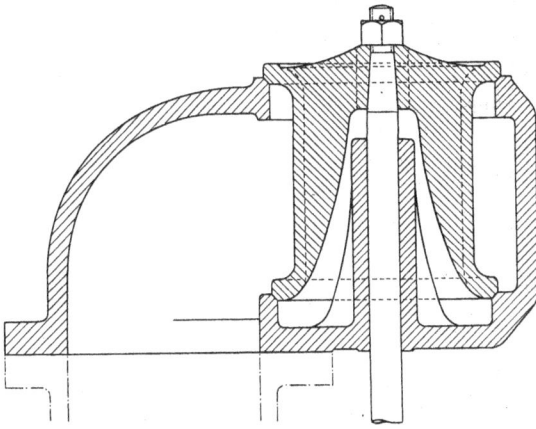

Ramsbottom double-beat regulator valve

did their early footplate work on locomotives fitted with this injector, have more than once 'enthused' to me over the trouble-free working. They were attached to the back of the ashpan and in consequence the overflow could not be seen from the footplate. But as one Crewe man put it to me: 'Once it was set, a flick of the throw-over handle of the water cock on the tender, and a sharp pull on the pull-out steam valve on the boiler were all that was required for their operation.' The excellent workmanship put into these fittings in itself contributed to their good operation. The steam pull-out valve seldom leaked, so that the injector was kept cool, and its position behind the ashpan, right in the air stream underneath caused by the movement of the locomotive, also assisted in keeping it cool. No steam locomotive man needs to be told that with a cold injector most of the troubles that can arise with that ingenious but often temperamental device never eventuate.

The blower and the ash ejector were worked by a single handle, which turned a rod (which actually formed the handrail) along the right-hand side of the boiler. At the smokebox end there was a two-way cock, and the handle on the back-plate of the boiler had three positions: when this was UP everything was shut off; when horizontal the blower was turned on, and when DOWN it operated the

technical descriptions of the locomotives published at the time they were first built.

Before leaving the boiler three other fittings must be mentioned. Although they were not peculiar to, or new on the 'Precursors'—they were, in fact, standard Crewe fittings—they were special to the L.N.W.R., and the excellent workmanship put into them contributed not a little to the efficient, trouble-free running of the locomotives themselves. These fittings were the Ramsbottom double-beat regulator valve, the Webb injector, and the combined blower and ash ejector. Taking the regulator first, this was a solid double-beat job, with no adjustment between the top and bottom seats. Its fitting was a specialist job. The valve was mounted on the top of a stand-pipe which stood up in the dome and turned a right-angle bend into the boiler, making a joint with the steam pipe about eighteen inches ahead of the dome. One can pass over the language that was sometimes used when one of those pipe joints had to be renewed. It involved sitting in the dome, with legs outstretched over the top tubes, and feeling for the bolts and nuts. They could never be seen, and could be located only by touch!

In the heyday of Crewe Works, which synchronised with the last days of Webb and continued well into the period of World War I, practically nothing in the way of proprietary fittings was used on North Western engines. All cocks, valves, and so on were designed and made on the premises; and although they included certain unorthodox features that would have been difficult to produce on a normal commercial basis, these had been mastered at Crewe and no troubles were experienced with them in service. One of these fittings was the Webb injector, shown in one of the accompanying drawings. Engineers trained at Crewe, who

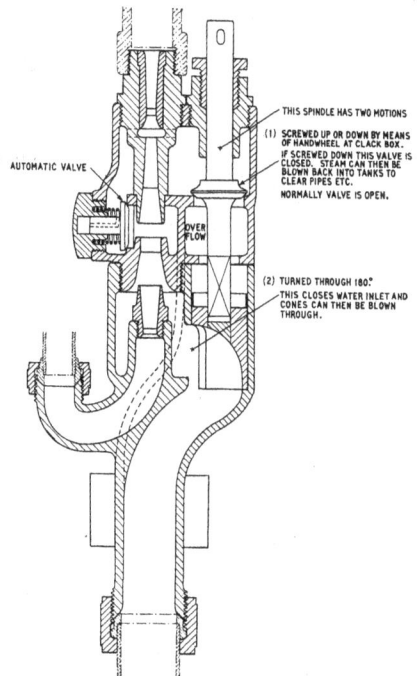

L.N.W.R. standard injector

J. N. Jackson, Chief Draughtsman, Crewe, under Webb, Whale, and Bowen-Cooke

George Whale, Chief Mechanical Engineer, 1903—1908

ash ejector. This latter had a pipe leading into the smokebox which branched into two and followed the curve of the smokebox at back and front. These curved tubes had a series of holes inclined upwards and outwards, and when steam was applied the jets from these holes stirred up the ashes so that they were caught by the blast and thrown out of the chimney in a continuous rain of cinders. It was an extremely effective device for keeping the smokebox clear of accumulated ash.

Turning now from the boiler to the machinery, one of the accompanying drawings shows the arrangement of the driving axle, including the centre bearing. The main journals were 8 in. diameter by 9 in. long, while the centre bearing was $7\frac{1}{4}$ in. in diameter. The absence of any eccentrics enabled the entire available space to be taken up with the massive built-up crankshaft. Although this latter, and the bearings provided for it were of a most generous proportion the main frames—for an engine designed to develop so high an output of power continuously—were on the light side. The frame-plates were only one inch thick, and there was a curious feature in the design of the frames, the origin of which may not be generally appreciated. The maximum length of main frame that

could be slotted out at Crewe was about 28 ft., so that any engine longer than this had to have an extension spliced on. In practice, this meant that all types from 4—4—0s upwards had to have this splicing, and Crewe made a virtue out of this necessity by making the splice come between the point of attachment of the cylinders to the frame and motion plate. The distance between the frame plates was 4 ft. 2 in. rearwards from the motion plate, and 4 ft. 0 in. between the forward extensions, between which were fixed the cylinders.

The Crewe drawing office of 1903 evidently saw no reason to change another speciality of Webb days—the design of the leading bogie. In the strictest sense of the term it was not a bogie at all, because the Webb four-wheeled truck fitted to the 'Jubilee' and 'Alfred the Great' 4—4—0s and to the 'Bill Baileys' had no centre pivot. It was designed just like the leading truck on many model locomotives of today that have to negotiate relatively sharp curves. It moved in radial guides from an imaginary pivot point about 1 ft. 3 in. ahead of the driving axle. The action is shown on the accompanying diagram, and it will be appreciated that it is more theoretically correct than the conventional bogie. On the 'Precursors', the centre line of the

20

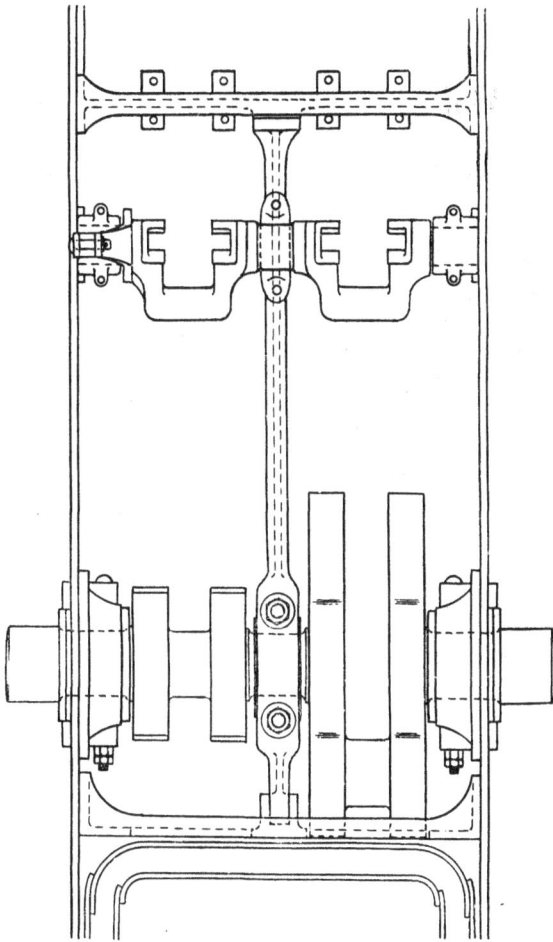

Plan, showing centre bearing on driving axle

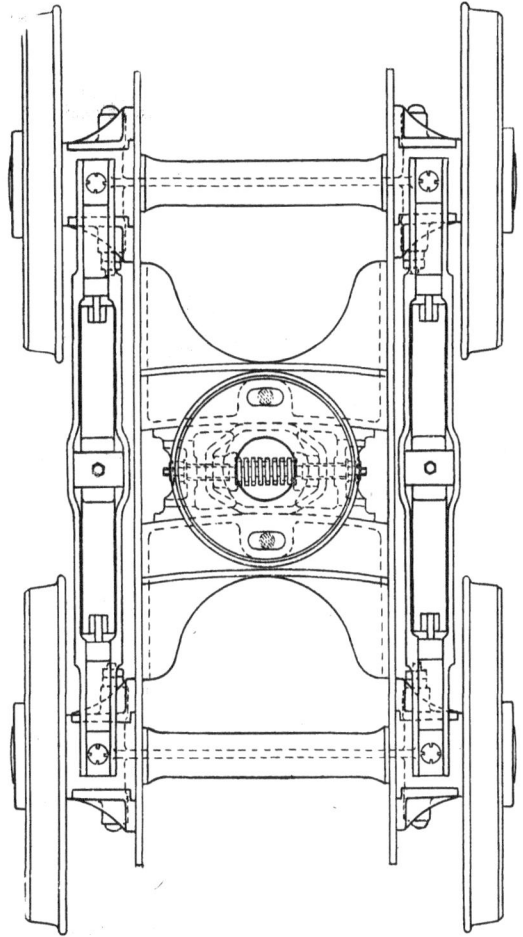

Plan of bogie, showing curved guides for radial motion

guides was on a radius of 10 ft. 9 in., whereas the distance between the centre line of the bogie and that of the driving axle was 12 ft. Of course, the construction of these radial guides was more difficult than that of an ordinary bogie with centre pivot; but such problems were taken in their stride by the Crewe Works of the 1900-22 period.

The cylinder and valve design, though conventional in some respects, was excellent in the provision it made for getting large volumes of steam through the inlet and exhaust ports. The Webb 'Jumbos' were generally acknowledged to be among the fastest-running engines on the North Western, though the 3-cylinder compound 'Teutonics', with a loose eccentric gear for their low-pressure cylinder, were very fast engines and frequently exceeded 85 m.p.h. But in view of the reputation of the 'Jumbos' it is interesting to compare certain of their cylinder proportions with those of the 'Precursors'. The basic dimensions were 17 in. dia. by 24 in.

stroke, against 19 in. dia. by 26 in. stroke: an increase, in the 'Precursor' of 35 per cent. But the maximum steam port area was more nearly doubled from 13.125 sq. in. to 23.44—an increase of 79 per cent. The valve-gear had the following dimensions:

Travel of valve in full gear	5 in.
Lap of valve	$1\frac{1}{16}$ in.
Lead of valve	$\frac{3}{16}$ in.
Inside clearance	NIL

At a time when the majority of British express locomotives, including such famous contemporaries of the 'Precursors' as the Great Eastern 'Claud Hamiltons' and the North Eastern 'R' class, had maximum valve travels of 4 in., or even less, the 'Precursor' valve-gear, combined with the very large port openings it gave, represented a distinctly advanced design. It had the great merit of enabling large volumes of steam to be got into and out of the cylinders, with consequent high output of power.

Taken all in all, George Whale in the specifica-

Up two-hour Birmingham express at south end of Watford tunnel: engine No. 2585 'Watt'

tion he had laid down, and Jackson in the way he had worked it out, had produced a modern express locomotive of admirable proportions, intended for very hard work on the road. A boiler that proved a prolific steam raiser, and a good cylinder lay-out were combined with a series of 'home-made' fittings such as the Ramsbottom regulator and Webb injector that 'worked' without fail. In giving the new regime all the credit they deserve for the fame the 'Precursors' subsequently earned, one must not overlook how much of their basic design was 'pure Webb'. Only the 'fads' were discarded, like the water-bottom to the ashpan. Otherwise the 'Precursor' could be closely described as a much enlarged 4—4—0 version of the 'Cauliflower', with a four-wheeled radial truck from the 'Jubilees' and 'Alfreds'. The new regime made no startling innovations. They built an engine that was in every way a synthesis of all that was best in the practice of Webb; and they built it in record time using the magnificent organisation and plant that Webb had established at Crewe. In one respect, however, Whale did break fresh ground, in that the tender was of an entirely new design with steel frames. It is astonishing to recall that Webb was using wood-framed tenders to the very end of his time at Crewe.

Three of the new engines were completed in March 1904 and two more in the following month.

Their names and numbers were:

513	*Precursor*
1395	*Harbinger*
1419	*Tamerlane*
2023	*Helvellyn*
2164	*Oberon*

In this beginning of the new era, connoisseurs of what might be termed the more personal side of the North Western locomotive practice were immediately reassured that tradition was secure in another respect: the names were being retained, and there was evidently to be no systematic numbering. There were no such things as published lists of engine names and numbers in those days; the enthusiasts had to compile their own lists from personal observations, and in later days it must have added a good deal of spice to 'spotting' expeditions to know that a 'Precursor' might be numbered anywhere between 1 and 2600! Four of the new 4—4—0s were named after engines of the original 'Precursor' class—Webb's 2—4—0 of 1874 with 5 ft. 6 in. coupled wheels; but the remaining engine of the batch, No. 1419 *Tamerlane*, took its name from a 3-cylinder compound of the 'Dreadnought' class, and indicated that scrapping of those engines had already commenced.

Tamerlane was the first engine of the class to enter the limelight of the 'British Locomotive

Practice and Performance' articles in *The Railway Magazine*. The late Charles Rous-Marten recorded her work with the utmost zest, and although his enthusiasm was not exactly justified by the performance his remarks are worth quoting, if for nothing else than to show the extent to which the stranglehold of double-heading had the North Western in its grip in those first years of the present century. In July 1904 he wrote:

'Mr. G. Whale's new express engines on the London & North Western Railway not only are very handsome and attractive-looking machines, but what is much better, are doing excellent work. Where they are concerned, that 17-coach piloting order is already a thing of the past. A few days ago I travelled from Crewe behind one of this class, No. 1419 *Tamerlane,* on the fast up express due at Euston at 9.15 p.m. The load, after Manchester and Liverpool portions had been united at Crewe, was computed as "eighteen coaches", *viz.* four 12-wheeled diners, reckoned as eight; six 8-wheelers, counted as nine; and one six-wheeled van, making the total load behind the tender 345 tons empty, or 360 tons including passengers, staff, luggage and stores.' Then, after giving some details of the run-

ning, he continued: 'Our final arrival at Euston was three minutes in advance of booked time, although we had left Crewe nearly a minute late. Our inclusive time from Crewe to Euston was 2 hr. 50 min. 43 sec. for the 158 miles, with a load of 360 tons, and *without a pilot.* Bravo, Mr. Whale!'

Some time before this, however, some excellent results had been obtained on a dynamometer car test run from Crewe to Rugby and back with the first engine of the class. As early as March 27, 1904 *Precursor* herself was fairly put through her paces in the haulage of a load of 375 tons. It was not a high-speed trial, but a test to prove the tractive ability of the new engine at what were then the critical speeds in the working of the express train schedules of the day, and to observe the capacity of the new boiler for continuous hard steaming. Although free-running downhill is a useful attribute in itself, on a line like the L.N.W.R., with its gradual rises and falls, there is an over-riding need for sustained power output at 55 to 60 m.p.h., and it was in this respect that *Precursor* was particularly tested. For example, after having slogged up the bank to Whitmore, no higher speed than 62 m.p.h. was reached descending to Stafford, and the maxi-

Up Excursion train passing Kilburn High Road, engine No. 2012 'Penguin'

23

Up Liverpool express near Kenton: engine No. 2164 'Oberon' (as rebuilt and superheated)

mum speed of the entire journey was only 67 m.p.h. in running down the bank between Lichfield and Hademore troughs.

On tris trial trip the curious little six-wheeled dynamometer car built by Mr. Webb was used; but the published results do not give any details of the drawbar pulls obtained. At speeds of 37 m.p.h. and upwards, 25 readings of indicated horsepower were taken and these varied between 936 and 1,174. The latter figure was obtained at a speed of 61 m.p.h. just to the south of Tamworth; but in the initial acceleration from Crewe three notably high figures were obtained on the 1 in 249 gradient to Betley Road, of 1,168 i.h.p. at 37 m.p.h., 1,142 at 40 m.p.h. and 1,151 at 41 m.p.h. The complete record, as originally published in *The Engineer,* is shown in the accompanying table.

In passing, I may add that on Rous-Marten's journey with *Tamerlane* and 360 tons, the attained speed at Betley Road was 47 m.p.h., against 41 on the test trip with *Precursor,* and Whitmore summit was passed in a full minute less. Nevertheless, the trial of March 27, 1904 indicated that Crewe had a locomotive capable of developing 1,000 indicated horsepower continuously, and while comparisons may be odious this performance, in the measure of

Up Manchester express on Bushey troughs: engine No. 1301 'Candidate'

continuous power output, was vastly better than anything that had been achieved in the comprehensive series of trials carried out with the first of the Smith-Johnson compounds on the Midland not many months previously.

Another batch of five locomotives was completed at Crewe in June 1904, namely:

2	Simoom
7	Titan
412	Alfred Paget
510	Albatross
659	Dreadnought

Again it is worth noting the engines from which those names were taken. In the order given above, they had previously been borne by a 2—4—0 'Precursor', a 'Dreadnought' compound, a 'Lady of the Lake' 2—2—2, a 'Precursor' and, of course, the

Engine No. 310 'Achilles', at Euston

pioneer of the 'Dreadnoughts'. The management of the line was not long in using the fine appearance of the new engines for publicity purposes. It was a year of intense railway competition, and in anticipation of a very serious challenge from the Great Central, which materialised in the remarkable run of the 3.25 p.m. from Marylebone in reaching Manchester in 230 min., the North Western accelerated their morning and evening crack trains from Euston to an overall time of 210 min.; and they advertised it by striking posters reproduced on pages 29 & 33. Those runs included a stop at Stockport, and involved the making of an average speed of 55.3 m.p.h. start-to-stop from Euston to Stockport. The performance of these engines is dealt with in some detail in the next chapter, and the present one is concluded by a list of the remaining 120 locomotives of the 'Precursor' class, 100 of which were built between October 1904 and May 1906, and the last 20 between June and August 1907. With their names and dates are also given the class of engine previously bearing the same name. From the list opposite it will be seen that many of these

'PRECURSOR' CLASS   OCT 1904—AUG 1907

Locomotive	Date built	Previous engines of same name in Class
639 Ajax	October 1904	D
648 Archimedes	,,	D Bl AP
685 Cossack	,,	P AG
60 Dragon	,,	P AG
106 Druid	,,	P AG
301 Leviathan	,,	D Bl AG
305 Senator	November 1904	P AG
643 Sirocco	,,	P AG
1102 Thunderbolt	,,	P AG
1117 Vandal	,,	D Bl AP
301 Achilles	December 1904	D Bl AG
333 Ambassador	,,	D DX
515 Champion	,,	P AG
622 Euphrates	,,	D
638 Huskisson	,,	D AP
303 Himalaya	January 1905	D
645 Mammoth	,,	D Bl AG
806 Swiftsure	,,	D
1120 Thunderer	,,	D
1137 Vesuvius	,,	D AP
323 Argus	February 1905	D
1104 Cedric	,,	P
1111 Cerberus	March 1905	P AG
1431 Egeria	,,	L
2064 Jason	,,	P AP
40 Niagara	,,	D
520 Panopea	,,	L
1469 Tantalus	,,	L AP
1737 Viscount	,,	P AG
2031 Waverley	,,	L
365 Alchymist	April 1905	D DX AG
1115 Apollo	,,	E Bl AP
1545 Cyclops	,,	E AG
1573 Dunrobin	,,	D
2061 Eglinton	,,	P AG
184 Havelock	May 1905	L
366 Medusa	,,	D AP Bl
519 Messenger	,,	E AP
1430 Victor	,,	E AP Bl
2120 Trentham	,,	E
113 Aurania	July 1905	E
300 Emerald	,,	P AP
302 Greyhound	,,	D AP
315 Harrowby	,,	P AG
688 Hecate	,,	E AP Bl
1509 America	August 1905	E
1617 Hydra	,,	E AP Bl
1723 Scorpion	,,	L AP
2062 Sunbeam	,,	E AP
2257 Vulture	,,	P AP Bl
311 Emperor	September 1905	E AP
374 Empress	,,	E AP
811 Express	,,	E
911 Herald	,,	D AG Bl
1114 Knowsley	,,	E AP Bl
1116 Pandora	,,	L
1510 Psyche	,,	L
1784 Python	October 1905	P AG
2166 Shooting Star	,,	E
2202 Vizier	,,	P
117 Alaska	,,	E
1301 Candidate	,,	P AG
1363 Cornwall	,,	8 ft. 6 in. 2-2-2
127 Snake	November 1905	E AP
229 Stork	,,	D AG Bl
1396 Harpy	,,	D AP Bl
1439 Tiger	,,	L
2007 Oregon	,,	E
2012 Penguin	,,	AP E

Locomotive	Date built	Previous engines of same name in Class
2115 Servia	,,	E
2576 Arab	December 1905	AG P
2577 Etna	,,	DX P
2578 Fame	,,	AG P
2579 Ganymede	,,	J66
2580 Problem	,,	L
2581 Peel	,,	L
2582 Rowland Hill	,,	AG Bl D
2583 Teutonic	January 1906	T
2584 Velocipede	,,	E
2585 Watt	,,	AP L
723 Coptic	February 1906	T
837 Friar	,,	AP E
1312 Ionic	,,	T
1387 Lang Meg	March 1906	P
1642 Lapwing	,,	AG P
234 Pearl	,,	AP P
526 Ilion	,,	J66
1311 Napoleon	,,	L
2017 Tubal	,,	AG DX J6
2513 Levens	,,	P
282 Alaric	April 1906	AP Bl
561 Antaeus	,,	AG
675 Adjutant	,,	AG
772 Admiral	,,	AG
804 Amphion	,,	—
988 Bellerophon	,,	AG DX
990 Bucephalus	,,	AG Bl
1433 Faerie Queene	,,	L
1650 Richard Trevithick	May 1906	GB
1787 Hyperion	,,	AG
1 Clive	June 1907	L
218 Daphne	,,	L
419 Monarch	,,	AP L
469 Marmion	,,	L
564 Erebus	,,	AP L
665 Mersey	,,	AP L
276 Doric	July 1907	T
754 Celtic	,,	T
802 Gaelic	,,	T
1011 Locke	,,	AP DX L
1364 Clyde	,,	L
2053 Edith	,,	L
2181 Eleanor	,,	L
807 Oceanic	August 1907	T
976 Pacific	,,	T
1297 Phalaris	,,	AG J6
1309 Shamrock	,,	J66
1516 Alecto	,,	AP J66
2011 Brougham	,,	J66
2051 Delamere	,,	AG Bl

Classes of previous engines bearing same name:

AP = Allan 2-2-2
AG = Allan 2-4-0
DX = DX 0-6-0 Goods
Bl = 'Bloomer' 2-2-2
L = 'Lady of the Lake' 2-2-2
P = 'Precursor' 5 ft. 6 in. 2-4-0
J6 = 6 ft. 'Jumbo' (Whitworth)
J66 = 6 ft. 6 in. 'Jumbo' (Precedent)
E = 'Experiment' 3-cyl. compound
D = 'Dreadnought' 3-cyl. compound
T = 'Teutonic' 3-cyl. compound
GB = 'Greater Britain' compound

Up Birmingham two-hour express near Kenton: engine No. 2585 'Watt'

names had been carried by three previous engines. Only three were renamed in the course of their careers, as follows:

No.	Original Name	New Name
412	*Alfred Paget*	*Marquis*
1363	*Cornwall*	*Brindley*
2583	*Teutonic*	*The Czar/Moonstone*

At the time the 'Precursor' No. 1363 was built the old 8 ft. 6 in. single *Cornwall* had been withdrawn. For traffic purposes she had been classed with the 'Lady of the Lake' 2—2—2s, and these were being systematically scrapped. When, fortunately, it was decided to preserve *Cornwall* the new 4—4—0 No.

1363 was named *Brindley*, which title had previously been carried by a 6 ft. 6 in. 'Jumbo'. *Teutonic* had the name defaced by a thick red line, and the new name, *The Tsar*, mounted on a second plate just above, on the outbreak of World War I in 1914. Mention of war draws attention to the name of engine No. 1311, and to readers of a later generation it might seem strange that one of our greatest national enemies should have been remembered. But the name *Napoleon* on the L.N.W.R. dates from the 'Lady of the Lake' class engine No. 565; and that engine, built in 1861, was undoubtedly named after our ally in the Crimea, the Emperor Napoleon III, and not he who spent his last days as our 'guest' at St. Helena! So far as can be traced, there was only one 'Precursor' name that was new, that of engine No. 804, *Amphion*.

CHAPTER 3

TRAIN SERVICE METAMORPHOSIS

IN the first months after their introduction the impact of the 'Precursors' upon the train working as a whole was not great. Individually they did splendidly; but to some extent Whale was the victim of his own drive. With the building of the 'Precursors' he had commenced a vigorous scrapping campaign, and in its early stages this left the

noticeable feature of the early running of the 'Precursors' was the lack of any high speed downhill. The uphill and level work was such as to make fast running on the favourable lengths unnecessary.

Some early performances of these engines may be summarised in tabular form, as shown below.

The run with *Tamerlane* was on the 10.45 a.m.

EARLY 'PRECURSOR' PERFORMANCE

Engine No.	Name	Load tons	Route	Dist. miles	Time min.	Max. speed m.p.h.
513	*Precursor* .	350	Crewe-Euston . . .	158	173½	66
2164	*Oberon* .	385	Willesden-Rugby	77.2	87	—
2164	*Oberon* .	385	Rugby-Crewe .	75.5	82½	—
2023	*Helvellyn* .	385*	Euston-Crewe .	158	173	70
1419	*Tamerlane* .	350	Euston-Stafford . . .	133.5	138½	72
685	*Cossack* .	205	Euston-Birmingham .	113	116	—
60	*Dragon* .	220	Euston-Birmingham .	113	118½†	—

*Less 23 tons slipped at Nuneaton
†despite westerly gale

running department seriously short of engines. In 1904, only the 'Precursors' and the 'Alfred the Great' compounds with modified valve gear were exempt from the notorious 'equal to 17' piloting rule. The great majority of trains still needed a second engine and it was as much the scrapping of the 'Lady of the Lake' 2—2—2s as anything else that created the locomotive famine. The 'Precursors' had four important down expresses from Euston as follows:

   8.30 a.m.   Irish Mail
  10.00 a.m.   Glasgow and Edinburgh
   5.30 p.m.   Belfast boat express
  11.50 p.m.   Glasgow sleeper

On these trains, and the 6.20 p.m. up from Crewe, they took loads 'equal to 21' without assistance, but on easier timed trains like the 3.2 p.m. up Scotsman from Crewe to Euston they took 'equal to 25'. The

from Euston, and was a fine performance, logged by Charles Rous-Marten. An abbreviated log published in December 1904 gave the following times:

Dist. miles		Actual	
		m.	s.
0.0	Euston . . .	0	00
31.7	Tring	38	20
46.7	Bletchley . . .	51	36
82.5	Rugby . . .	86	20
110.0	Tamworth . .	113	26
116.3	Lichfield . . .	119	19
—		sigs.	
133.5	Stafford . . .	138	25

With a 350-ton load this was very good going, and was mainly the result of fine hill-climbing. The minimum speeds were 55 m.p.h. between Watford and Tring, and 55½ m.p.h. at Roade. It will be

Up Manchester express passing Bushey: engine No. 2023 'Helvellyn'

seen that the average speed between Tring and Lichfield was well over 60 m.p.h. for 84 miles on end. I have not seen any early records of work with loads 'equal to 25'; on these trains the tonnage was 420 to 430, but some later examples of performance in this category are given subsequently in this book. The timetable alterations of 1905, however, reduced the number of trains loading up to such tonnages by dividing many services into two parts. On some of these trains 'Precursors' were used for relatively light trains, but by the summer there were over sixty of them at work, and so far as the Southern Division was concerned the locomotive famine was virtually at an end. From 1905 the maximum load for a 'Precursor' was reduced to '20½'. This was strictly enforced and, as it seemed a point of honour that they should never be piloted, there were times when through carriages which had been attached at intermediate points en route had to be run separately, rather than make the main train up to more than '20½'.

Within the revised limit of '20½' coaches the 'Precursors' did much splendid work. One of the finest runs on record for the year 1905 was made on the accelerated evening express from Euston to Liverpool, booked to run the 192¼ miles to Edge Hill non-stop in 208 min.; the load was 'equal to 18'—350 tons behind the tender—and the engine

No. 1117, *Vandal*. The start was exceedingly fine, passing Willesden Junction, 5.4 miles, in 8¾ min., and Watford, 17.5 miles, in 21 min. The initial time was so brisk that one suspects the train was banked in rear to Camden. Be that as it may, the speed through Watford was unusually high, 65 m.p.h., and the 14.2 miles up to Tring took only 14 min. 35 sec. This was remarkable work for a 'Precursor' hauling as much as 350 tons, and involved holding the speed to not less than 60 m.p.h. as far as the ascent at Berkhamsted, and making a minimum speed of 56 m.p.h. at Tring summit. After such a fine start the driver could afford to run much more easily. There were signal checks at Denbigh Hall just north of Bletchley, outside Crewe, and again at Minshull Vernon; but despite these hindrances Edge Hill was reached 1¼ min. early, in 206 min. 50 sec. from Euston. The net time was 198¾ min., equal to an average speed of 58 m.p.h. throughout.

With an even heavier load of 400 tons, Rous-Marten clocked an equally fine run by No. 520, *Panopea*, on the 10 a.m. down Scotsman. The start was not so fast as on the Liverpool train just described, and the time was 23 min. to passing Watford. Speed did not fall below 50 m.p.h. on the climb to Tring, and good brisk work continued to bring the train into Rugby 2½ min. early, in 90 min. 24 sec. from Euston. The continuation was equally good, yielding a time of 79¾ min. for the 75½ miles from Rugby to Crewe, and arriving 3¼ min. early. It is certainly a remarkable tribute to the 'Precursors' that a load of 400 tons could be worked at an average speed of 54.7 m.p.h. from Euston to Rugby, and from there to Crewe at an average of 56.8 m.p.h.

It goes without saying that to achieve work of this quality, with what was after all a relatively small engine, the firing must have been excellent. It has been said by some, whose sympathies lie elsewhere than Crewe, that these engines, and the 'George the Fifths', would steam under the efforts of a navvy. No skill was needed, just the physical strength to keep piling on the coal. Although the 'Precursors' and the 'Georges' required a rather simpler technique than the six-coupled engines, the fireman had still to fire with his brains as much as with the shovel. With the 'Precursors', the most usual practice was to put on six shovelfuls at each round, with an additional five every second or third

round. The six shovelfuls at each round were placed as follows: one in each forward corner of the firebox, and two in each back corner. Then at every second or third round one shovelful would be put roughly halfway down each side of the box, one straight forward to the front and two under the door. The fire was kept well banked up under the door, because it was found this helped the coal to shake gradually forward and cover the middle of the box evenly. Contrary to what is sometimes imagined, the 'Precursors' were regularly run well linked up, cutting off at about 25 per cent for normal fast express work.

On the two-hour Birmingham expresses the 'Precursors' did some running that would have been regarded as phenomenal a few years earlier. It is true that the loads were not heavy; but when delays had occurred, or when there was otherwise incentive to run, the drivers certainly put their new locomotives to good use. On the 2.45 p.m. up from New Street one afternoon the authorities were evidently anxious to put on a good show for Rous-

'Precursors' in a poster campaign

An unidentified 'Precursor' on the up Irish Mail near Colwyn Bay

Marten. A locomotive inspector was put on to ride on the footplate, and although the load was no more than 170 tons behind the tender some quite remarkable work was done. In the early days of the two-hour service there was great insistence on punctuality, and to assist in this a determined effort was made to keep down the loads. Unfortunately, this sometimes led to serious overcrowding of the carriages, and on this occasion Rous-Marten recorded that the train was packed from end to end. As the competence of the 'Precursors' was proved, again and again, by runs like the one about to be described there was considerable relaxation as to the number of carriages run, and things became more comfortable for the passengers.

On this run the engine was No. 310, *Achilles,* and the speed was 70 m.p.h. before the train was 4 miles out of Birmingham. Continuing at 75 to 77 m.p.h., they passed Coventry, 18.9 miles, in 17¾ min., and although checked almost to a stand by signal in Rugby station, they reached that point, 30½ miles, in 27 min. 19 sec. Very fast running followed, at 72 to 80 m.p.h. all the way from Weedon until checked approaching Bletchley, and again at Stoke Hammond box. After that there was a very swift recovery, and the outstanding feat of the whole journey followed. Speed was worked up to 72½ m.p.h. and this was sustained without any variation up the 1 in 335 gradient to Tring. The idea of 72 m.p.h. being sustained up such a gradient was then considered absolutely novel, and Rous-Marten was justifiably enthusiastic. But so far as

power output was concerned, it was not anything out of the ordinary, and involved an equivalent drawbar horsepower of about 750. In years to come we shall regard as commonplace the speeds of 85 to 90 m.p.h. maintained by the new electric locomotives up the 1 in 177 of Madeley bank with loads of 450 to 500 tons. Today they are still something of a phenomenon, though technically they are no different from the achievement of *Achilles* in 1905 —namely, the product of a powerful new locomotive hauling a load well within its maximum capacity.

So far as fully detailed logs are concerned, two runs on the up 'West Coast Corridor', then due to arrive in Euston at 10.45 p.m., gave a good idea of what was expected of the 'Precursors' in their early days. This train had an easier timing than most of the principal up expresses, in deference to its weight; but both engines did remarkably well. The start of *Harbinger,* with such a load as 435 tons, was remarkable for an engine of these moderate dimensions, and although no maximum and minimum speeds are quoted in the record the engine must have been doing about 70 m.p.h. at both Weedon and Wolverton. Although there are several intermediate gradients between Rugby and Bletchley the overall effect of the line is roughly level, and times of 39¾ and 40¼ min. over this 35.8 miles inevitably invite comparison with Great Western starts from Paddington to Reading. It would not be often, one would imagine, that a Great Western four-coupled engine would pass Reading in 40 min. with a 400-ton load in those days!

L.N.W.R. RUGBY—WILLESDEN JUNCTION

Engine No.		1650	1395
Engine Name		Richard Trevithick	Harbinger
Load tons E/F		385/405	414/435
Dist. miles		Sch. min.	Actual m. s.	Actual m. s.

Dist. miles		Sch. min.	Actual m. s.	Actual m. s.
0.0	RUGBY	0	0 00	0 00
7.2	Welton	—	12 15	12 17
12.8	Weedon	—	17 35	17 43
19.7	Blisworth	—	24 05	24 20
22.6	Roade	28	27 08	27 25
30.1	Wolverton	—	34 00	34 21
35.8	BLETCHLEY	42	39 47	40 18
50.8	Tring	59	56 15	58 30
58.0	Boxmoor	—	63 38	66 16
65.0	WATFORD Jc.	74	70 01	72 38
71.1	Harrow	—	75 42	78 32
77.1	WILLESDEN Jc.	87	81 41	84 42

Naturally there was some falling off on the long rise to Tring, and *Harbinger,* with her 435-ton load, dropped over a minute on the point-to-point scheduled time. But there was some brisk running downhill in conclusion, and both engines finished well within schedule. To Bletchley, there had been nothing to choose between the two performances; but *Richard Trevithick* was driven much harder up to Tring, and had established a lead of nearly 3 min. on passing Boxmoor. When the tonnage system of reckoning train loads was introduced, in October 1913, the maximum load for any train was laid down as 420 tons tare, and on all ordinary express services from that time onwards the 'Precursor' limit was fixed at 350 tons. But a special regulation applied to the down and up 'Corridor' expresses— 2 p.m. from Euston and 7.32 p.m. from Crewe. On these two trains the 'Precursors' were allowed to handle the maximum of 420 tons, so on the run tabulated, *Harbinger* was actually within her load. What days they were! The demands upon L.N.W.R. locomotives were indeed unique in their severity.

When the novelty of such new standards of locomotive performance had passed, and more than a hundred of the 'Precursors' were in service, runs clocked in the years 1906 to 1909 assumed an almost monotonous excellence—if one may use such an expression. I have not seen detailed logs of any performance on the Irish Mails between Chester and Holyhead, but the running south of Crewe on each and every express bore the stamp of a reliability such as the North Western had rarely known before. At first, the idea of piloting any train hauled by a 'Precursor' was abhorrent: something that was just not done! And this sentiment caused some problems in running extras. But by the year 1906 there was a return to realities, and one could occasionally see pilots ahead of both 'Precursors' and the six-coupled 'Experiments'. Nevertheless, there were times, especially on the Northern Division, when the Operating Department was the victim of the new-found locomotive efficiency. A great many trains were made up to tonnages between 350 and 400 and, with such loads, there was not such a margin of engine power available for recovery of lost time as in former days, when practically every train of any weight was double-headed.

Eng. No.	Name	Load tons	Section	Dist. mls.	Time min.
2513	Levens	355	Euston-Crewe	158	169¼
311	Emperor	365	,,	158	171¼
2513	Levens	370	,,	158	171¼
311	Emperor	385	,,	158	171
1509	America	375	Stafford-Willesden	128	135½

The foregoing table gives a few examples, in summary form, of characteristic runs with heavy trains on the Southern Division. The times in some cases include the effects of incidental checks.

The Birmingham non-stops, with loads varying between 250 and 300 tons, were relatively easy to

Up express leaving Crewe, hauled by No. 7 'Titan'

Engine 106 'Druid' on down mail train near Rugby

L.N.W.R. EUSTON—BIRMINGHAM

Run No.		1	2	3	4
Engine No.		1784	184	303	40
Engine Name		*Python*	*Havelock*	*Himalaya*	*Niagara*
Load tons gross		250	255	270	270*
Dist. Miles		Actual m. s.	Actual m. s.	Actual m. s.	Actual m. s.
0.0	EUSTON	0 00	0 00	0 00	0 00
2.4	Loudoun Road	4 59	5 15	5 02	5 21
—		—	p.w.s.	p.w.s.	—
5.4	WILLESDEN	8 24	9 36	9 11	8 42
11.4	Harrow	15 19	16 14	16 15	14 53
—		sigs.	—	p.w.s.	—
17.5	WATFORD	22 22	22 45	23 31	21 05
21.0	Kings Langley	26 12	26 20	27 15	24 32
24.5	Boxmoor	30 02	sigs.	31 01	28 11
28.0	Berkhamsted	33 54	sigs.	34 48	31 55
31.7	Tring	38 18	38 36	38 56	35 49
36.1	Cheddington	42 32	42 51	43 08	39 55
40.2	Leighton Buzzard	46 10	46 23	46 36	43 16
46.7	BLETCHLEY	51 59	52 05	52 16	48 49
52.4	Wolverton	57 14	57 20	57 20	53 50
59.9	Roade	64 58	64 53	64 52	61 05
62.8	Blisworth	68 07	67 56	68 01	64 05
69.7	Weedon	74 27	74 16	74 19	70 17
75.3	Welton	80 03	79 47	79 48	75 39
—		—	—	sigs.	SLIP
82.5	RUGBY	87 02	86 52	87 51	83 02
—		—	sigs.	—	—
89.1	Brandon	93 29	93 57	94 53	90 30
94.0	COVENTRY	97 52	98 33	99 10	94 50
97.5	Tile Hill	101 42	102 21	102 52	98 25
99.5	Berkswell	103 53	104 27	105 00	100 26
102.8	Hampton	107 09	107 35	107 54	103 26
109.1	Stechford	113 39	113 28	113 32	108 58
111.0	Adderley Park	115 50	115 26	115 45	111 07
—		—	sigs.	—	—
112.9	BIRMINGHAM	118 55	119 08	118 50	115 05
	Net time min.	118	116	115	115
Speeds	m.p.h.	—	—	—	—
Watford		60	64½	59	64½
Tring		52½	51	53	55
Cheddington		69	70½	74	76½
Roade		53	54	54	56½
Weedon		66	64½	66	67
Hillmorton		68	67	—	65
Brandon		63½	64½	71½	69
Beechwood Tunnel		53	56½	54	60

*Load reduced to 245 tons at Rugby

work, and the net times constantly achieved showed average speeds of little below 60 m.p.h. throughout. In studying details of these runs, it is interesting to see how rarely any really fast running was made downhill. The drivers seemed to aim at maintaining a very even pace, both uphill and downhill. I have tabulated a collection of four runs, on three of which the same load was conveyed from Euston to Birmingham. On the fourth a coach was slipped at Rugby, and this involved a much slower run through that station, taking the cross-overs at entrance and exit from the down platform line.

On the first run, with a load of 250 tons, engine No. 1784, *Python*, made an excellent start, passing Willesden in the smart time of 8 min. 24 sec. There was a slight signal check at Bushey, but after that it was very placid going. Apart from the slack through Rugby, the speeds did not vary more than from 52½ up to 70 m.p.h., and Birmingham was reached a minute early. On the second run engine No. 184, *Havelock*, had two permanent way checks in the early stages, and it was good work in the circumstances to pass Watford in 22¾ min. From there on to Rugby the going was very similar to that of *Python,* but drawing slightly ahead through a faster climb to Roade. There were further checks, at Brandon and in the approach to Birmingham, but enough was in hand for an arrival nearly a minute ahead of time. The third run, with engine No. 303, *Himalaya,* was also an excellent piece of work with a 270-ton load, and these three runs showed net average speeds of 57.3, 58.3 and 58.8 m.p.h. The fourth, slipping a coach at Rugby, was the finest run of all. Engine No. 40, *Niagara,* made a good start out to Willesden, and the combination of good hillclimbing and a fast descent from Tring put this engine well ahead of all others by Bletchley. There were no checks at all on this journey, and fast running after Rugby, with a minimum of 60 m.p.h. on the 1 in 330 rise from Coventry to Beechwood Tunnel, resulted in Birmingham being reached 5 min. early. On all these runs the weather conditions were far from favourable, with strong adverse winds prevailing throughout.

An example of performance over a route not often logged in detail is tabulated herewith on the 6 p.m. express from Liverpool to Newcastle, which was worked by the 'Precursor' 4—4—0 No. 2584, *Velocipede,* from Liverpool to Leeds. The load on

Another striking 'Precursor' poster

L.N.W.R. 6 p.m. LIVERPOOL—LEEDS

Load: 6 coaches, 155 tons gross
Engine: No. 2584 *Velocipede*

Dist. miles		Sch. min.	Actual m. s.	Speeds m.p.h.
0.0	LIME STREET	0	0 00	—
1.4	Edge Hill . .		4 25	—
—			sigs.	—
3.6	Broad Green .		7 55	—
5.7	Huyton . .		10 00	66
8.9	Rainhill . .		13 15	55½
11.9	*St. Helens Jc.* .		15 55	79
—			sigs.	—
14.8	EARLSTOWN Jc. . .		18 40	—
18.9	Kenyon Jc. .		22 55	—
27.6	ECCLES . .		30 40	68 (max)
31.4	MANCHESTER EXCHANGE .	38	36 30	
1.7	Miles Platting .		5 15	—
6.6	Ashton . .		12 25	—
8.1	STALYBRIDGE .		14 35	—
15.4	Diggle . .		25 55	39*
19.0	Marsden . .		30 55	slow
—			sigs.	
26.1	HUDDERS-FIELD . .	43	41 15	
2.7	Bradley . .		4 30	
—			sigs.	
4.9	MIRFIELD . .		8 30	
8.0	DEWSBURY .		13 15	
12.5	Morley . .		21 20	36*
17.1	LEEDS . .	31	28 40	

*minimum speeds on banks
Net times: 34 min., 38 min. and 25 min.

this occasion was no more than light, but the running was smart and well within schedule time. This journey is subject to the most extraordinary changes in the physical characteristics of the line. It begins with the straight and largely level course of the historic Liverpool & Manchester Railway, and then continues on mountain gradients with much curvature over the Pennine 'gable'. The final stretch from Huddersfield into Leeds is again heavily graded, and generally unsuited for fast running.

The start out of Liverpool, through the vertical-sided rock cuttings to Edge Hill, is continuously at 1 in 93, after which the line is level to a point a mile east of Huyton. After the signal check at Broad Green, speed was worked rapidly up to 66 m.p.h. before tackling the 1½ miles at 1 in 95 that leads to Rainhill. There is then a level plateau rather more than 2 miles long, and it was here that the memorable engine trials took place in 1829. Then comes a steep descent at 1 in 91 to St. Helens Junction, and speed at this point was all but 80 m.p.h. Onwards to Manchester, the line is virtually level, but it was certainly smart work to have gained time between Liverpool and Manchester despite two signal checks. It is a continuous hard grind from Manchester to the western end of

C

A novel headboard for the Euston—Rhyl non-stop:
209¼ miles in 237 minutes

Standedge Tunnel, at Diggle, but not by any means a straightforward run. The immediate start savours more of South Devon so far as gradients are concerned with a climb at 1 in 59-47 out to Miles Platting. Then comes a heavy slack at Stalybridge, to cross over on to the Friezland line. From this point, the ascent is mostly at 1 in 100 to 1 in 125, and here *Velocipede* sustained 39-40 m.p.h. The 3 miles of level through Standedge Tunnel, including the passing of the unique water troughs that are *inside* the tunnel, was taken at moderate speed, and the winding descent towards Huddersfield is no place for speeding. Nevertheless, all was set for an arrival in 38 min. from Manchester, when a succession of adverse signals caused a loss of 3¼ min. The last stage into Leeds is infested with speed restrictions, difficult junctions and heavy gradients, and the only opportunity for the driver to show off the capacity of his engine comes in the climb from Dewsbury to Morley Tunnel, on 1 in 138, where speed was worked smartly up to 36 m.p.h. Although the overall times were not spectacular, it was an

interesting example of 'Precursor' performance on a crosscountry route.

In the year 1906, the 'Precursors' made a brief appearance on the main line between Crewe and Carlisle. After their first introduction in 1904, attention was concentrated upon getting the working south of Crewe into good order, and during 1904 and 1905 the Northern Division was left to carry on as before, with a great amount of double-heading. But by the summer of 1906 there were 110 'Precursors' on the road, together with 15 of the new 'Experiments', and some of the new 4—4—0s could then be spared for the Carlisle road. The 'Precursors' did extremely well, though there were times when they fell prey to slipping on the banks. The summer of 1906 seems to have been a wet one, and with the new engines taking large loads unassisted there was occasional loss of time in bad weather conditions. What I have written earlier in this chapter about the Operating Department suffering from the new-found efficiency of the locomotive stud will be appreciated the more from a reference to the extraordinarily close scheduling of express trains over the Carlisle road at the height of the August holiday season. On the morning of August 4, 1906, the following was the *booked* succession of trains into Carlisle. As it worked out, some of these were divided:

1.12 a.m.	3.32 a.m.
1.35 ,,	3.42 ,,
1.45 ,,	3.53 ,,
1.56 ,,	4. 5 ,,
2.14 ,,	4.15 ,,
2.24 ,,	4.33 ,,
2.39 ,,	5.30 ,,
3. 1 ,,	5.40 ,,
3.10 ,,	5.50 ,,
3.22 ,,	6. 3 ,,

What a feast this would have provided for any railway enthusiast keen enough to keep watch through the night and to record the engines bringing these trains in, and the Caledonian engines taking them forward. It would also have been interesting to have known what the timekeeping was like. At that time the great majority of those trains would have arrived in Carlisle double-headed. A few would no doubt have been worked by 'Precursors' and one or two 'Experiments' would probably have been in evidence. It was a matter of prestige then that these new locomotives should not be assisted, though with the 'Precursors' no one seemed to mind taking rear-end banking assistance from Tebay up to Shap Summit. But the great majority of these trains would still have been worked by the old brigade—Webb four-cylinder compound 4—4—0s, and the trusty little 'Jumbos'.

A splendid example of actual running was noted by R. E. Charlewood on the down 'Corridor', then leaving Preston at 6.25 p.m. and allowed 103 min. for the 90 miles to Carlisle. An abridged log is tabulated herewith.

L.N.W.R. 6.25 p.m. PRESTON—CARLISLE
Load: 310 tons gross
Engine: 4—4—0 No. 1363 *Cornwall*

Dist. Miles		Sch. min.	Actual m. s.	Speeds m.p.h.
0.0	PRESTON .	0	0 00	—
21.0	LANCASTER .	22	22 48	70 (max)
27.3	CARNFORTH .	29	28 13	69/56
34.6	Milnthorpe .		35 31	—
40.1	Oxenholme .	43	41 33	—
47.2	Grayrigg . .		52 42	31½
53.2	Tebay . .	61	60 47	
			61 57	
58.7	*Shap Summit* .	71	72 36	
90.1	CARLISLE .	103	101 10	

Particularly in respect of the running between Preston and Carnforth, this was a remarkable trip. There was no suggestion of nursing the engine in readiness for the climb to Shap, and some really fast work was done on the level in order to pass Lancaster in such time as 22 min. 48 sec. In later years, when the 'George the Fifth' class was making such a name for itself on the down 'Corridor', the schedule was 1 min. easier, with 23 min. to Lancaster and 104 min. to Carlisle. The minimum speed of 31½ m.p.h. on Grayrigg was reasonably good, but not exceptional for a load of 310 tons. All the same, it must be recorded that the 'Precursors' did not always do as well as this, and in that same summer Charlewood clocked No. 1301 *Candidate* on the 1.45 min. from Preston with a load of 325 tons, and nearly 3 min. was dropped on the fast schedule of 102 min. Although the climb of Grayrigg bank had been equally good, with a minimum speed of 31½ m.p.h., the start was much slower and it took 63¾ min. to reach the stop at Tebay. The time to Carlisle was 104¾ min. Both runs, by *Cornwall* and *Candidate,* were made in wet weather. The former engine, No. 1363, had her name changed to *Brindley* when it was decided to preserve the famous 8 ft. 6 in. 2—2—2 *Cornwall.*

One of the best 'Precursor' runs on record over the Northern Division was made in the middle of the night, on the 1 a.m. up from Carlisle with a load of 330 tons. Once again the weather was very bad, with a strong south-westerly wind and heavy rain. From these records it would seem that the summer of 1906 had some strong points of similarity to that of 1965! The engine was No. 2580, *Problem,* and she climbed the 31.4 miles to Shap Summit in 48 min. 53 sec. Thereafter, the 37.6 miles down to Lancaster took 33½ min. and

A 'Precursor' No. 234 'Pearl', booked for the down Sunny South Special northward from Willesden, coupled to the 2 p.m. West Coast 'Corridor', and ready to leave Euston

The 2 p.m. 'Corridor' near Kenton, hauled by No. 1309 'Shamrock'

the last 21 miles into Preston 23 min. 17 sec., making up an excellent overall time of 105 min. 40 sec. from Carlisle. Good though these runs were, the 'Precursors' were quickly superseded as Northern Division express engines by the new 'Experiments'. By the time the summer service of 1907 was introduced there were 35 of these latter engines at work—enough to provide for all the regular expresses north of Preston—and the 'Precursors' were gradually moved elsewhere. From that time onward they were rarely seen north of Preston, until L.M.S.R. days when some were drafted to the Furness section, and others did occasional duty as main-line pilots working from

Oxenholme. Some notes on this phase of 'Precursor' working are given in a later chapter of this book, dealing with post-grouping days.

It has sometimes been stated that the hard work done by the 'Precursors' was at the expense of heavy coal consumption. The Interchange trials of 1909, in which two of these engines were matched against Great Northern 'Atlantics', certainly does not bear this out. On the L.N.W.R., the test trains worked included the 10 a.m. 'Scotsman' from Euston to Crewe, which was loaded to the 'Precursor' maximum of 'equal to 19½', and booked to make a running average speed of 52½ m.p.h. The late Sir William Stanier, when Chief Mech-

An up express, 'Precursor' hauled, near Bushey

The down Irish Mail leaving the Britannia tubular bridge

TRIALS ON THE L.N.W.R.

Engine	L.N.W.R. No. 510 Albatross	G.N.R. No. 1449
Total number of trips .	26	26
Average load per trip .	290 tons	320 tons
Train miles run . .	4113	4113
Ton miles run (excluding engine) . .	1,194,250	1,317,448
Coal burned per train mile	40.73 lb.	41.08 lb.
Coal burned per ton mile .	0.140 lb.	0.128 lb.

TRIALS ON THE G.N.R.

Engine	G.N.R. No. 1451	L.N.W.R. No. 412 Marquis
Average load (16 trips Doncaster to King's Cross and back 312 miles) .	237¾ tons	236½ tons
Coal consumed (ex Houghton Colliery) Per train mile . .	34.6 lb.	36.5 lb.
Per ton mile (excluding engine) . . .	0.145 lb.	0.154 lb.
Oil and Tallow per 100 train miles	4.12 lb.	4 53 lb.
Speed	53.12 m.p.h.	52.73 m.p.h.

anical Engineer of the L.M.S.R., was kind enough to look out for me such records as remained of these trials, and the average results of 26 competitive runs on the L.N.W.R.—*Albatross v* G.N.R. No. 1449, and 16 return trips from Doncaster to King's Cross and back; *Marquis v* G.N.R. No. 1451—were as tabulated.

From the above, the results, especially from *Albatross*, were very good, with an average coal consumption of only 40.73 lb. per mile over more than 8,000 miles of fast running. They make also a very interesting comparison between wide and narrow fireboxes on the same duties.

A very heavy up North Wales excursion near Old Colwyn: engine No. 2115 'Servia'

CHAPTER 4

THE 'EXPERIMENT' CLASS

IN the eyes of the Locomotive Department at Crewe, the 'Precursors' were essentially Southern Division engines. They were concentrated upon the traffic south of Crewe, though this, of course, included all the crack workings to Liverpool and Manchester. Following the large-scale introduction of the 'Precursors', the policy was to get the Southern Division right, eliminate piloting, and continue the double-heading of all the fastest and heaviest trains north of Crewe. Then, for the first time since the introduction of the ill-starred Webb 'Precursors' of 1874, Whale put in hand the design of a special type of express locomotive for the Northern Division. It could, I suppose, be said that the 6 ft. 3 in. 2—4—0 'Whitworths'—the 'six-foot Jumbos', as they were commonly known—were essentially Northern Division engines; but the larger-wheeled 'Jumbos', the 6 ft. 9 in. 'Precedents', were so regularly used in the North and so frequently coupled to a 'Whitworth' on the fastest trains, that the latter engines could on no account

be classed as *the* Northern Division express locomotives. So far as the Webb compounds were concerned, with the exception of the unsatisfactory 'Experiment' class, which did most of their work on the Irish Mails, all varieties seemed to work on both sections of the line, north and south of Crewe. The ten 2—2—2—2s of the 'John Hick' class were intended by Mr. Webb for the Northern Division; but were such poor tools that they were soon transferred to secondary duties elsewhere.

And so the design of the second 'Experiment' class was gradually worked out at Crewe. The underlying idea was to have a locomotive of similar capacity to the 'Precursors', but having that little extra in tractive effort and adhesion to suit the conditions on the mountain section. Before discussing the design of the locomotives themselves, some reference to the road itself is necessary, so that the factors affecting the engine working may be better appreciated. The northern section of the West Coast main line, from Crewe to Carlisle, is 141

The Whale 'Experiment': built Crewe, April 1905

Up sleeping car express, soon after sunrise, on Bushey troughs: engine No. 507 'Sarmatian'

miles long. For the first 78 miles, to Carnforth, the gradients are generally no more difficult than those of the Southern Division. There are some sharp pitches, such as the rise from Winwick Junction to Golborne, and on the Boars Head bank which comes immediately after Wigan and includes 2 miles at 1 in 104. But these gradients are not long enough to cause any real difficulty; and if an engine has been thrashed sufficiently hard up Boars Head bank to cause some drop in the boiler pressure, or water level, or both, there follows an easy downhill run to Preston, and some enforcedly slow running at 15 m.p.h. through the latter station, which gives some chance of a complete recovery on the footplate.

Nevertheless, with the sharp, though short, intermediate gradients and the need to ease the speed a little over some of the junctions, it needed good work with a heavy train to cover the 51 miles from Crewe to Preston within the hour. After that, there was no respite for the next 70 min. For nearly 30 miles north of Preston the line is virtually dead level. There is a sharp drop for a mile from Lancaster Old Junction to the Castle station, but this is not of much use for speed recovery, for officially a restriction was imposed at the junction itself. A level stretch might be considered to provide easy going: but any steam locomotive man will agree that such a stretch, coming in the middle of a long, fast stretch, can be very trying. In steam days on the East Coast route, when the crack double-home

turns were being worked between Kings Cross and Newcastle, the drivers and firemen of the Gresley 'Pacifics' all agreed that 'the roughest bit' was the magnificent level stretch from York to Darlington! In North Western days, one had to run at 60-65 m.p.h. on the level north of Preston to keep time, and if the engine was a bit shy for steam the road did not help the crew to pull things round. Yet this was just the very place where one could well be nursing the engine a little, for beyond Carnforth there began the 30-mile ascent to Shap Summit.

In that 30 miles there is a vertical rise of 885 ft., and at the time of which I am now writing the 10 a.m. express from Euston to Glasgow was allowed only 39 min. to climb the 31.4 miles from Carnforth to Shap Summit. Some smart work was needed to keep these strenuous uphill times, and after nearly 80 miles of express running from Crewe the effort was required just when conditions on the footplate were likely to have deteriorated. Unless things had been very expertly managed, the fire could be dirty, and steam pressure below maximum, with the result that the ascent to Shap could be an ordeal. This, of course, was well recognised, and it was not only the fast express passenger trains that needed consideration. The freight traffic over Shap was heavy, and two locomotive depots existed, at Oxenholme—on the Grayrigg Bank—and at Tebay, just at the foot of the Shap incline itself, where assistance could always be obtained. But to stop for a pilot at Oxenholme was the last

The neat and compact appearance of the 'Experiments' is well shown in this official photograph of No. 66

thing drivers of the Scotch expresses wished to do. It would have been a confession of failure, in all but those instances of definite and recognised over-loading. As related in the previous chapter, a load of 'equal to 20½' was the maximum normally worked with any express train on the L.N.W.R; but while the 'Precursors' worked such loads un-assisted on the Southern Division it was too much to expect, in 1904-5 at any rate, that any engine would take such a load unassisted over Shap.

What loads Whale and his men expected to take over Shap with the new 'Experiments' has never been made really clear. At that period in steam locomotive design no engineer could predict, with any certainty, what the performance of a new class was likely to be. The drawing offices advanced by rule of thumb methods based on the established work of earlier locomotives, and so far as nominal tractive effort was concerned the only difference between the 'Precursors' and the 'Experiments' lay in the coupled-wheel diameter—6 ft. 9 in. against 6 ft. 3 in. Those dimensions were, of course, with new tyres, and as in the case of the two varieties of 'Jumbo' it was customary to refer to the new engines as the '6 ft. 6 in. 4—4—0s' and the '6 ft. 0 in. 4—6—0s'. On the basis of the wheel diameters with new tyres the nominal tractive effort, at 85 per cent. boiler pressure, was 17,250 lb. for the 'Precursor' and 18,630 lb. for the

'Experiment'. The cylinders and valve details were the same, though there would be some variation in the actual valve movements owing to the difference in length of the connecting rods: 7 ft. on the 'Precursor', and 6 ft. 6 in. on the 'Experiment'.

The fundamental difference between the two designs lay, of course, in the boiler. In writing of the 'Precursor', I have emphasised the similarity in boiler proportions between those of the new 4—4—0s and those of the 'Jumbos' and 'Cauli-flowers'. The 'Experiment' boiler, on the other hand, was something quite new, though this would scarcely be appreciated when taking a superficial look at the two engines standing side by side. Unlike his contemporaries on the Caledonian, the North Eastern and the London & South Western, George Whale was not concerned with building a mammoth locomotive. His requirement was a variant of the highly successful 'Precursor' for Northern Division conditions, using as many stan-dard parts and tools as practicable. The 'Experi-ment' has been criticised as a rather half-hearted attempt at a main-line 4—6—0 express locomotive; but actually it was extremely sound in conception and design. In practice, they proved a curious mix-ture of success and near-failure, and the reason for this lay in the design of the boiler.

In producing the compact 4—6—0 version of the 'Precursor' the three pairs of 6 ft. 3 in. coupled

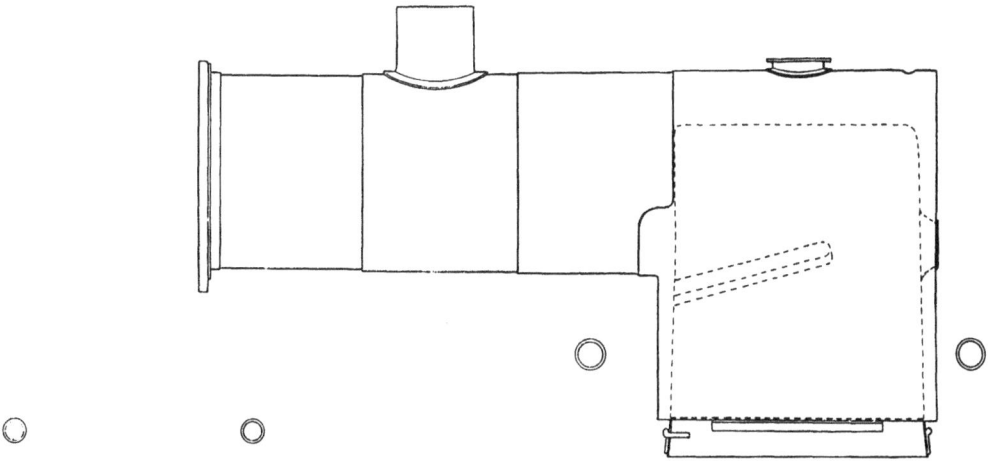

Diagram of 'Precursor' boiler

wheels were pitched at no more than 6 ft. 9½ in. centres. The firebox back-plate was actually ahead of the rearmost pair of coupled wheels, so that the injector, in its usual place on the back of the ashpan, was just ahead of the rear coupled axle. The shape of the firebox was virtually dictated by the position of the coupled axles, and the result was a shallow level grate, with an area of 25 sq. ft. The same flanging blocks as for the 'Precursor' were used, but although the barrel was slightly longer, having a length of 13 ft. 0 in. between the tube plates as against 12 ft. 2¼ in., there was a slight rearrangement of the tubes, giving a total of 279, against the original 309 of the 'Precursor'. A crowding of the tubes can give a large heating surface, but at the

same time nullify the effect by restricting the circulation of the water. In one respect the 'Experiment' boiler might have been expected to be less free in steaming than that of the 'Precursor'. The longer the tubes the less effect the blast in the smokebox has in creating draught in the firebox, and although the difference between 12 ft. 2¼ in. and 13 ft. is not very great, there would be a difference, and on the wrong side.

But the factor that most heavily prejudiced the early performance of the 'Experiments' was the technique needed in firing that very shallow grate. It was something entirely new on the North Western, and involved shooting the coal almost horizontally from the firedoor in order to keep the

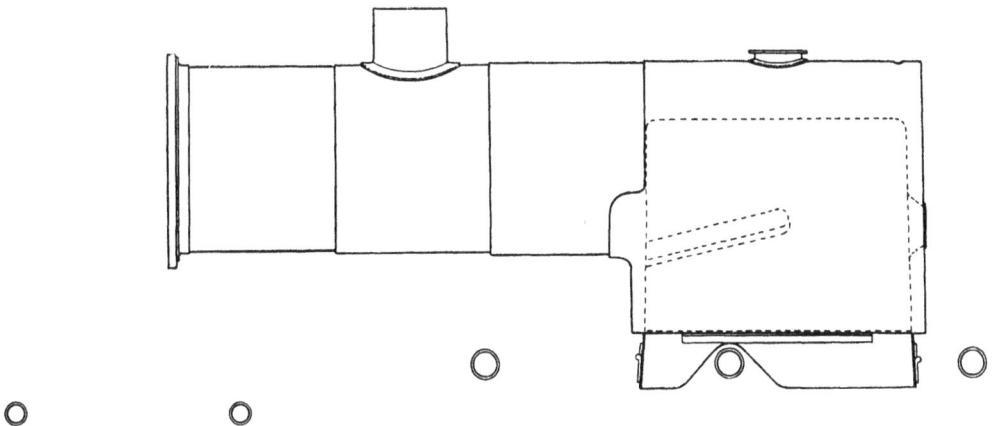

Diagram of 'Experiment' boiler

Down Liverpool express near Kenton: engine No. 1526 'Sanspareil'

front part of the grate covered. Firemen found it difficult to *see* the effects of what they were doing, and they would allow holes to develop in what was, of course, the hottest part of the fire. In course of time they discovered that the most effective way to keep a good, even fire in the forward part of the grate was so to inject the coal that it hit the tube plate and then fell back on to the grate. To do this successfully required a certain knack, and an engineer who was trained at Crewe once made this comment to me: 'The shovel was a long narrow one, with a long handle, and the secret was to bang that shovel, held level, on the firehole doorplate, the while sliding the shank smartly through the guiding hand. Once this had been mastered there was nothing to fear.' It must be admitted, however, that my friend was referring to days when there were not only the 105 'Experiments', but hundreds of the superheated 'Prince of Wales' 4—6—0s running. The knack was a well-known technique on the L.N.W.R. It was very different when the first 'Experiments' came out in 1905; then not even the locomotive inspectors knew the trick, and I do not suppose the men in the drawing office who designed that firebox could give much help either!

The first engine of the class, No. 66, *Experiment*, was completed at Crewe in April 1905, and four more were turned out in June of that year. These were:

306	*Autocrat*
353	*Britannic*
372	*Germanic*
507	*Sarmatian*

At the time these engines were constructed, Crewe was at the very zenith of its production programme with the 'Precursors', and the building of no more than five 'Experiments' gave an opportunity for them to be thoroughly tried out on the Carlisle road before the works began on quantity production. Mr. Whale has been criticised for the choice of name for the pioneer engine, particularly in that it was linked by number as well as name to one of the least successful of Webb's prototypes. Whatever Webb's No. 66 of 1882 may have been, Whale's No. 66 of 1905 was certainly not an 'experiment' in the accepted sense of the term. She was a soundly conceived prototype, sufficiently successful for so tough and practical a railwayman as Whale himself to build 105 of the class, and to provide the foundation for the Bowen-Cooke superheated version of the 'Prince of Wales' class. And, while on the subject of names, those of the four 'Experiments' built in June 1905 all came from scrapped 'Experiment' class compounds except for *Autocrat*, which was originally on a 'Dreadnought'.

The first recorded performance of an 'Experiment' was a very fine one, though perhaps not entirely representative. When Charles Rous-Marten was travelling for professional purposes the railway companies concerned usually put on a special show for him, and on this particular occasion Inspector Adam Brown accompanied the crew on the footplate. The train was the 10 a.m. Scotch express from Euston, conveying portions for both Edinburgh and Glasgow, and it is an interesting commentary upon the train service arrangements of that time that after remarshalling at Crewe the Edinburgh portion left first—a light train worked by a 6 ft. 6 in. 'Jumbo'. Despite division of the train the Glasgow portion, strengthened by the addition of various through carriages, weighed 320 tons, and was hauled by No. 66, *Experiment*. The start from Crewe was very brisk, with speeds of 67 to 70 m.p.h. all the way from Winsford to Weaver Junction, and a top speed of 74 m.p.h. at Moore troughs. Warrington (24 miles) was passed in 25¼ min., Wigan (35¾ miles) in 37 min., and Preston in 54 min. 26 sec. This was good. The next 21 miles on to Lancaster took 23 min. 21 sec., but on coming into the fell country the train encountered some rough weather, with strong side-winds and drizzling rain. Under these conditions, no better minimum speed than 32 m.p.h. could be achieved on Grayrigg bank, although in 1905 such a speed, with a load of 320 tons, would have been thought something exceptional.

Euston—Perth express climbing Shap:
engine No. 1553 'Faraday'

Then it appeared that the first part of the train had got into dire trouble on Shap, for the Glasgow portion was stopped at Tebay—right at the foot of the incline—and held there for no less than 9 min. The time for the 104.1 miles from Crewe to Tebay was 118½ min. start to stop, or just outside the schedule of 117 min. laid down for the ordinary run of the 10 a.m. from Euston. In the circumstances, and having particular regard to the very unfavourable weather, one would have expected to see a rear-end bank engine taken; but *Experiment* was taken up unassisted, and the outcome can best be described in Rous-Marten's own words: 'When we ultimately got away from Tebay it was under the formidable disadvantage of having to start dead on the bank, while the rails were in the worst possible condition, through mist and drizzle, and the side gale was blowing hard. A good deal of preliminary slipping was the unavoidable consequence, but *Experiment* soon regained the mastery, and proceeded to climb the five miles at 1 in 75 in a manner that was decidedly brilliant. Throughout

Engine No. 2027 'Queen Empress'

the whole distance the tendency was for the speed to increase; sometimes it kept at exactly the same point for several successive quarter-miles, then slightly rose, but never once receded. After covering several successive quarter-miles in 33 seconds each, the final two before the summit were done each in 32.6 sec., representing a speed of 27.7 miles an hour. When it is considered that this was achieved from a dead start on the bank, without assistance of pilot or pusher, it will be recognised as very strong testimony to the excellence of Mr. Whale's new locomotive type in respect of hill climbing with a heavy load. Owing to the bad slipping at the outset on the greasy rail, we took 14 min. from the Tebay start to the summit.' To attain and sustain 27½ m.p.h. on a 1 in 75 gradient in such conditions of loading and weather was certainly an outstanding feat, deserving all the praise Rous-Marten gave it.

But then another extraordinary and unexpected facet of 'Experiment' performance was revealed. Rous-Marten goes on to tell how they made a very fast run to Carlisle, covering the 31.4 miles from the summit to the stop in 29 min. 41 sec. With that tantalising vagueness which characterised his writings when he felt it desirable to skate round some particular effort, he commented: 'The speed was sometimes very high. Indeed, the freeness of the running of the six-coupled engine could hardly have been surpassed by any four-coupled or even

Engine No. 2646 'Boniface'

Engine No. 1703 'Princess May', carrying the name formerly borne by a Webb compound. At the time No. 1703 was built, November 1906, 'Princess May' was actually the 'Princess of Wales', and in 1910 became 'Queen Mary'

by a single-wheeler.' But he did not say what the maximum speed was! Some little time later, however, he revealed that it had been $93\frac{1}{2}$ m.p.h., and the next few years were to show that this was by no means a freak performance. Whether the 'Precursors' could have done the same, given their heads, we do not know; but the fact remains that on their own showing the 'Experiments' were the fastest engines yet to run on the L.N.W.R. As far as I can trace, they were the *only* engines ever to reach 90 m.p.h. and over, even including the superheater engines that followed them. I think the 'Claughtons' could have equalled or surpassed those 'Experiment' figures; but so far as I am aware no actual record of more than 88 m.p.h. stands to their credit.

During the summer and autumn of 1905 the five 'Experiments' were almost exclusively on the Carlisle road. They took the Glasgow portion of the 10 a.m. from Euston and the down 'Corridor' (2 p.m. from Euston), and from these two trains the return workings were the 8.42 p.m. and 1 a.m. from Carlisle. They also had the 4.12 p.m. up 'Corridor', probably working north on the sharply-timed morning semi-fast from Crewe in order to pick up this important return working. Despite the enthusiasm of Rous-Marten, that other very experienced and

critical observer, R. E. Charlewood, was not at all impressed. He used to contribute an article to *The Railway Magazine* at the close of each year, commenting upon the train services and locomotive performance of the past summer on the L.N.W.R. Concerning the results from 1905, he wrote: 'It must be admitted that it was thanks to the fast downhill speed, rather than to any wonderful hill-climbing abilities, that the "Experiments" performed the most exacting of their tasks.' The ascent to Shap from the Carlisle side could be just as exacting, even though the maximum steepness of the gradient was not more than 1 in 125. Starting 'cold' from Carlisle, with a fire that could easily be a bit 'green', that ascent could be a laborious affair, as when *Experiment* herself, with 350 tons, on the 8.42 p.m. up took $54\frac{1}{2}$ min. to pass Shap summit, 31.4 miles.

Thirty more 'Experiments' were built at Crewe between January and December 1906, and another ten were added in the autumn of 1907. These forty engines are listed in the table opposite.

With more of these new engines available, some were drafted on to Southern Division duties. On the heaviest trains they were considered 'one coach better' than a 'Precursor', and engine No. 1987, *Glendower*, was allocated to the 'show-piece' of the

Locomotive		Date rebuilt	Previous engines of same name	
565	City of Carlisle .	Jan. 1906	D	
893	City of Chester .	,,	D	
1074	City of Dublin .	,,	D	
1357	City of Edinburgh .	,,	D	
1669	City of Glasgow .	,,	D	
165	City of Lichfield .	Feb. 1906	D	
828	City of Liverpool .	,,	D	
978	City of London .	,,	D	
1405	City of Manchester .	,,	D	
1575	City of Paris . .	,,	D	
1986	Clanricarde .	Sept. 1906	AP	
1987	Glendower .	,,	DX	AP
1988	Hurricane .	,,	AG	
1989	Lady of the Lake .	Oct. 1906	L	DX
1990	North Western .	,,	AG	J66
1991	Palmerston .	,,	L	
1992	President .	,,	Bl	AG
1993	Richard Moon .	,,	GB	
1994	Scottish Chief .	,,	GB	
1995	Tornado .	,,	L	
61	Atalanta .	Nov. 1906	L	AP
222	Ivanhoe .	,,	L	
291	Leander .	,,	L	AP
667	Mazeppa .	,,	L	AP
1304	Prometheus .	,,	L	AP
1676	Prince of Wales* .	,,	L	
1709	Princess May .	,,	GB	
2027	Queen Empress .	,,	GB	
2052	Stephenson .	Dec. 1906	L	AP
2269	William Cawkwell .	,,	GB	
496	Harlequin .	Sept 1907	L	AP
830	Phosphorus .	,,	L	
902	Combermere .	,,	L	
937	Princess Alice .	,,	L	
1014	Henry Bessemer .	,,	GB	
1135	Prince George .	,,	GB	
2112	Victoria .	,,	L	
1361	Prospero .	Oct. 1907	AG	J6
1526	Sanspareil .	,,	J6	
2161	Jeanie Deans .	,,	T	

*renamed Shakespeare in 1911

Engine No. 222 'Ivanhoe', on the Lancashire and Yorkshire line near Kirkham

record of maximum and minimum speeds was made on either journey; but with *Westmorland* the minimum speed at Tring was 50 m.p.h.—a grand effort in itself—and the maximum near Wembley was 75 m.p.h. *Glendower* had a slight signal check approaching Tring, but even with this and the concluding check for permanent way work, a minute was gained upon the schedule time of 87 min. Runs like this amply explain why the locomotive authorities at Crewe were happy enough to build many more 'Experiments' after the earlier batches had been tried out (see page 46).

About this time, some coal trials were carried out between Euston and Crewe comparing the performance of 'Experiments' with 'Precursors'. Both entire line—the 2 p.m. down 'West Coast Corridor' express, as between Euston and Crewe. *Glendower* was shared by two famous Camden drivers, Dave Button and Peter Jarvis, and from 1908 onwards to see that engine turned out for the 'Corridor' was to appreciate the full dignity and majesty of a black engine, and just what the term 'Premier Line' meant in that spacious decade.

By the courtesy of Mr. Eric L. Bell, I am able to include a log of *Glendower's* running on the up 'Corridor', as between Rugby and Willesden, when the load was no less than 440 tons behind the tender. This was a tremendous tonnage for a small non-superheated 4—6—0 around the year 1910; but beside it is an even finer run with the sister engine, No. 1534 *Westmorland*, when an average speed of 56.6 m.p.h. was made with a slightly smaller load of 415 tons. The net average speed with *Glendower* was 55.2 m.p.h. No continuous

Engine No. 353 'Britannic', fitted with bogie shields

THE L.N.W.R. 'PRECURSOR' FAMILY

L.N.W.R. RUGBY—WILLESDEN JUNCTION

Engine No. Engine Name Load tons gross		1534 *Westmorland* 415		1987 *Glendower* 440	
Dist. Miles		Actual m.　s.	Av. Speed m.p.h.	Actual m.　s.	Av. Speed m.p.h.
0.0	RUGBY　.　.　.　.　.	0　00	—	0　00	—
4.3	*Milepost 78¼*　.　.　.　.	8　36	—	8　32	—
7.3	Welton　...　.　:　.　.	12　03	52.2	12　08	50.0
12.9	Weedon　.　.　.　.　.	17　28	62.2	17　42	60.4
19.8	Blisworth　.　.　.　.　.	24　03	62.8	24　34	60.3
22.7	Roade　.　.　.　.　.	27　11	55.5	27　47	54.2
27.8	Castlethorpe　.　.　.　.	31　58	63.9	32　49	60.8
30.2	Wolverton　.　.　.　.　.	34　05	68.2	34　59	66.6
35.9	BLETCHLEY　.　.　.　.	39　55	58.7	40　59	57.0
42.4	Leighton Buzzard　.　.　.	46　50	56.5	47　56	56.1
46.5	Cheddington　.　.　.　.	51　17	55.3	52　25	54.8
—		—	—	sigs.	—
50.9	Tring　.　.　.　.　.	56　27	51.2	57　57	46.7
54.6	Berkhamsted　.　.　.　.	60　27	55.5	62　09	52.9
58.1	Boxmoor　.　.　.　.　.	63　43	64.3	65　35	61.2
61.6	King's Langley　.　.　.	66　51	66.9	68　55	63.1
65.1	WATFORD　.　.　.　.	69　56	68.0	72　10	64.5
66.6	Bushey　.　.　.　.　.	71　18	65.9	73　34	64.3
69.3	Pinner　.　.　.　.　.	73　52	62.3	76　19	58.8
71.2	Harrow　.　.　.　.　.	75　30	69.6	p.w.s.	—
74.5	Wembley　.　.　.　.　.	78　17	71.2	—	—
77.2	WILLESDEN JUNCT.　.　.　.	81　54	—	86　03*	—

*Net time: 83¾ min.

types were expertly handled and the advantage, though slight, seemed to lie with the 'Experiments'. Nevertheless, there was not the same reliability about the working of the six-coupled engines, particularly over Shap, and advantage was frequently taken of the availability of bank engines at Oxenholme. A number of 2—4—0s either of the 6 ft. or 6 ft. 6 in. varieties of 'Jumbos' were set aside for this duty, and the pilots worked through between Oxenholme and Carlisle so as to be available for return workings. Stops at Shap Summit were avoided, and it was in the running of an up express double-headed with a 'Jumbo' and an 'Experiment'

that a maximum of 90 m.p.h. was clocked.

Nevertheless, although the 'Experiments' had not been able to eliminate piloting in the north in the same way as the 'Precursors' had succeeded in the south, they became widely appreciated as a general service passenger engine, and an order for 60 more of them was put in hand at Crewe in the autumn of 1908. This order had barely been started when Mr. Whale retired at the end of 1908, and only the first two engines of the new series had been completed. Whale was succeeded by C. J. Bowen-Cooke, who had previously been Running Superintendent of the Southern Division, with his headquarters at Rugby. In that office he had been in a particularly good position to appreciate the practical working efficiency of the various types of locomotives on the line. Furthermore, unlike Whale, he was not *only* a running man, but an engineer of very wide interests. So one can be fairly sure that if he had harboured any doubts about the usefulness of the 'Experiments' he would have taken early steps to curtail or cancel altogether the locomotives of that large order for 60 which had not been started. It seems certain that Bowen-Cooke was quite content to add this large number of 'Experiments' to the locomotive stock of the L.N.W.R. The names and numbers of these 60 engines are given on page 49.

Down express near Shilton: engine No. 1703
'Northumberland'

The 10 a.m. Euston to Glasgow and Edinburgh express on Bushey troughs, hauled by engine No. 1412 'Bedfordshire'

THE TWO DAY SCOTCH EXPRESSES

The 2 p.m. West Coast 'Corridor' express near Denbigh Hall, Bletchley, hauled by engine No. 1987 'Glendower'

Glasgow portion of the 10 a.m. from Euston passing Shap Summit: engine No. 1357 'City of Edinburgh'

The 2 p.m. 'Corridor' leaving Euston, hauled by engine No. 1987 'Glendower'

SIXTY 'EXPERIMENT' CLASS 4-6-0s
1908–1910

Locomotive			Date built	Names previously borne by	
322	Adriatic	. .	Dec. 1908	T	
884	Greater Britain	.	,,	GB	
887	Fortuna	.	Jan. 1909	L	
1020	Majestic	.	,,	L AP DX	
1483	Red Gauntlet	.	,,	L	
1490	Wellington	.	,,	L	AP
1553	Faraday	.	,,	J66	
1571	Herschel	.	,,	J66	
2076	Pheasant	.	,,	J6	
2116	Greystoke	.	,,	J6	AG
2621	Ethelred	.	Feb. 1909	L	
2622	Eunomia	.	,,	L	
2623	Lord of the Isles	.	,,	L	
2624	Saracen	.	,,	L	AP
2625	Buckland	.	,,	J66	
2626	Chillington	.	,,	AG J66	
2627	President Lincoln	.	Mar. 1909	J66	
2628	Banshee	.	,,	AP DX J6	
2629	Terrier	.	,,	AG DX J6	
2630	Buffalo	.	,,	DX J66	
1406	George Findlay	.	April 1909	GB	
1413	Henry Cort	.	,,	JH	P
1477	Hugh Myddleton	.	May 1909	JH	
1498	Thomas Savery	.	,,	JH	
1566	John Penn	.	,,	JH	
1603	Princess Alexandra	.	,,	L	
1649	Sisyphus	.	,,	J66	
1661	Wordsworth	.	,,	AG J66	
1781	Lightning	.	,,	AP J66	
2022	Marlborough	.	,,	J66	
2637	Babylon	.	June 1909	New name	
2638	Byzantium	.	,,	,,	
2639	Bactria	.	,,	,,	
2640	Belisarius	.	,,	,,	
2641	Bellona	.	,,	,,	
2642	Berenice	.	,,	,,	
2643	Bacchus	.	,,	,,	
2644	Berengaria	.	,,	,,	
2645	Britomart	.	July 1909	,,	
2646	Boniface	.	,,	,,	
1412	Bedfordshire	.	Nov. 1909	,,	
1418	Cheshire	.	,,	,,	
1420	Derbyshire	.	,,	,,	
1455	Herefordshire	.	,,	,,	
1611	Hertfordshire	.	,,	,,	
1616	Lancashire	.	,,	,,	
1624	Leicestershire	.	,,	,,	
1652	Middlesex	.	,,	,,	
1689	Monmouthshire	.	Dec. 1909	,,	
1703	Northumberland	.	,,	,,	
71	Oxfordshire	.	,,	,,	
275	Shropshire	.	,,	,,	
677	Staffordshire	.	,,	,,	
1002	Warwickshire	.	,,	,,	
1534	Westmorland	.	,,	,,	
1471	Worcestershire	.	Jan. 1910	,,	
1561	Yorkshire	.	,,	,,	
1618	Carnarvonshire	.	,,	,,	
1621	Denbighshire	.	,,	,,	
1658	Flintshire	.	,,	,,	

The first 30 of these new engines mostly took their names from 'Lady of the Lake' class singles which were being scrapped at the time, but more significantly from 'Jumbos' of both the 6 ft. and 6 ft. 6 in. varieties. It was indeed a sign of the times that some of these splendid little engines had started to go to the scrap-heap. But the names of the last 30 'Experiments' were all new. At last, it seemed, the rate of new construction was outstripping the rate of scrapping. In connection with engines 2637 to 2646, all of which had names commencing with 'B', there were three fine names of old that might have been revived at this time: *Basilisk, Baronet* and *Briareus*. They were last used on 'Bloomers'; but they disappeared completely from the L.N.W.R. list when those engines were scrapped.

By that time, the early difficulties in handling them seem to have been mastered, and in 1909 and 1910 they were doing a good deal of solid reliable work. Like the 'Precursors', they worked very high weekly mileages. The first comprehensive set of data on which their day-to-day performances could be assessed was published in *The Railway Magazine* by Cecil J. Allen. At the time when Bowen-Cooke succeeded to the chieftainship at Crewe, Allen was travelling frequently on the Glasgow portion of the 10 a.m. from Euston between Crewe and Carlisle. This train then had a fairly smart timing of 159 min. for the 141-mile run, with 127 min. to pass Shap Summit, 109.6 miles. The minimum load was one of seven coaches, representing a gross load of about 205 tons behind the tender. This gave no difficulties, but it was frequently increased. The normal formation included a through carriage from Birmingham to Glasgow, and at times of heavy traffic that 'carriage' often consisted of a train in itself, with its own dining car. The 'Experiments' took up to ten coaches successfully on this booking; but with 11 it was usually the practice to provide pilot assistance. The 2 p.m. 'Corridor' from Euston was much harder. It conveyed a minimum load of about 370 tons from

Engine No. 2638 'Byzantium', at Willesden

49

Crewe to Preston, and 305 tons onwards to Carlisle. Its running time was 163 min., which, if allowance is made for stopping and restarting at Preston, was equivalent to a non-stop run in 161 min.

On six runs with the morning express from Crewe, in all cases non-stop to Carlisle and taking no assistance at any point, the following performances are on record.

Engine (No. and Name	Load tons	Actual time m. s.	Net time min.
978 *City of London*	205	155 00	154
1676 *Prince of Wales**	205	162 45	155
1534 *Westmorland* .	205	155 50	155¾
1020 *Majestic* .	285	158 10	158¼
565 *City of Carlisle*	285	162 35	159¼
887 *Fortuna* . .	310	156 45	156¾

* Afterwards renamed *Shakespeare*

It is perhaps significant, however, that not one of the six engines, even on the more lightly loaded trains, kept the booked point-to-point time from Carnforth up to Shap Summit. This train was allowed 39 min. for that heavily adverse length of 31.4 miles, and on the six runs mentioned above, in order, the times were: 39 min. 50 sec., 42 min., 42 min., 45 min. 5 sec., 46 min. 35 secs., and 46 min. 55 sec. The fifth run included a permanent way slack intermediately, but all the other runs were unchecked. On the last of the six runs *Fortuna*

126¾ min. The run then finished with a fast descent to Carlisle, including a maximum speed of 86½ m.p.h. The detailed log of this interesting journey is discussed in the next chapter.

To see 'Experiment' performance in its true perspective it is interesting to study three runs on the 5.19 p.m. from Crewe (the 2 p.m. from Euston). It is to some extent taking the story out of chronological order by introducing comparisons with the work of the Bowen-Cooke superheater engines; but when the *George the Fifth* and the *Prince of Wales* were introduced they were the pride of the line, and very closely watched and nursed locomotives. I shall have a great deal to say about them in later chapters; but here I am comparing their work on this most celebrated of Scotch expresses with that of an 'Experiment', and all three engines were hauling very heavy trains. The logs are below, as between Crewe and Preston.

A study of these figures shows that there was very little in it, and in continuing from Preston, with reduced loads of 330, 330 and 340 tons, the three engines passed Lancaster, 21 miles, in 24 min. 20 sec., 23 min. 25 sec., and 24 min. exactly. The real difference came on the mountain section, where the 'Experiment' stopped for a pilot at Oxenholme, whereas the two superheater engines went up not only unassisted, but at considerably higher speeds than were usual with the 'Experiments' on 200-ton trains. In 1909 and 1910 the 'Experiments' were to be set the toughest tasks in their careers, and an analysis of these runs, together with some further

Engine No.				353	819*	2663*
Engine Name				*Britannic*	*Prince of Wales*	*George the Fifth*
Class				(Exp.)	—	—
Load tons full				400	400	410
Dist. Miles			Sch. min.	Actual m. s.	Actual m. s.	Actual m. s.
0.0	CREWE . . .		0	0 00	0 00	0 00
4.8	Minshull Vernon			8 40	8 15	8 40
11.8	Hartford . . .			16 00	14 45	15 35
18.8	Preston Brook .			22 45	22 00	22 25
24.0	WARRINGTON . .		26	28 05	27 10	27 30
31.0	Golborne . . .			35 50	35 10	36 00
35.8	WIGAN . . .		40	41 20	40 30	41 40
41.6	Coppull . . .			50 20	49 00	49 50
50.9	PRESTON . . .		59	60 00	59 20	59 55

*Superheater engines

made her fast overall time by remarkable running as far as Carnforth and, by covering the 78.2 miles from Crewe to the former point in 79¾ min., she was 8¼ min. early on commencing the climb to Shap. Practically all this time in hand was lost by a very slow ascent, and the Summit was passed in

runs in ordinary service, are made in the next chapter. Under the stimulus of severe competition, and handled by men of exceptional keenness and skill, there is no doubt that these engines did very well. It is equally certain that they were performances well above average.

'Pride of the line': engine No. 1987 'Glendower' at Euston, with Driver Peter Jarvis on the footplate

The nameplate of No. 372 during World War I, with 'Germanic' defaced in red, and 'Belgic' superimposed

Engine No. 1471 'Worcestershire' photographed at Laira sheds, Plymouth, after working the
G.W.R. 'Cornish Riviera Express' in August 1910

CHAPTER 5

INTERCHANGE TRIALS

IN locomotive history there is no more fascinating subject than a study of tests of one design against another. If it were a case of straight scientific trials, as conducted by the British Railways Board in the last days of steam, much of the sporting and human interest would be lost; but on the London & North Western Railway in 1909 and 1910 the circumstances were very different. In those years Crewe locomotives were involved in five distinct sets of interchange trials, and while three of these were carefully engineered by Mr. Bowen-Cooke, as part of his widespread investigations towards the future standard motive power of the L.N.W.R., the other two were arranged at the request of other railway companies to help settle domestic problems of their own. The five interchange trials were:

was concerned centred upon the work of the 'Experiments'. There is no doubt that the writings of Rous-Marten and R. E. Charlewood in *The Railway Magazine* had not placed these engines generally in a favourable light. The success of the 'Precursors' had been so absolute that the evident shortcomings of the 'Experiments' on certain occasions tended to give a somewhat distorted view of the position as a whole. The only interchange trial with an 'Experiment' that Bowen-Cooke himself engineered was that with the Caledonian, comparing the Crewe engine with a much larger and nominally more powerful inside-cylinder 4—6—0, using a boiler pressure of 200 lb. per sq. in., and with Stephenson's link motion against Joy's radial gear. The 'Cardean' class 4—6—0s were then non-

Year	Competing Rly. Co.	L.N.W.R. Loco. Type	Rival Loco. Type	Routes worked
1909	G.N.R.	'Precursor'	Large 'Atlantic'	Euston—Crewe Kings X—Doncaster
1909	L.B.S.C.R.	'Precursor'	Marsh 'I3' Tank	Rugby—Brighton
1909	Caledonian	'Experiment'	'Cardean'	Crewe—Carlisle Carlisle—Glasgow
1909	N.B.R.	'Experiment'	Reid 'Atlantic'	Preston—Carlisle
1910	G.W.R.	'Experiment'	Non-superheater 'Star'	Euston—Crewe Paddington—Plymouth

The 'Precursors', No. 412, *Marquis,* on the Great Northern, and No. 7, *Titan,* in running the 'Sunny South Special' throughout from Rugby to Brighton had a relatively easy passage and, as recorded in Chapter 3, both *Marquis* and the engine running against the visiting G.N. 'Atlantic' between Euston and Crewe—No. 510, *Albatross*—showed up quite well in coal consumption against the much larger Doncaster locomotive. But in these exchange trials most of the interest so far as the L.N.W.R.

superheated, with slide valves.

The trial against the North British 'Atlantic' was, one gathers, intended as a 'show up' of the inadequacies of Reid's huge new locomotives which, when non-superheated, were not an unqualified success. On the Waverley route, with loads above 250 tons or so, they needed double-heading, and the North British management would have liked to have had a North Western engine and worked it between Carlisle and Edinburgh. But as the L.N.W.R. load-

The G.N.R. Atlantic No. 1449 leaving Euston with the 10 a.m. Scotch express

A LOCOMOTIVE EXCHANGE OF 1909

The 'Precursor' No. 412 'Marquis' leaving King's Cross with the 1.30 p.m. Leeds express

ing gauge was higher than that of the North British, there was not enough clearance to permit an 'Experiment' to run and, instead, a North British 'Atlantic' was set to run between Carlisle and Preston, so that its performance on Shap could be observed. This trial took place on special trains in a single day. Both engines made one return trip from Carlisle to Preston and back, with a train of 290 tons. The result, not unexpectedly, was a 'walk-over' for the 'Experiment'. She was hauling a train below her normal maximum load, was a picked engine, and had a driver and fireman who were thoroughly familiar with the road. The North British men had never been over the line before, and even with a pilotman they were at a disadvantage and used far more coal than the 'Experiment'. From the North Western locomotive point of view the event had no significance; it had been arranged to oblige the management of a friendly neighbour.

The 'Experiment' trials against Caledonian and Great Western locomotives were a very different matter, and before discussing the results it will help to place them in perspective if the finest standards of 'Experiment' performance in ordinary service on the L.N.W.R. are analysed first. To begin with, I have tabulated the very fine run clocked by Cecil J. Allen on the Glasgow portion of the 10 a.m. from Euston, with engine No. 887, *Fortuna*, between Crewe and Carlisle.

Up Scotch express near Tebay; engines 2643 'Bacchus' and 561 'Antaeus'

The start was remarkable, with a top speed of $77\frac{1}{2}$ m.p.h. descending Preston Brook bank, and although the minimum speed after Wigan is not quoted in the original record it cannot have fallen much, if anything, below 40 m.p.h. on Boars Head bank to give such an average as 48.6 m.p.h. from Wigan to Coppull. Preston was passed at the usual very slow speed, and this is clearly reflected in the slow average onwards to Barton. But then there followed some unusually fast running on the level towards Lancaster, with a sustained speed of 67 m.p.h. Careful attention was paid to the 50 m.p.h. at Lancaster Old Junction, and a flying attack was made on the ascent to Shap. But, having passed Carnforth $8\frac{1}{4}$ min. early, the driver and fireman justifiably took things easily on the climb. The minimum speeds were $30\frac{1}{4}$ m.p.h. on Grayrigg bank and $21\frac{1}{4}$ m.p.h. on Shap. Although these figures cannot be described as poor for a relatively small non-superheated 4—6—0 hauling a load of 310 tons, the uphill schedules of the L.N.W.R. in those days were such that almost 8 min. were lost between Carnforth and Shap Summit. Then came a fast descent to Carlisle, with a top speed of $86\frac{1}{2}$ m.p.h.

With loads of about 300 tons, the times made by *Fortuna* on this trip were little below the 'Experiment' average and, considered in relation to gradient and the dimensions of the locomotives concerned, they must be regarded as quite good. There were very few locomotive types in Great Britain at that time that would have done as well, even though many of these were much larger and heavier than the 'Experiments'. But the North Western set its own standards of hill-climbing, and the fact remains that in ordinary service there is not a single case on record of an 'Experiment' keeping the point-to-point time of 39 min. from Carnforth to Shap Summit, with the 10 a.m. from Euston, or, unassisted, the 42 min. of the 2 p.m. It may be argued that the bookings of these trains

L.N.W.R. 1.12 p.m. CREWE—CARLISLE
Load: 44 axles, 310 tons full
Engine: 4-6-0 No. 887 *Fortuna*

Dist. miles		Sch. min.	Actual m. s.	Av. speed m.p.h.
0.0	CREWE . . .	0	0 00	—
4.8	Minshull Vernon .		7 55	36.4
11.8	Hartford . .		14 00	69.0
18.8	Preston Brook .		19 55	71.0
24.0	WARRINGTON .	27	24 20	70.7
31.0	Golborne . .		31 10	61.6
35.8	WIGAN . . .	40	36 00	59.7
41.6	Coppull . .		43 10	48.6
50.9	PRESTON . .	58	52 05	62.6
55.7	Barton . .		58 50	42.7
63.6	Scorton . .		66 15	64.0
71.9	LANCASTER . .	81	74 10	63.0
78.2	CARNFORTH . .	88	79 50	66.8
85.5	Milnthorpe .		88 00	53.7
91.0	Oxenholme . .	101	95 25	44.5
98.1	Grayrigg . .		108 35	32.4
104.1	Tebay . .	117	115 25	52.8
109.6	*Shap Summit* .	127	126 45	29.1
111.6	Shap . . .		129 30	43.7
123.1	PENRITH . .	141	139 50	66.8
130.2	Calthwaite . .		146 45	61.7
136.1	Wreay . .		151 40	72.0
141.0	CARLISLE . .	159	156 45	60.2

were uneven, as witnessed by *Fortuna's* spectacular gain on time from Crewe to Carnforth. It is not without significance that in more recent times, during the heyday of the 'Royal Scots', the same train was allowed 89 min. to pass Carnforth, and then 43 min. up to Shap Summit. A comparison of the times of *Fortuna* with two other good 'Experiment' runs enables us to assess something of the optimum capacity of these engines in climbing from Carnforth to Shap Summit.

in the height of the chimney and dome, and in the width across the eaves of the cab. This latter dimension was not greater than that of the largest Caledonian express locomotives, but the width occurred at a greater height. One can be fairly sure that J. F. McIntosh would have taken advantage of any extra height allowable in such engines as the 'Cardean' class 4—6—0s; but the height from rail to top of chimney in these latter engines was 12 ft. 11 in., against 13 ft. 6 in. on the 'Experi-

Engine No.						1020	887	2116
Engine Name						*Majestic*	*Fortuna*	*Greystoke*
Load tons gross						285	310	340
Dist. miles						m. s.	m. s.	m. s.
0.0	Carnforth	.	.	.	.	0 00*	0 00*	0 00*
7.3	Milnthorpe	.	.	.	.	7 35	8 10	7 31
12.8	Oxenholme	.	.	.	.	14 55	15 35	14 28
19.9	Grayrigg	.	.	.	.	27 55	28 45	26 01
25.9	Tebay	.	.	.	.	34 55	35 35	33 05
31.4	Shap Summit	.	.	.	.	45 05	46 55	44 18
Min. speeds: m.p.h.:	Grayrigg	.	.	.		30½	30¼	33¼
	Shap	.	.	.		23½	21¼	20¼
Average speed:	Carnforth—Summit	.		.		41.7	40.1	42.5

*Times from passing Carnforth at 65–70 m.p.h.

The performance of *Greystoke* on the 2 p.m. from Euston was perhaps rather exceptional. The 'Experiments' usually took the pilot from Oxenholme with loads of this magnitude, but on the other hand the ascent of Grayrigg bank was the finest of all. The average speeds of the three engines from Oxenholme to Grayrigg work out at 32.3, 31.9, and 36.3 m.p.h., and it is evident that *Greystoke* was developing about 900 equivalent drawbar horsepower at Grayrigg summit. Having regard to *Fortuna's* tremendous sprint from Crewe to Carnforth, and *Greystoke's* hill-climbing ability as displayed on so difficult a train as the down 'Corridor', the performance characteristics of the 'Experiments' must be considered as thoroughly satisfactory—due regard being paid to their size and weight.

The capacity of these engines for heavy sustained hill-climbing was tested very severely in the exchange with the Caledonian Railway in 1909. No details are available as to how engine No. 1405, *City of Manchester*, did between Carlisle and Glasgow, and at this stage in history there must be very considerable doubt as to whether No. 1405 ever *did* run on the Caledonian. Her going north was certainly reported in the railway press at the time, but her profile, in cross-section, seriously encroaches upon the Caledonian loading gauge both

ments'. The profile of the L.N.W.R. engine in relation to the Caledonian loading gauge is shown in the diagram on page 56. In view of the encroachment, it would seem most unlikely that the civil engineer would have permitted an 'Experiment' to run to Glasgow.

On the L.N.W.R. line No. 2630, *Buffalo*, did some grand work. On the 12.58 p.m. up from Carlisle, with tare loads of 360 tons, both this engine and the Caledonian 4—6—0, *Cardean*, were set the somewhat staggering task of passing Shap Summit in 47 min. from Carlisle, inclusive of a 5 min. stop at Penrith. This was a normal requirement of the timetable, albeit not usually with so heavy a load; but on July 6, 1909 with *Cardean*, and on July 9, 1909 with *Buffalo*, all-out attempts were made to keep time with maximum load trains. With larger cylinders and a much larger boiler, *Cardean* naturally had the better of it; but *Buffalo* nevertheless produced what was probably the maximum ever from an 'Experiment'. Here, again, I am indebted to the late Sir William Stanier, who had a search made among the old records, from which I have 'reconstructed' the log in order to make some assessment of the power output involved. In brief, *Buffalo* climbed the 17.9 miles from Carlisle to Penrith in 24¾ min. start to stop, and then went on to pass Shap Summit, 13.6 miles driven and fired, they could do splendid work uphill; that they could also run very fast was demonstrated from the outset by Rous-Marten's experience with engine No. 66. It is nevertheless true that, taken all round, the 'Experiments' did not get off to a very good start, and this shaky reputation remained with them.

So we come to the momentous interchange trial with the Great Western Railway in the summer of 1910. Bowen-Cooke was a close student of foreign locomotive practice, and the results of the locomotive exchanges of 1909 had certainly confirmed his belief in the advantage to be gained from high-degree superheating, on the lines advocated by Dr. Schmidt. The early results from the first North Western superheater engine, the *George the Fifth*, were phenomenal; but for the future top-line motive power of the L.N.W.R. Bowen-Cooke was looking a great deal further than merely superheated versions of the 'Precursors' and the 'Experiments'. At the same time he had to watch the factor of dead weight on the track, because the civil engineer, like most of his contemporaries, was loath to sanction any appreciable increase over existing standards. Bowen-Cooke, in the meantime, had been very impressed with the performance of the Maffei 4-cylinder compound 4—6—0s then working in Bavaria, particularly in their beautiful riding, and absence of hammer-blow due to all four cylinders driving on the one axle. He hoped that by designing

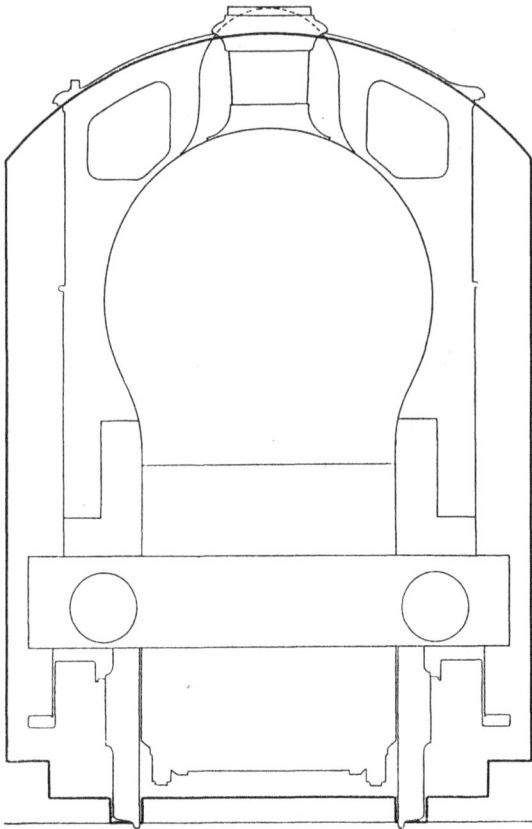

Profile of 'Experiment' class 4-6-0, with Caledonian loading gauge superimposed

from the restart, in 19¾ min. *Cardean's* times were 23½ and 18½ min. respectively.

The accompanying log shows my reconstruction of the work of *Buffalo* on that memorable ninth of July. From this it seems clear that a speed of about 43 m.p.h. must have been sustained continuously on the 1 in 125 gradient between Clifton and Shap Summit, and this would have needed the output, tremendous for a locomotive of the size of an 'Experiment', of 1,260 equivalent drawbar horsepower. The engine was clearly not exhausted by this effort, for she was taken pell-mell down to Carnforth to recover the slight amount of time that had been inevitably lost in the ascent. The total running time of 74 min. from Carlisle to Carnforth was a magnificent piece of 'Experiment' running, including as it did the effects of slowing down and stopping at so critical a point as Penrith. Taken together, the work of *Britannic* described in the preceding chapter, and that of *Fortuna, Greystoke* and *Buffalo*, is enough to establish the 'Experiments' as very worthy northern counterparts of the 'Precursors'. There is no doubt that, when expertly

L.N.W.R. 12.58 p.m. CARLISLE—PRESTON

Load: 362 tons tare, 385 tons full
Engine: 4–6–0 No. 2630 *Buffalo*

Dist. Miles			Sch. min.	Actual m. s.	Sp'ds. m.p.h.
0.0	CARLISLE	. .	0	0 00	—
1.4	*No. 13 Box*	. .		3 10	—
4.9	Wreay	. .		8 55	36.5
13.1	Plumpton	. .		19 25	46.8
17.9	PENRITH	. .	24	24 45	
1.1	*Eamont Jct.*	. .		3 00	—
3.3	Milepost 48	. .		5 55	45.3
4.3	,, 47	. .		7 12	46.7
5.3	,, 46	. .		8 31	45.6
6.3	,, 45	. .		9 52	44.4
7.3	,, 44	. .		11 14	43.9
8.3	,, 43	. .		12 37	43.4
9.3	,, 42	. .		14 21	42.9
10.3	,, 41	. .		15 25	42.9
11.5	Shap	. .		17 10	44.4
13.5	*Shap Summit*	. .	18	19 45	46.3
19.0	Tebay	. .	24	25 00	62.9
32.0	Oxenholme	. .	38	37 45	61.2
44.9	CARNFORTH	. .	51	49 15	67.3
51.2	LANCASTER	. .	58	56 30	52.1
—			—	sigs.	
72.2	PRESTON	. .	80	83 45	

The 1910 Locomotive Exchange: G.W.R. 4-6-0 No. 4005 'Polar Star' leaving Euston, with the 12.10 p.m. Liverpool and Manchester express

a locomotive devoid of all hammer-blow, he would be permitted to use a greater dead weight. After all, the ultimate effect of a locomotive upon the track and bridges is a combination of static and dynamic loading.

Then at this interesting point in L.N.W.R. locomotive history there came a request, from the Great Western Railway of all companies, for an interchange trial between non-superheater 4-6-0s. It is most important that the background to the trials of August 1910 should be clearly understood, because a great deal of nonsense has been written about the event. Some writers, jumping to quite unwarranted conclusions, have assumed that it was a continuation of the policy of holding interchange trials in the previous summer by Mr. Bowen-Cooke and have written as though that very eminent engineer was a simpleton who believed an 'Experiment' could compete on level terms with a Great Western 'Star', and had issued a 'challenge' accordingly. I need not dwell here upon the serious and acrimonious discussions among the higher management of the G.W.R. that had goaded Churchward into asking for this interchange trial. For his part, Bowen-Cooke was very interested to have a 'Star' at work between Euston and Crewe for a fortnight, because it was the nearest English

equivalent to the big 4-cylinder 4—6—0 that he himself was planning. But one doubts if the railway political implications were fully appreciated at Crewe. If they had been, it is most unlikely that the trials would ever have taken place.

Churchward was being severely criticised from within the G.W.R. management for the high cost of his 4—6—0 locomotives. Some inside information had reached Paddington about the cost of the 'Experiments', which were very much cheaper to build than the 'Stars'. Churchward's object in asking for the exchange was to show his board how very much better than the 'Experiments' his engines were, and it was arranged for the trials to take place in the heaviest traffic period of the whole year —a fortnight in mid-August. Quite apart from any questions of train loads or engine capacity, there was no comparison between the relative difficulty of the duties chosen for test purposes. On the North Western it was nothing more than a straightforward spin up and down the main line between Euston and Crewe. One could scarcely imagine an easier road for a stranger to learn; there were no fewer than *five* sets of water troughs in the distance of 158 miles, and the average speeds of the trains worked did not exceed 55 m.p.h.

On the Great Western the visiting driver had to

Engine No. 1471 'Worcestershire', at Exeter, after working the 11.50 a.m. 'Torquay diner' from Paddington

work over no less than 300 miles of strange route. The programme included the working of a two-hour Bristol express, in addition to such onerous tasks as the down 'Cornish Riviera', and the 11.50 a.m. 'Torquay Diner', as that train was then popularly known. The main line to Bristol is straightforward enough; but the shortened route to the west, including the winding length of the Berks and Hants line, the heavy slacks at Westbury and Frome, Whiteball bank and, finally, the extraordinary curves and gradients of the South Devon line, was a tough enough proposition for the regular men with locomotives of ample power, let alone for a strange driver 'up against it' in more senses than one. A handicap that was appreciated from the start of the preliminary runs was the spacing of the water troughs. On the North Western, from the start of a run from Euston to Crewe, the first troughs came no more than $15\frac{1}{2}$ miles out, and the intervals between successive sets were then 39, $28\frac{1}{2}$, $29\frac{1}{2}$, and 35 miles. On the Great Western, the first set came at Aldermaston, 44 miles out, and the subsequent intervals were 52 (to Westbury) and 40 to Cogload. On a non-stop run to Plymouth, there was only one set in the very difficult 87 miles from Cogload to North Road—those between Exminster and Starcross.

In any steam locomotive working, nothing can cause greater anxiety, or give rise to a feeling of greater frustration, than to be short of water. This was brought home to me more vividly perhaps than at any other time when I was riding on the footplate on a hard northcountry job, and first one, and then the second injector failed. We had stopped to report our plight, and while the fireman was away at the signal-box telephone the driver said: 'It's a *terrible* thing when you can't get water into the boiler'; and the emphasis he put on that one

word 'terrible' spoke more than pages of technical description. Then in the 1910 exchanges, there was another factor which should not really have arisen. Camden shed was instructed to send an 'Experiment' to Old Oak Common. The issues at stake were certainly not communicated to the shed foreman, and at the height of the summer traffic he sent the engine he could best spare! This was No. 1471, *Worcestershire*. She was new out of the shops in January 1910, and by August she had run something like 45,000 miles. She was far from a specially selected engine, and was not even in the first flight of Camden express engines. And with all the disadvantages of water supply and route, this was the engine which was to compete against the flower of the G.W.R.!

Now North Western men would not in the ordinary way have blinked an eyelid at having to work a fast, important train with a high-mileage engine. They would set their teeth, roar and rattle along, and get there on time. But you can't 'roar' if you are running short of water, and the hapless driver and fireman on *Worcestershire* had to make various out-of-course stops for water. On the West of England trains they had to stop at Savernake on the down journey, and on one up working they were piloted throughout from Exeter to Savernake. Naturally, there was considerable loss of time. This suited Churchward's purpose admirably, because the competing G.W.R. engine—the celebrated No. 4003, *Lode Star*—was punctual on all her trains throughout the test period. But despite their unhappy position, the driver and fireman of *Worcestershire* never gave up, and on their last journey they had so mastered the technique of running over the West of England main line as to be able to make a non-stop run from Paddington to Exeter, with the 11.50 a.m. 'Torquay Diner'. The

G.W.R. 11.50 a.m. PADDINGTON—EXETER

Engine: L.N.W.R. 4—6—0 No. 1471 *Worcestershire*
Load: to Westbury 385 tons tare, 415 tons full
to Taunton 357 tons tare, 385 tons full
to Exeter 250 tons tare, 270 tons full

Dist. Miles		Sch. min.	Actual min.	Av. Sp. m.p.h.
0.0	PADDINGTON.	0	0	—
9.1	Southall	11	12½	43½
18.5	Slough	20	23	54
24.2	Maidenhead	25½	29	57
31.0	Twyford	31½	36¼	56½
36.0	READING	37	41½	57
53.1	Newbury	56	62	50
70.1	Savernake	73½	82	51½
95.6	WESTBURY (Slip)	97½	107½	60
108.5	*Milepost 122¾*		125½	43
115.3	Castle Cary	120	132½	58½
137.9	*Cogload Jnc.*	144	155	60½
142.9	TAUNTON (Slip)	149	160½	54½
153.8	*Whiteball Box*		175	45¼
173.7	EXETER	180	193½	64½

accompanying log of the run was given to me by the late C. B. Collett, when he was Chief Mechanical Engineer of the Great Western Railway. This log deserves close study because it clearly reveals the technique of the driver in his successful attempt to get through to Exeter non-stop.

His immediate start out of Paddington with the 415-ton train was splendid; but then, on dead level track, the average speed from Southall to Reading was no more than 55½ m.p.h. This was not up to normal 'Experiment' standards, let alone representative of the work of men who had the honour of the L.N.W.R. in their hands. Obviously they had their eyes on Aldermaston troughs, to top right up, and have enough water to climb to Savernake satisfactorily. *Worcestershire* lost 6 min. on schedule out to Newbury, and really did not do badly at all to make an average speed of 51½ m.p.h. from there up to Savernake. Then one could imagine a North

Western man really giving the engine her head, down to Westbury. Here was a stretch where an 'Experiment' could 'fly' to some purpose, displaying its traditional swiftness on favourable stretches of line; but still more time was lost, probably because the engine was being worked under the easiest of steam to conserve water supply. At Westbury, the load was reduced to 358 tons, and some considerably harder running followed. Only a single minute was lost on schedule in the 42.3 miles from Westbury to Cogload Junction, and then, with a load still further reduced to 270 tons by slipping a portion at Taunton, there came a splendid finish. Speed can have been little, if anything, below 30 m.p.h. at Whiteball summit, and there was some very fast running down to Exeter, with speeds of 75 to 80 m.p.h. sustained over much of the distance between Tiverton Junction and Stoke Canon. Nevertheless, the arrival at Exeter was 13½ min. late, and once again the G.W.R. partisans had every reason to rejoice.

In view of the manifest difficulties that prevailed throughout on the footplate, the overall average speed of 54 m.p.h. from Paddington to Exeter was a magnificent achievement, and one I feel has never been accorded the recognition it deserves. At the time, a most extraordinary statement was published by the Rev. W. J. Scott, in *The Railway Magazine*, to the effect that on arrival at Exeter 'the engine was found to be badly strained'. Now Scott was in the confidence of many of the high officials of the G.W.R., and may have been told exactly what was wrong; but I cannot think it could have been anything mechanical, or the driver would never have run as he did between Taunton and Exeter. She may have developed a hot bearing somewhere, though such troubles were few and far between with the Whale engines. The most likely explanation is leaky tubes. Another account read: 'Throughout the test weeks the "Experiment" had to be flogged unmercifully in the attempt to keep

'Polar Star' on the 10 a.m. Scotch express at
Bushey troughs

'Worcestershire' leaving Paddington on the
11.50 'Torquay diner'

The new L.N.W.R. dynamometer car of 1908

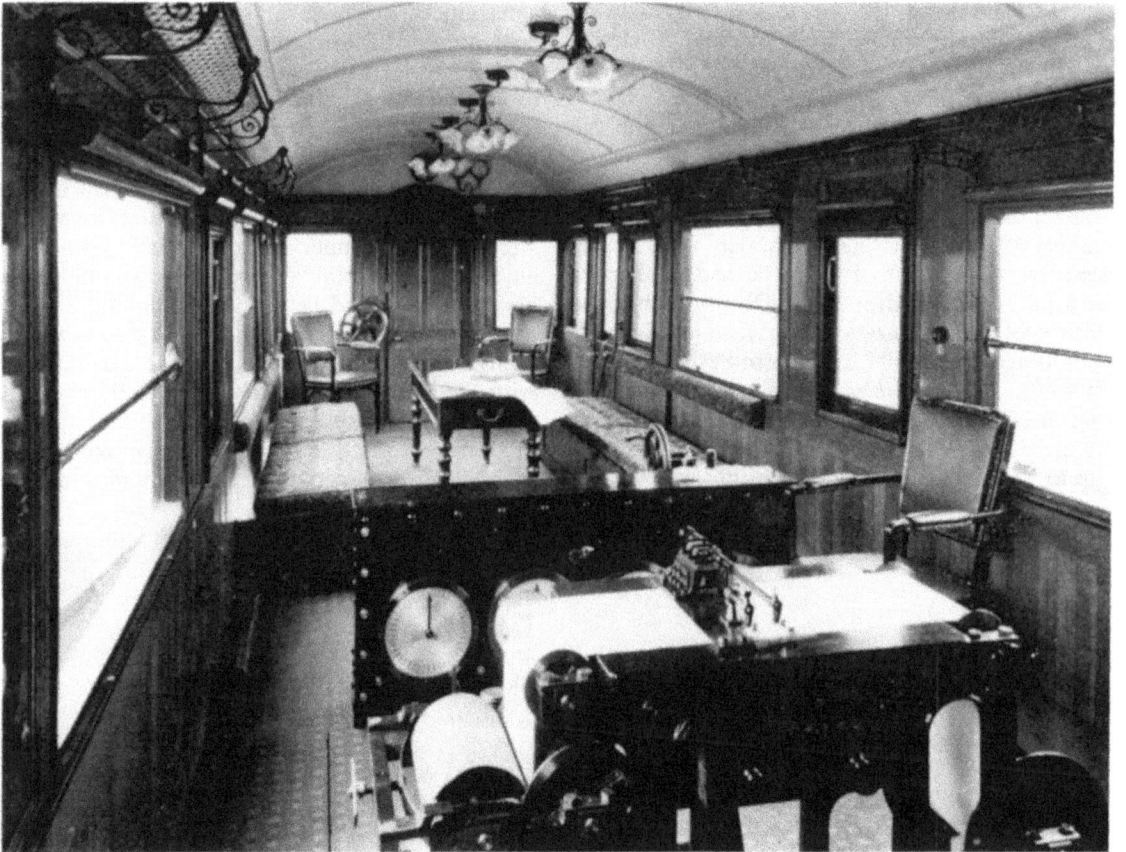

Interior of the new dynamometer car showing the integrator apparatus in the foreground

'Marquis' at full speed on the Great Northern Railway near Potters Bar

The G.N.R. Atlantic No. 1449 working down to Crewe on a Sunday morning train at Bushey

time; her coal consumption was tremendous; and finally she returned to Crewe in a badly strained condition.' Such an assessment is certainly not borne out by the facts of her last and most successful run. What 'Experiments' could do when they were *really* flogged is shown by the tremendous effort of No. 2630, *Buffalo,* on the 12.58 p.m. from Carlisle to Preston, described earlier in this chapter.

Unfortunately, the daily press became interested in this interchange trial, and as it was the holiday season, when there was little in the way of ordinary news to report, some newspapers 'splashed' the results, with much colourful comment, to the great disadvantage of the L.N.W.R. The irony of it was that just as *Worcestershire* was not a top flight representative of the 'Experiment' class, neither were the 'Experiments' themselves representative of Crewe's best at that time. In July 1910, the first L.N.W.R. superheater engine, No. 2663, *George*

the Fifth, had been completed at Crewe, and on Sunday, July 24, a magnificent test run was made from Euston to Crewe. The superiority of the 'Georges' over the 'Experiments' in haulage ability, coal and water consumption, and general performance was well-nigh sensational, as will be shown in subsequent chapters; and if a 'George the Fifth' and not an 'Experiment' had been used in the comparative trials against the G.W.R., there is little doubt that an astonishing situation would have been created. For it is quite certain that a 59-ton 'George the Fifth' would have been able to handle both the 'Cornish Riviera Express' and the 'Torquay Diner' with the loads presented to *Worcestershire,* and keep time comfortably. Then what would the commentators have said! Having made this assertion, it is now time to turn from the 'Experiments' to some of the most amazing engines that have ever run in Great Britain.

*Engine No. 2582 'Rowland Hill', named after the Postmaster-General who inaugurated the Penny Post, in 1840;
a photograph displaying the fine proportions of the 'Precursors'*

TRANSITION :
'PRECURSOR' TO 'GEORGE THE FIFTH'

*One of the most famous of the 'Georges'. A picture in 'photographic grey' of the 5,000th engine built
at Crewe, the 'Coronation'*

CHAPTER 6

THE 'GEORGE THE FIFTH' CLASS

WHEN C. J. Bowen-Cooke succeeded George Whale as Chief Mechanical Engineer in January 1909, the motive power position on the L.N.W.R. was vastly different from that which confronted Whale in May 1903. By the beginning of 1909, nearly all the Webb 3-cylinder compounds had been scrapped; there were 130 'Precursors' and 47 'Experiments' at work, while many of the 'Alfred the Great' class 4-cylinder compound 4—4—0s had been greatly improved by the fitting of an independent reversing gear and a separate set of valve motion for the high-pressure cylinders. Crewe was just getting into its stride with the large order for 60 'Experiments' and, by the beginning of July 1909, 40 of these new engines were on the road. Compared to the situation that existed little more than five years earlier, in March 1904, when *Precursor* was completed at Crewe, the express passenger locomotive stocks were respectively:

March 1904:	166 6ft. 6in. Jumbos
	90 6ft. 0in. Jumbos
	60 Lady of the Lake singles
	100 3-cylinder compounds
	80 4-cylinder compounds
July 1909:	142 6ft. 6in. Jumbos
	66 6ft. 0in. Jumbos
	5 3-cylinder compounds
	80 4-cylinder compounds
	130 Precursors
	85 Experiments

While the strength had been reduced by the scrapping of some 50 'Jumbos', the principal change was the replacement of 60 'Ladies' and 100 3-cylinder compounds by 130 'Precursors' and 85 'Experiments'. The five remaining 3-cylinder compounds were all of the 'John Hick' class, and were virtually a 'write-off' so far as main-line passenger work was concerned. Furthermore, by the virtual elimination of double-heading on the main line south of Crewe, there was no longer the desperate shortage of engines that had prevailed at the height of Whale's 'scrap and build' programme. The working of the traffic was in a sound state, though both 'Precursors' and 'Experiments' had to be worked very hard on the heaviest and fastest duties, and their capacity clearly left no margin for acceleration, or more economical operation by the conveyance of heavier loads with one engine. Nevertheless, while enhancement of locomotive power was necessary, the situation was not immediately urgent and Bowen-Cooke could afford to do some experimenting.

The interchange trials of 1909 (Chapter 5) were one outward sign of the forward thinking in progress at Crewe, while Bowen-Cooke's wide acquaintance with locomotive practice on the Continent, and his remarkably detailed knowledge of notable engine designs, meant that the net was being cast much wider than the confines and experience of the L.N.W.R. itself. While many British engineers of that period were attracted to French and American practice, it was the work of Schmidt and Maffei in Germany to which Bowen-Cooke gave the closest attention.

Douglas Earle-Marsh, the Locomotive Superintendent of the London, Brighton & South Coast Railway, was one of the first British engineers to try the Schmidt superheater and, as the working of the Brighton 4—4—2 tank engine No. 23 came to have such a decisive influence upon future practice at Crewe, the origin of the Brighton application is worth recalling. Marsh was originally on the Great Northern Railway, and his first express engine for the L.B.S.C.R. was a very close copy of the well-known Ivatt large-boilered 'Atlantics' of the G.N.R. Then, in 1907, evidently not satisfied with the technical staff available at Brighton, he brought in B. K. Field, who had been chief locomotive draughtsman at the Stoke works of the North

Staffordshire Railway. Field was appointed chief draughtsman at the Locomotive and Carriage Works at Brighton, and immediately began, in his own modest way, to exert a profound influence upon the locomotive practice of the L.B.S.C.R. In 1907, Marsh was in the midst of a not-very-successful programme of 4—4—2 tank engine construction. His suburban engines of Classes 'I1' and 'I2' were virtually failures, and when Field arrived at Brighton the 'I3' was on the drawing-boards—a tank engine version of the Billinton 'B4' express passenger 4—4—0. In this case, Marsh was on much surer ground, because the 'B4' was an excellent design and well proved in service.

Field was not a little surprised that Marsh was concerned with nothing more enterprising than a tank engine version of an express passenger design of 1899, non-superheated, with slide valves and unrepresentative of any advance in practice over the ensuing eight years. He at once suggested to Marsh that the building of the new 4—4—2 tank engines presented an opportunity of thoroughly modernising the design by putting on Schmidt superheaters, piston valves, and, a subtle touch, such alterations in outward style as would stamp the new engines as an original Marsh product rather than a mere tank engine version of a well-known Billinton design. Marsh was delighted with the idea, and while the first 'I3' tank No. 21 was built as originally intended, the second was superheated. The Brighton people were out for economy in working, and so while the superheater engines had 21 in. diameter cylinders, against 19 in. on the saturated members of the class, the former engines had 160 lb. per sq. in. boiler pressure while the saturated ones had 180. The first superheated 'I3' went into service in 1908 and, allied to the use of

C. J. Bowen-Cooke, Chief Mechanical Engineer, 1909 to 1920

the Schmidt superheater, it also had piston valves, with the Schmidt segmental piston valve rings. Furthermore, the superheater was very large in relation to the tube heating surface.

At once this engine began to show quite remarkable economy in fuel consumption over all other Brighton express types; but it is important to note and appreciate that Marsh, on the advice of B. K. Field, used a fairly high degree of superheat, albeit with a considerable reduction in boiler pressure as compared with the saturated engines of the 'I3' class. This was entirely in accordance with the precepts of Schmidt, though not every British engineer who was experimenting with superheated

The first L.N.W.R. superheater, engine No. 2663 'George the Fifth'

The 'Precursor' No. 7 'Titan' during the locomotive exchange of 1909, at Brighton, ready to work the Sunny South Special through to Rugby

steam in that decade followed in the same way. On the Great Western, for example, Churchward retained his high boiler pressure of 225 lb. per sq. in. but used a very moderate degree of superheat. He was anxious not to throw away heat in the exhaust, and his development of the superheater at Swindon, from the trial of the Schmidt apparatus on one of the 'Saint' class 4—6—0s, was designed to provide just enough superheat to cover the long range of expansion he was using in his new standard locomotives, and to exhaust the steam at a temperature little above the point of condensation. Bowen-Cooke wanted more power, as well as economy in the working of the heavy L.N.W.R. express traffic. The experimental running of the Brighton engine No. 23 on the 'Sunny South Special', throughout from Brighton to Rugby, was of intense interest to all concerned at Crewe, because it demonstrated without any doubt the economies in both coal and water consumption that Schmidt claimed for his superheater, and how it contributed to a very free-running engine.

No coal consumption figures have ever been quoted for the Brighton engine No. 23, nor for the 'Precursor' No. 7, Titan, that was run in competition; but the fact that the 'I3' ran through from East Croydon to Rugby without taking water intermediately tells its own tale. The round trip of 264 miles from Brighton to Rugby and back was accomplished on one heaped bunkerful of coal, about $3\frac{1}{4}$ tons; this indicated a consumption of about 27 lb. per mile, and the water consumption would be no more than 22 gallons per mile. If, on the other hand, Titan was running up to normal 'Precursor' standards, she would, with a moderate train of this weight, have been using about 40 lb. per mile. As described in Chapter 3 of this book, in the trials against the Great Northern 'Atlantic' engine, No. 510, Albatross, working on her own line with an average load per trip of 290 tons, used 40.7 lb. per mile, while on the G.N.R., with an average load of 237 tons, engine No. 412, Marquis, used $36\frac{1}{2}$ lb. per mile. The superiority of the Brighton engine over Titan was just what one would expect a well-designed superheater engine with piston valves to show over a non-superheater engine, and the comparison certainly convinced the powers-that-be at Crewe that Schmidt's claims were fully justified.

On the other side, there are stories of Titan having to be flogged so hard as to arrive at Brighton with a red-hot smokebox door. These can be put down as figments of some partisan imagination,

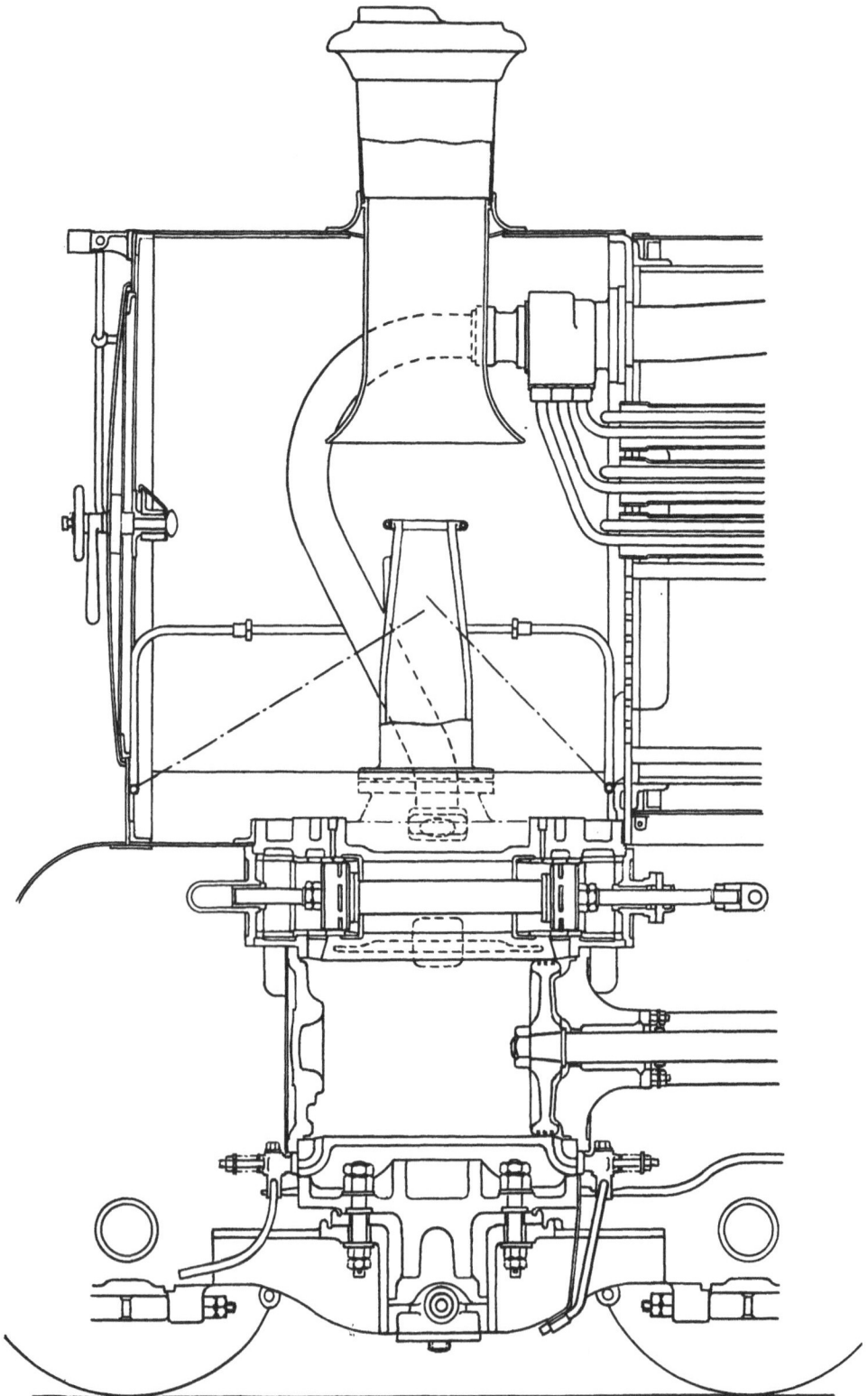

'George the Fifth' class, longitudinal section of the smokebox and cylinder

Engine No. 1681 'Ptarmigan' on arrival at Euston from Liverpool

Engine No. 2271 'J. P. Bickersteth' on the 2 p.m. 'Corridor' near Kenton

4-4-0 BOILERS
HEATING SURFACES in Sq. Ft.

Engine	'Precursor'	Queen Mary	George the Fifth
Flue tubes . . .	1848.4	1800.7	1385.4
Superheater elements .	—	—	302.5
Firebox . . .	161.3	161.3	161.3
Total . . .	2009.7	1962	1849.2
Boiler pressure lb. per sq. in. . . .	175	175	175

PROPORTIONS OF SUPERHEATERS

Engine	G.W.R. Super-heated 'Star'	Brighton 'I3' 4-4-2T	L.N.W.R. 'George the Fifth'
Tube heating surface sq. ft. .	1686.6	850	1385.4
Superheater element heating surface sq. ft. .	262.6	305	302.5
Ratio Superheater to tubes . .	0.155	0.358	0.219
Boiler pressure lb. per sq. in. . .	225	160	175

'George the Fifth' class 4-4-0, front end

'George the Fifth' class, cab view

because in relation to what the 'Precursors' were regularly called upon to do every day on the Liverpool and Manchester expresses from Euston, the 'Sunny South Special', with its 250-ton load, was a 'boy's job'. If a leak should have developed in the smokebox door and caused some burning of the metal, one can be sure it was nothing to do with the vigour of the engine working. If it had been, then the engines of the crack Liverpool and Manchester expresses would have become incandescent! The man who drove *Titan* during the exchange was P. Clow, of Rugby—'Peter the Dandy', as he was nicknamed—who shared with R. Walker the driving of the 8 p.m. Tourist express from Euston during the last days of the Race to the North in 1895, with the Webb 3-cylinder compounds *Coptic* and *Adriatic*.

Following the locomotive exchanges of 1909, Bowen-Cooke set the Crewe drawing office to work on the design of an 'improved Precursor'. The addition of superheating increases considerably the first-cost of a locomotive, not only in the superheater itself, but in the accessories needed in the form of mechanical lubrication. The undoubted advantages had to be set against the increased cost, and arrangements were, therefore, made for the construction of two new engines, one using saturated steam and the other superheated, but otherwise identical. Unlike the first Brighton essay into superheating, both engines would carry the same boiler pressure, and both engines would have the same improved front-end. The saturated engine would be in every way an improved 'Precursor', with the same diameter of cylinders, and 175 lb. per sq. in. boiler pressure, but using piston instead of slide

valves, and very generous port ope was to be the same as the 'Precurs was fitted with an extended smoke feature is sometimes thought to l accommodate the superheater, but drawing is enough to show that thi greater smokebox volume tends to pulsations of draught on the fire, d haust, and when a locomotive is wor low speed there is less tendency to about, and so cause holes to develop.

The new engines were completed a June 1910, No. 2663 superheated, and saturated. They synchronised closely wi ginning of a new reign in Great Britain, a great satisfaction of the L.N.W.R. and the public who took an interest in locomoti 2663 was named *George the Fifth* and N *Queen Mary*. The respective dimensions boilers are naturally of great interest, and th on page 68 sets out a comparison between th Mr. Bowen-Cooke's two new engines alon those of the 'Precursor'.

So far as the *George the Fifth* is concerned, particular point of interest is the relation of su heater element heating surface to the tube heat surface, because this gives a clear indication of t degree to which the steam is superheated above th temperature of formation. The comparative dimensions of the superheaters in the three express locomotives already discussed in this chapter are set out in the table on page 68.

Against a steam temperature of about 550 deg. Fah. on the Great Western superheater 4—6—0s, the North Western engines worked at about 650

Glasgow portion of 10 a.m. ex-Euston, with through portion from Birmingham next to the engine:
'Queen Mary' class 4-4-0 No. 2271 'J. P. Bickersteth', photographed near Farington

Engine No. 1681 'Ptarmigan' on arrival at Euston from Liverpool

Engine No. 2271 'J. P. Bickersteth' on the 2 p.m. 'Corridor' near Kenton

4–4–0 BOILERS
HEATING SURFACES in Sq. Ft.

Engine	'Precursor'	Queen Mary	George the Fifth
Flue tubes . . .	1848.4	1800.7	1385.4
Superheater elements .	—	—	302.5
Firebox . . .	161.3	161.3	161.3
Total . . .	2009.7	1962	1849.2
Boiler pressure lb. per sq. in. . . .	175	175	175

PROPORTIONS OF SUPERHEATERS

Engine	G.W.R. Super-heated 'Star'	Brighton 'I3' 4–4–2T	L.N.W.R. 'George the Fifth'
Tube heating surface sq. ft. .	1686.6	850	1385.4
Superheater element heating surface sq. ft. . .	262.6	305	302.5
Ratio Superheater to tubes . .	0.155	0.358	0.219
Boiler pressure lb. per sq. in. . .	225	160	175

'George the Fifth' class 4-4-0, front end

'George the Fifth' class, cab view

because in relation to what the 'Precursors' were regularly called upon to do every day on the Liverpool and Manchester expresses from Euston, the 'Sunny South Special', with its 250-ton load, was a 'boy's job'. If a leak should have developed in the smokebox door and caused some burning of the metal, one can be sure it was nothing to do with the vigour of the engine working. If it had been, then the engines of the crack Liverpool and Manchester expresses would have become incandescent! The man who drove *Titan* during the exchange was P. Clow, of Rugby—'Peter the Dandy', as he was nicknamed—who shared with R. Walker the driving of the 8 p.m. Tourist express from Euston during the last days of the Race to the North in 1895, with the Webb 3-cylinder compounds *Coptic* and *Adriatic*.

Following the locomotive exchanges of 1909, Bowen-Cooke set the Crewe drawing office to work on the design of an 'improved Precursor'. The addition of superheating increases considerably the first-cost of a locomotive, not only in the superheater itself, but in the accessories needed in the form of mechanical lubrication. The undoubted advantages had to be set against the increased cost, and arrangements were, therefore, made for the construction of two new engines, one using saturated steam and the other superheated, but otherwise identical. Unlike the first Brighton essay into superheating, both engines would carry the same boiler pressure, and both engines would have the same improved front-end. The saturated engine would be in every way an improved 'Precursor', with the same diameter of cylinders, and 175 lb. per sq. in. boiler pressure, but using piston instead of slide

valves, and very generous port openings. The boiler was to be the same as the 'Precursor', except that it was fitted with an extended smokebox. This latter feature is sometimes thought to be necessary to accommodate the superheater, but a glance at the drawing is enough to show that this is not so. A greater smokebox volume tends to even out the pulsations of draught on the fire, due to the exhaust, and when a locomotive is working hard at low speed there is less tendency to tear the fire about, and so cause holes to develop.

The new engines were completed at Crewe in June 1910, No. 2663 superheated, and No. 2664 saturated. They synchronised closely with the beginning of a new reign in Great Britain, and to the great satisfaction of the L.N.W.R. and the travelling public who took an interest in locomotives, No. 2663 was named *George the Fifth* and No. 2664 *Queen Mary*. The respective dimensions of the boilers are naturally of great interest, and the table on page 68 sets out a comparison between those of Mr. Bowen-Cooke's two new engines alongside those of the 'Precursor'.

So far as the *George the Fifth* is concerned, the particular point of interest is the relation of superheater element heating surface to the tube heating surface, because this gives a clear indication of the degree to which the steam is superheated above the temperature of formation. The comparative dimensions of the superheaters in the three express locomotives already discussed in this chapter are set out in the table on page 68.

Against a steam temperature of about 550 deg. Fah. on the Great Western superheater 4—6—0s, the North Western engines worked at about 650

Glasgow portion of 10 a.m. ex-Euston, with through portion from Birmingham next to the engine:
'Queen Mary' class 4-4-0 No. 2271 'J. P. Bickersteth', photographed near Farington

Engine No. 2663, in shop grey, fitted with indicator shelters ready for the very fast trial runs of July 1910

deg., and the very large superheaters of the Brighton 4—4—2 tanks would probably have realised equally high temperatures, despite the lower boiler pressure. While Marsh designed an engine that would be of comparable power to the non-superheated 'I3', and the 'B4' tender 4—4—0s, but would work with much greater economy in fuel and water, Bowen-Cooke utilised superheating to get enhanced power, and while the *Queen Mary* had the same-sized cylinders as the 'Precursors', the *George the Fifth,* as originally built, had 20 in. cylinders—an increase of more than 10 per cent in nominal tractive effort.

I have mentioned earlier, however, that the two new engines, 2663 and 2664, had improved front-ends. First of all, the maximum steam port area was increased from 23.44 sq. in. to no less than 31.35 sq. in. This in itself would contribute to the free running of the engine, but the valve gear dimensions were remarkable for that period in that the maximum travel of the valves in full gear was $5\frac{1}{2}$ in.—only $\frac{1}{4}$ in. short of that of the Gresley 'A4 Pacifics'. The other leading valve dimensions were:

Lap of valve	$1\frac{1}{4}$ in.
Lead	$\frac{3}{16}$ in.
Exhaust Clearance	$\frac{1}{16}$ in.
Max. travel	$5\frac{1}{2}$ in.
Dia. of piston valve	8 in.

The combination of high-degree superheating, giving a greatly increased fluidity to the steam, with large steam and exhaust passages, gave the *George the Fifth* an advantage over the 'Precursors' far greater than the mere increase of cylinder diameter from 19 to 20 in., and on Sunday, July 24, 1910 a test run was made from Crewe to Euston and back with the new dynamometer car. This handsome vehicle had been completed at Wolverton in August 1908, and was used on one occasion in 1909 during the trials of the Great Northern 'Atlantic', No.

1449, between Euston and Crewe. If the trial run of the *Precursor* in March 1904 had ushered in a new era of locomotive performance on the L.N.W.R., the test with the *George the Fifth* in July 1910 set the standard at a considerably higher level. To work a train of 357 tons tare non-stop from Euston to Crewe at an average speed of slightly over 60 m.p.h. was entirely novel.

Before discussing this performance in detail, there are certain other features of the new locomotives themselves that are of interest. The use of a continuous splasher over the coupled wheels was a superficial change—which, in later years, enabled a 'George the Fifth' to be readily distinguishable from those 'Precursors' which were rebuilt with superheaters and piston valves. But one clear point of difference between 'Precursors' and 'Georges' lay in the size of the bogie wheels. On the 'Precursors' they were 3 ft. 9 in. diameter, and as these engines had slide valves the cylinders could be inclined. But on the 'Georges', with 8 in. piston valves immediately above the cylinders, the latter were horizontal, which precluded the use of bogie wheels larger than 3 ft. 3 in. The drawing on page 66 shows the arrangement of cylinders, valves, and the slides for the 'radial truck'—as in the 'Precursors' and 'Experiments', it was not a true bogie. The small bogie wheels rather detracted from the appearance of the 'George the Fifths', in comparison with the 'Precursors'; otherwise they were very fine-looking engines.

The valve gear, as will be seen from the drawing on page 74, had an indirect drive through a rocking shaft. This diagram also shows the extent to which the connecting rod was enlarged to provide the pin point for the jack link for the Joy valve gear. The 'George the Fifth' class, despite the greatly increased power they were expected to develop, had exactly the same bearing and frame design as the 'Precursors', with the same dimensions for the journals, and main frame plates only 1 in. thick. As originally built, they had pyrometer gauges in the cab to indicate the temperature of the steam on leaving the superheater, and a superheater damper under the control of the driver. This latter device was sometimes used to advantage when starting away cold, with a fire that could be somewhat 'green', and boiler pressure apt to fall. Then the driver would close the damper, and deflect the exhaust gases from the superheater flues to the small tubes only. This would cause a fall in steam temperature that would quickly rally the boiler and, once the steaming was normally free, the superheater would be opened again to raise steam temperature. Observations on the comparative performance of the two engines *George the Fifth* and *Queen Mary* continued during the summer and early autumn of 1910. No specific test results with the *Queen Mary* have ever been published; but from all accounts she was a very good engine, considerably superior in everyday performance to the 'Precursors'. So satisfactory, indeed, was her work that nine more engines of this non-superheated class were built at Crewe in October-November 1910, their names and numbers being:

238	*F. W. Webb*
896	*George Whale*
1195	*T. J. Hare*
1550	*Westminster*
1559	*Drake*
2151	*Newcomen*
2271	*J. P. Bickersteth*
2507	*Miles MacInnes*
2512	*Thomas Houghton*

Of these names, *Drake* and *Newcomen* had previously been borne by 6 ft. 6 in. 'Jumbos'; but all the rest were new. It was interesting to see that Bowen-Cooke availed himself of the earliest opportunity to honour his two great predecessors in office, just as Webb himself had done in 1872, when the first new engine completed at Crewe after he had assumed the chieftainship was named *John Ramsbottom*. One can quite understand that in the strained situation of 1903 no one then wished to name an engine after Mr. Webb. Seven years later the situation could be seen in broader perspective, and Bowen-Cooke's gesture was well appreciated.

In the meantime, the superheater engine, No. 2663, *George the Fifth*, was doing some remarkable work. The round trip from Crewe to Euston and back with the dynamometer car and a load of 357 tons, set up some new records both for sustained high speed with a fairly heavy train, and for sustained output of power. It is nevertheless argued sometimes, by those who would deprecate the work

of Crewe locomotives, that the dynamometer car runs with the first locomotive of a new design often set standards that were not reached in ordinary day-to-day service. In the case of the 'George the Fifth' class superheater 4—4—0s, however, the data I have been able to gather together over the years relating to their work on the main line between Euston and Crewe shows quite clearly that, while the test run of July 24, 1910 was a very good performance, it would not have been regarded as anything out of the ordinary by 1914 and 1915. What made the occasion of such vital importance to the locomotive department at Crewe was the manner in which it demonstrated that a big effort could be sustained from start to finish of a 158-mile run.

The engine, it must be remembered, was then brand new, and only just nicely run-in. It was still in 'shop grey', and things were taken fairly easily on the southbound journey. It was on the return trip, non-stop from Euston to Crewe, that the big effort was made. Times were recorded at only a few intermediate points, and strategic locations like Tring and Whitmore do not appear in the log; but the details published at the time give complete records of the indicated horsepower registered. Indicator cards were taken at 37 places, including an equal number on both adverse and favourable stretches of the line, and from these it is easy to appreciate how a very fast overall time came to be made, even though some of the uphill speeds were not exceptional. The skeleton log of the run was as follows:

DYNAMOMETER-CAR TEST RUN: July 24, 1910
Load: 357½ tons tare
Engine: No. 2663 *George the Fifth*

Dist. miles		Actual time min.	Av. speeds m.p.h.
0.0	EUSTON	0	—
5.4	Willesden Jnct.	10	31½
46.7	Bletchley	51	60½
62.8	Blisworth	65½	66½
82.5	RUGBY	83½	65½
97.1	Nuneaton	98½	58½
110.0	Tamworth	108¾	75½
116.3	Lichfield	114	72
133.6	Stafford	130½	63
158.0	CREWE	156½	56½

The work between Willesden and Tring was no more than moderate by the standards established by these engines in later years, with a sustained speed of 51 m.p.h. on the 1 in 335 gradient past

Harrow and Pinner; nothing more than 60 m.p.h. at Watford Junction, and a minimum of 52 m.p.h. at Tring. This involved outputs of indicated horse-power varying between 1,001 and 1,201; but whereas in 1904 *Precursor* had been eased on all the favourable sections of line the *George the Fifth* was taken along in terrific style, and outputs of 1,202 and 1,110 i.h.p. were recorded at speeds of 74½ and 77½ m.p.h. respectively. The complete record of indicated horsepower is given in the accompanying table:

In 1914, Sir Henry Fowler, Chief Mechanical Engineer of the Midland Railway, read a paper on superheating before the Institution of Civil Engineers and, in the subsequent discussion, C. J. Bowen-Cooke gave details of the test run with the *George the Fifth* (see foot of page).

It is, of course, the figures for coal consumption which are of the greatest interest, and for a hard, sustained run such as the down journey on July 24 the figure of 45.7 lb. per train mile is very reason-able. It is interesting to compare this with results obtained with the first of the 'Royal Scots' in 1927, thus:

TEST RUNS: EUSTON—CREWE

Engine	2663	6100
Load, behind tender, tons tare	357	496
Average speed, m.p.h.	60.5	54.4
Coal, lb. per mile	45.7	46.4
Coal, lb. per sq. ft. of grate area per hour	123.1	81.08
Coal, per gross ton mile lb.	0.100	0.075
Mean i.h.p.	1,082	1,070

The rate of firing in relation to the grate area is naturally very much higher on the small grate of the *George the Fifth*, while the coal consumption per gross ton mile is easily explained by the con-siderably higher speed run on the test journey of

L.N.W.R. HORSEPOWER RECORDS

Engine No. 2663 *George the Fifth*

Approximate Location				Speed m.p.h.	I.H.P.
Willesden	.	.	.	51	1001
Sudbury	.	.	.	53	1016
Pinner	.	.	.	51½	1033
—	.	.	.	51	1071
—	.	.	.	54	1041
Watford	.	.	.	60	—
—	.	.	.	59	1044
Boxmoor	.	.	.	57	1097
—	.	.	.	55	1201
Milepost 30	.	.	.	52	1078
Sears Crossing	.	.	.	78½	—
Bletchley	.	.	.	74	1167
—	.	.	.	74½	1123
Wolverton	.	.	.	77½	998
—	.	.	.	67	1101
—	.	.	.	60	1074
Roade Cutting	.	.	.	58	1115
Weedon	.	.	.	68½	1222
—	.	.	.	64	1099
—	.	.	.	62	1172
Kilsby Tunnel	.	.	.	62	1165
Hillmorton	.	.	.	70	—
Rugby	.	.	.	36	—
—	.	.	.	52½	1102
—	.	.	.	64	1229
—	.	.	.	62½	1178
Nuneaton	.	.	.	77½	1111
—	.	.	.	77½	1094
—	.	.	.	74½	1202
—	.	.	.	70	1116
—	.	.	.	63	1153
Lichfield	.	.	.	61	1099
—	.	.	.	69	1028
—	.	.	.	64	1069
—	.	.	.	64	995
Stafford	.	.	.	slack	—
—	.	.	.	51	999
—	.	.	.	57	1127
—	.	.	.	60	1135
—	.	.	.	63	1202
—	.	.	.	62	1223
Whitmore	.	.	.	60	1113
Betley Road	.	.	.	77	—

LONDON AND NORTH WESTERN RAILWAY—LOCOMOTIVE PERFORMANCE

George the Fifth, Crewe to London and Return Trip, July 24, 1910

Train and engine tons	Mean speed m.p.h.	Coal per mile lb.	Mean i.h.p.	Coal Consumption lb.			Journeys
				Per sq. ft. of grate area per hour	per i.h.p. hour	per gross ton-mile	
454.23	56.0	39.6	936	99.0	2.37	0.087	Crewe to London
454.23	60.5	45.7	1082	123.1	2.56	0.100	London to Crewe

Crewe to London: Crewe—Rugby, 53.75 m.p.h.; Rugby—London, 58.25 m.p.h.; Mean 56 m.p.h.
London to Crewe non-stop: 60.5 m.p.h.

1910. But in relation to the actual work done, there is nothing in it between the relative economies of the two locomotives. The mean drawbar horse-power on the run with the 'Royal Scot' engine was only 763. The *George the Fifth* in new condition had a thermal efficiency fully equal to the *Royal Scot*, when that engine was also new; and having achieved such splendid results in 1910, Bowen-Cooke was amply justified in recommending the adoption of superheating as a standard feature on future Crewe express passenger locomotives.

In addition to the coal consumption figures already quoted from the discussion at the Institution of Civil Engineers in 1914, Bowen-Cooke had some interesting comments to make generally on the results of superheating on the L.N.W.R. He said: 'The subject of superheating has been taken up not only by those responsible for the engineering side of the locomotive question, but also by those interested in the commercial working of railways. Anything in the shape of a 25 per cent. saving was a bait that was taken greedily by the general manager or anyone on the commercial side. Super-heating has been found to be more than a bait, and to be a benefit of real value.'

Turning to questions of engineering detail associated with superheaters, Bowen-Cooke spoke, among other things, of his experience with super-heater dampers, wear of elements, mechanical lubrication, and boiler repairs. After considering very carefully the question of providing an auto-matic damper, he had come to the conclusion that it was not necessary, and he therefore fitted a control-lever with which the driver could work the damper when required. The suitability of such an arrangement was proved, he thought, by the long life of the superheater tubes. As to the wear of superheater elements, he mentioned that in the case of one of his engines, after completing 224,441 miles of heavy main-line work, the superheater elements were taken out and found to be in such good condition that they were all replaced, with one exception. He had a section made of the one tube taken out, and this was displayed at the meet-ing. It was noticeable that there was very little sign of wear in that part of the tube where most would be expected; in fact, the wear and tear occurred chiefly at the ends of the tubes, where they came to and from the header-castings.

The two experimental engines, *George the Fifth* and *Queen Mary*, were very carefully examined so far as boiler repairs were concerned. The two en-gines came into Crewe for general repairs after they had covered 95,826 and 97,604 miles respectively, and they showed very little difference. Of course, both boilers were working at the same pressure, and in such conditions they had come to the conclusion at Crewe that superheating made no appreciable

The 'Corridor' at full speed near Kenton: engine No. 1294 'F. S. P. Wolferstan'

Up Liverpool and Manchester express passing under the Metropolitan Railway bridge near Kenton: engine No. 882 'Canada'

difference to the cost of boiler maintenance. But so far as coal consumption was concerned, the difference was astonishing. The two engines, 2663 and 2664, worked turn and turn about on the heaviest and fastest express trains on the main line between Euston and Crewe for several months, and the saving in coal worked out as high as 26.7 per cent. in favour of No. 2663. On a series of specific test runs between Preston and Carlisle, the saving in favour of No. 2663 was 25.77 per cent.

A further nine engines of the 'George the Fifth' class were built at Crewe in November, December and January 1910-11. Their names and numbers were as given alongside.

Engine		Date completed
1059	*Lord Loch*	November 1910
1294	*F. S. P. Wolferstan*	,, ,,
1583	*Henry Ward*	,, ,,
1725	*John Bateson*	,, ,,
2155	*W. C. Brocklehurst*	,, ,,
2025	*Sir Thomas Brooke*	December 1910
228	*E. Nettlefold*	January 1911
445	*P. H. Chambres*	,, ,,
2168	*Henry Maudslay*	,, ,,

The superheater engines steamed so freely that, on the last of the above-mentioned batch, No. 2168, it was decided to increase the cylinder diameter to $20\frac{1}{2}$ in., and this became the standard dimension for the entire class in the future.

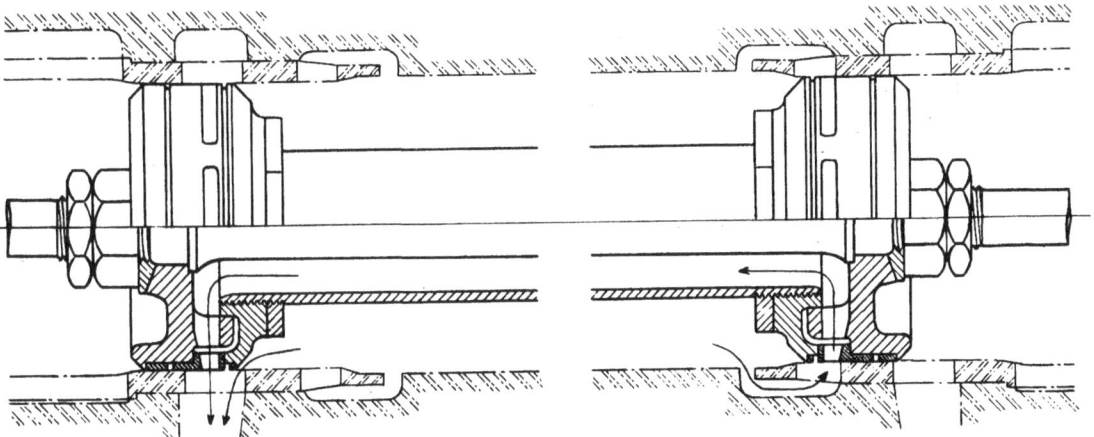

Standard design of piston valve with trick ports

73

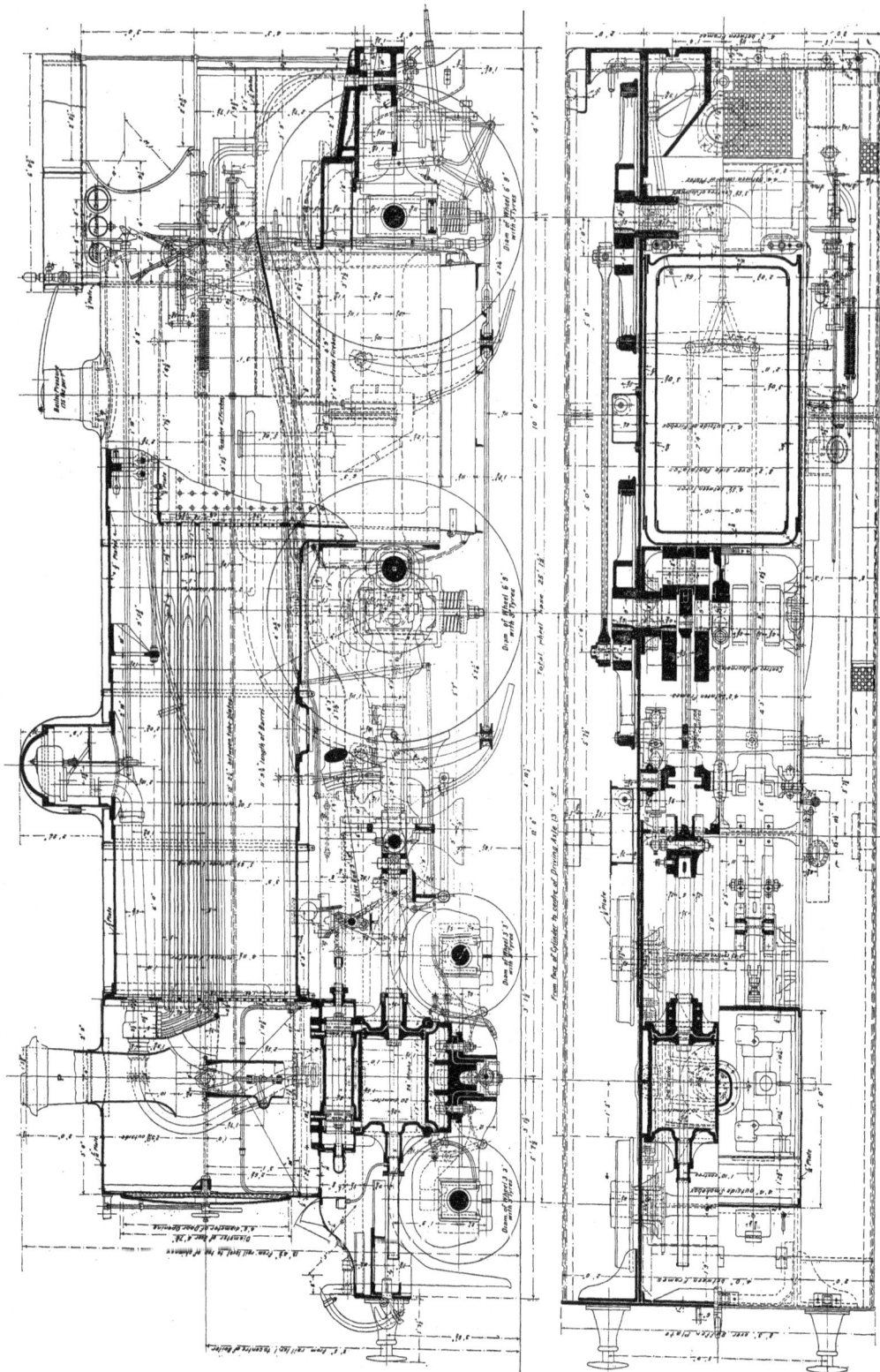

4-4-0 Passenger Express Engine London & North Western Railway, fitted with Schmidt's Superheater and Piston Valves.

'George the Fifth' class 4-4-0 with variable blastpipe

A scene on No. 6 platform Euston prior to departure of the 'Corridor': engine No. 1706 'Elkhound'

In the discussion upon the Fowler paper in 1914, there was no reference to the design of piston rings, which were of Schmidt's patent type, with double admission, through the use of 'trick' ports, as shown in the diagram on page 73. These gave excellent results when new, but in later years— many years later in fact—they were found to be a source of considerable weakness. As the mileage of the locomotives since general overhaul mounted up, wear on the rings gave rise to a serious leakage of steam past the piston valves, and on the 'Royal Scots', which originally had the simple type of Schmidt ring, without trick ports, the coal consumption from this one cause was sometimes nearly

The pioneer engine, No. 2663 'George the Fifth,' at Willesden shed, in 1922

The 5.30 p.m. Fleetwood boat express near Kenton: engine No. 1417 'Landrail'

80 per cent. more than when the engines were newly out of the shops. To what extent the 'George the Fifths' and other L.N.W.R. superheater engines suffered from this same disadvantage cannot be stated quantitatively; but the weakness was undoubtedly there, and helped to substantiate the reputation for heavy coal consumption that stigmatised Crewe locomotives in general in post-grouping days. But when in proper fettle the 'George the Fifths' could rise to phenomenal heights of performance, and at coal consumption rates that were not extravagant in themselves and vastly better than the majority of contemporary British locomotives.

That Bowen-Cooke was ready to pursue any course that would yield more economical working of locomotives is shown by his experiments in the use of variable blast pipes. These had a central cone which could be raised or lowered by a device like a small reversing screw on the driver's side of the cab. The blast could thus be sharpened or softened according to running conditions. The drawing of the variable blastpipe is dated December 1910, and as such it applied particularly to the new 4—6—2 superheater tanks, the first of which appeared in January 1911. But a drawing has also been published showing a 'George the Fifth' so equipped, and part of it is reproduced on page 74. The

engine in question is shown with 20 in. cylinders, and if this can be accepted as evidence it pin-points the actual engines so equipped to two only, namely those turned out from Crewe subsequent to the date of the variable blastpipe drawing and prior to the change to $20\frac{1}{2}$ in. cylinders as standard. These two engines were:

228   *E. Nettlefold*
445   *P. H. Chambres*

both completed at Crewe in January 1911, the same month as the first of the 4—6—2 tanks appeared.

Although the variable blastpipe is another way of obtaining the result achieved automatically by the Great Western jumper-cap, I do not think its use on the L.N.W.R. can be traced directly to the interchange trial of August 1910. Four months prior to the exchange, Bowen-Cooke had stated: 'The question of a variable blastpipe, so that the back pressure could be reduced as opportunity offered, was worthy of great consideration in connection with the question of the economical working of locomotives.' There are, however, no records of the device being fitted to any other L.N.W.R classes of locomotives.

The numbers, names and building dates of the remaining 70 engines of the class were as follows:

'GEORGE THE FIFTH' CLASS: 1911–1916

No.	Name	Date built	Class of engine previously bearing same name	No.	Name	Date built	Class of engine previously bearing same name
956	*Dachshund*	April 1911	—	1713	*Partridge*	„	AG Bl
1489	*Wolfhound*	„	—	1730	*Snipe*	Oct. 1911	AG
1504	*Boarhound*	„	—	1733	*Grouse*	„	—
1513	*Otterhound*	May 1911	—	1777	*Widgeon*	„	—
1532	*Bloodhound*	„	—	1799	*Woodcock*	„	AG
1628	*Foxhound*	„	—	82	*Charles Dickens*	Jan. 1913	J66
1662	*Deerhound*	„	—	752	*John Hick*	Feb. 1913	JH
1706	*Elkhound*	„	—	1138	*William Froude*	„	JH
1792	*Staghound*	„	—	2124	*John Rennie*	„	P
2495	*Bassetthound*	„	—	2154	*William Siemens*	„	JH
1800	*Coronation*	June 1911	—	2282	*Richard Arkwright*	„	JH
502	*British Empire*	„	—	89	*John Mayall*	Mar. 1913	J66
868	*India*	„	—	132	*S. R. Graves*	„	J66
882	*Canada*	„	—	681	*St. George*	„	AG.J6
1218	*Australia*	„	—	845	*Saddleback*	„	AP
2081	*New Zealand*	„	—	1193	*Edward Tootal*	„	J66
2212	*South Africa*	„	—	2279	*Henry Crosfield*	„	J66
2291	*Gibraltar*	„	—	404	*Eclipse*	April 1913	AG.J6
2177	*Malta*	July 1911	—	1188	*Penmaenmawr*	„	AG.J66
2498	*Cyprus*	„	—	1481	*Typhon*	„	AG.J6
361	*Beagle*	„	—	1680	*Loyalty*	„	—
888	*Challenger*	„	—	2086	*Phaeton*	„	AP.J66
1360	*Fire Queen*	„	—	2197	*Planet*	„	—
1394	*Harrier*	Aug. 1911	—	2242	*Meteor*	May 1913	AP.J66
1623	*Nubian*	„	—	2428	*Lord Stalbridge*	„	—
1631	*Racehorse*	„	—	104	*Leamington Spa*	June 1915	—
1644	*Roebuck*	„	AP	226	*Colwyn Bay*	„	—
2089	*Traveller*	„	—	363	*Llandudno*	May 1915	—
2220	*Vanguard*	„	—	789	*Windermere*	„	AP.AG
2494	*Perseus*	„	—	984	*Carnarvon*	„	—
1371	*Quail*	Sept. 1911	AG	1086	*Conway*	June 1915	AG
1417	*Landrail*	„	—	2106	*Holyhead*	„	—
1472	*Moor Hen*	„	—	2153	*Llandrindod*	„	—
1595	*Wild Duck*	„	—	2233	*Blackpool*	„	—
1681	*Ptarmigan*	„	AG	2370	*Dovedale*	July 1915	—

Notes: No. 1680, *Loyalty*, was named in honour of a visit of King George V and Queen Mary to Crewe in 1913.

No. 956, *Dachshund* was renamed *Bulldog* in 1914.

AP = Allan 2–2–2
P   = 'Precursor' 2–4–0
J6   = 6 ft. 'Jumbo'
AG = Allan 2–4–0
JH = 'John Hick' compound
J66 = 6 ft. 6 in. 'Jumbo'

2 p.m. West Coast 'Corridor' express near Kenton: engine No. 1706 'Elkhound'

The 10 a.m. Euston to Glasgow near Euston Junction: engine No. 1672 'Moorhen'

The 2 p.m. West Coast 'Corridor' near Kenton: engine No. 228 'E. Nettlefold'

CHAPTER 7

OUTSTANDING PERFORMANCE

For the Locomotive Department, 1911, 1912, 1913 and 1914 were vintage years on the London & North Western Railway. There was no acceleration of passenger train service beyond the high standards established in the previous decade, but on the main line, south of Crewe particularly, individual engine performance rose to heights that take some believing today. In the years after grouping, when the products of Crewe were to some extent in eclipse, there was a tendency to discount some of the better known achievements of L.N.W.R. locomotives on the grounds that they were isolated instances and could not be regularly repeated. This, of course, was entirely incorrect, and indeed the authoritative data now available show that some of the most legendary feats were themselves surpassed, not once but many times, in ordinary day-to-day running. Towards these achievements there is no doubt that the double-admission, trick-ported piston valves contributed a good deal, by permitting the free entry of a large gulp of steam at each stroke. It is true that on high mileage engines the trick ports were apt to become restricted, due to the formation of carbon deposits; but when new, or otherwise in good trim, the flow of steam into the cylinders was very free.

Many of the logs by which the performance of the 'George the Fifth' class engines on the Southern Division can be most clearly assessed relate to the running of two heavy and fast down expresses worked by engines and men from Crewe North shed—the 10.30 a.m. Liverpool and Manchester express and the 5.30 p.m. Fleetwood boat express. In the ordinary way, the Anglo-Scottish expresses and the Irish Mails did not demand such hard work, and no logs have come to my notice of work on the heavy and fast evening dining-car expresses from Euston to Liverpool and to Manchester. It would have been most interesting to have had records of the running of these two trains. The

5.55 p.m. to Liverpool ran non-stop to Edge Hill, at an average speed of 55.4 m.p.h. It was a 'single-home' turn for Edge Hill men, who worked up on the 11 a.m. from Lime Street, and was a 'star turn' in every way. One engine, in the finest condition, was used on the job for weeks, or even months at a stretch, and the 'link' consisted only of two pairs of enginemen, who worked the train on alternate days. The 6.5 p.m. to Manchester, booked non-stop from Euston to Wilmslow at an average speed of 55 m.p.h., was a 'double-home' turn for Crewe North shed. The engine and men worked up to London on one of the early morning sleeping-car trains; then the men lodged at the Camden enginemen's hostel until evening, when they worked through to Manchester, and eventually back to Crewe with a semi-fast train.

The yardstick of maximum performance from the 'George the Fifth' class, so far as contemporary published information was concerned, was established by a run logged by Cecil J. Allen at the end of November 1911 on the 10.30 a.m. from Euston to Crewe. A total of 40 new engines of the class was built between April and October 1911, and the locomotive featuring in this very fine run was completed at Crewe in September—No. 1595, *Wild Duck*. In passing, it may be regarded as an interesting coincidence that the locomotive making what was for long regarded as one of the greatest runs between Euston and Crewe should have borne virtually the same name—albeit in a less glamorous form—as the engine holding the world speed record for steam. 'Wild Duck' and 'Mallard' are, of course, one and the same bird. The 10.30 a.m. from Euston to Crewe was allowed 171 min. for the run of 158 miles, an average speed of 55.5 m.p.h., and with maximum load trains the 'Precursors' could maintain time. But the circumstances that led to the remarkable effort of *Wild Duck* was a most inglorious start out of Euston, in which the train

79

stalled on Camden bank, and had to be assisted in rear by a yard engine.

Very many years later that great enthusiast, the late W. H. Whitworth, told me how puzzled he had been at the time as to why the engine had stalled. He knew the driver, Greenhalgh of Crewe North, and asked him what happened. Expert photographer and railwayist though he was, Whitworth was no engineer (actually he was a dentist), and the driver explained by actions rather than words. His homely description of the affair, if quoted verbatim, would undoubtedly earn for me the Order of the Blue Pencil; but bowdlerised it was something like this: 'This perisher—indicating one control—wouldn't come, and this adjectival thing wouldn't go, and there we b—— well stuck!' All very amusing, but not very informative; but having passed Willesden 11 min. late as a result of this affair, he set about things so vigorously as to pass Rugeley on time. Only a momentary signal stop at Crewe South prevented an arrival 2 min. early! Cecil J. Allen had every justification for the ecstasies of praise he bestowed upon the driver and fireman, and upon the 'George the Fifth' class locomotives in general. But although the brilliant recovery of lost time lent a particular interest and

excitement to this run the actual engine performance was not anything out of the ordinary in those halcyon years of Crewe locomotive prowess.

Despite his expressive description of the circumstances in which *Wild Duck* stalled on Camden bank when Cecil J. Allen was a passenger, Driver Greenhalgh, like most of his kind, was a true artist of an engineman, and my friend E. V. M. Powell has told me of another occasion, with the same engine, when he was stopped on Camden bank, by signal. This time the train was the 6.15 p.m. ex-Euston, on a Sunday evening, in the spring of 1914, again with a load of over 400 tons ('equal to 20½'), and booked non-stop to Crewe. Powell, in the course of his pupilage at the Works, was third man on the footplate. They were roaring up the bank in characteristic style when Euston No. 4 Box suddenly threw his signals to danger as they were actually passing the box. A carriage door was swinging open. While it was being shut, and the train examined to see that all was well, Greenhalgh sent Powell and the fireman to distribute ashes on the rails for about an engine's length ahead.

When he got the right-away from the guard, Greenhalgh kept the vacuum brake of the train on while releasing the steam brake on the engine; he

Llandudno—Manchester express near Colwyn Bay, hauled by engine No. 2233 'Blackpool'

then put the engine into mid-gear and opened the regulator slightly. What happened then is most vividly told in Powell's own words: 'Greenhalgh then started to blow the brake off the train. As soon as the driver felt the weight of the train on the engine, he opened the regulator a little more and started to unwind the reversing gear very slowly. The engine held the train, and seconds passed. Then with a terrific shudder the engine started to move. A few seconds later there was a tremendous blast from the chimney, and then another, and another. We were away, and without a slip! Jack Greenhalgh saw that we were Right Time at Crewe. That was all that mattered on the L.N.W.R. in those days: "Right Time."'

In those years the drivers of the 'George the Fifth' class engines had matters so comfortably in hand even on the fastest trains that one rarely saw a maximum effort sustained for any length of time. There was no need. But run after run shows that the *Wild Duck* standard of hill-climbing, particularly in the work between Willesden and Tring, was frequently equalled. I have tabulated first of all five runs on non-stop trains between Euston and Crewe, wherein the dynamometer-car test run of July 24, 1910 and the run of *Wild Duck*, in 1911, are set alongside what might be termed three ordinary runs. Of these latter, those of *India* and *Henry Crosfield* were on the 10.30 a.m.; the third was on the 12.10 p.m. with 4 min. additional time allowed

L.N.W.R. EUSTON—CREWE NON-STOPS

Run No.		1	2	3	4	5
Train (ex-Euston)		3.3*	10.30 a.m.	12.10 p.m.	10.30 a.m.	10.30 a.m.
Engine No.		2663	868	1294	1595	2279
Engine Name		*George the Fifth*	*India*	*F.S.P. Wolferstan*	*Wild Duck*	*Henry Crosfield*
Load tons gross		365	370	410	410	445
Dist. Miles		Actual m. s.	Actual m. s.	Actual m. s.	Actual m. s.	Actual m. s.
0.0	EUSTON	0 00	0 00	0 00	0 00	0 00
1.3	Chalk Farm	4 30	4 35	4 50	13 20	4 50
5.4	WILLESDEN JUNCT.	10 00	10 15	10 55	19 55	10 45
11.4	Harrow	16 45	16 30	17 35	26 30	17 45
17.5	WATFORD JUNCT.	23 30	22 40	24 20	32 55	24 45
		—	p.w.s.	—	—	—
24.5	Boxmoor	30 45	30 45	31 35	40 05	32 25
31.7	Tring	38 45	42 00	39 40	47 40	40 35
36.1	Cheddington	42 45	46 15	sigs.	51 35	44 55
46.7	BLETCHLEY	51 00	55 20	54 40	60 10	54 05
52.4	Wolverton	55 45	60 20	60 35	64 50	59 10
59.9	Roade	63 30	67 20	68 30	71 40	66 25
69.7	Weedon	71 30	76 15	78 25	80 50	75 50
75.3	Welton	76 30	81 30	84 05	86 15	81 20
		—	sigs.	—	—	—
82.5	RUGBY	83 30	89 30	91 45	93 30	89 15
91.4	Shilton	93 15	100 00	102 20	103 40	100 10
97.1	NUNEATON	98 30	105 15	107 55	109 00	105 55
102.3	Atherstone	102 30	109 50	113 05	113 25	110 40
110.0	TAMWORTH	108 45	116 50	120 10	119 50	117 20
116.3	Lichfield	114 00	122 40	126 15	125 20	123 00
		—	p.w.s.	—	—	p.w.s.
124.3	Rugeley	121 30	132 20	134 20	132 55	132 30
133.6	STAFFORD	130 30	141 25	144 35	142 15	142 45
138.9	Norton Bridge	136 30	147 45	151 25	148 40	149 15
147.6	Whitmore	145 00	157 00	161 20	157 55	158 45
150.1	Madeley	147 30	159 35	164 20	160 40	161 35
153.3	Betley Road	150 15	162 35	167 20	163 20	164 25
		—	sigs.	—	sig. stop	—
158.0	CREWE	156 30	169 10	174 00	170 45	169 50
	Net times min.	156½	160¼	172½	—	167¼
Average speds m.p.h.						
	Willesden—Watford	53.8	58.5	53.5	55.8	51.8
	Watford—Tring	55.9	checked	55.6	57.8	53.9
	Tring—Welton	69.7	66.3	check	67.7	64.2
	Shilton—Tamworth	72.1	66.3	62.5	69.2	65.2
	Norton Bridge—Whitmore	61.4	55.8	52.1	55.8	54.3

*Dynamometer car special.   Times taken to nearest ¼ minute

F

Fleetwood boat express (13 coach load) near Kenton, hauled by engine No. 1623 'Nubian'

to Crewe. The engine concerned in this last-mentioned run, No. 1294, *F. S. P. Wolferstan*, was one of the first of the class to be stationed at Camden, and in its early days it was worked exclusively by Drivers David Button and Peter Jarvis, either on the 12.10 p.m. or on the 2 p.m. 'Corridor'—'single-home' to Crewe and back. These two drivers could be reckoned to get the finest work out of any engine but nothing exceptional was needed on this run.

In studying the runs as a group, it will be seen that *India* streaked away from *George the Fifth* at the start. The driver of No. 868 knew he had two permanent way slacks to come and he immediately began to get time in hand. In the end, despite four checks of varying severity, he reached Crewe 2 min. early, with a net time of 160¼ min. to his credit. The next significant point to be noticed is that on No. 3 run, with the 12.10 p.m., although this driver had 175 min. in which to reach Crewe, he passed Tring in only one minute more than the test trip, despite a load 45 tons greater. After that, of course, there was no need to hurry. Having recovered from the effects of the unfortunate stop on Camden bank, *Wild Duck* got going to some purpose and her time was the fastest of all between Watford and Tring,

and included a sustained minimum speed of 56 m.p.h. on the 1 in 335 gradient. Beyond Tring, however, the test run with *George the Fifth* came into its own, and although *Wild Duck* was taken along in great style the test run showed an advantage of 4 min. between Tring and Betley Road. Nevertheless, the effort of *Wild Duck*, with its average of 63.1 m.p.h. including Rugby and Stafford slacks, was an altogether outstanding one. The last run in the table shows splendidly sustained performance throughout with a much heavier load of 445 tons. The official maximum tare load for a 'George the Fifth' on these fast timings was 400 tons; but the North Western drivers would cheerfully tackle considerable overloads when necessary; as in this case, when the excess was 23 tons tare.

The 5.30 p.m .from Euston was generally considered to be one of the hardest turns, because the booked time to passing Rugby was 87 min., against 91 min. with the 10.30 a.m. The 5.30 p.m. slipped a portion at Nuneaton, and the working times were easier from Rugby northward; but the drivers seemed to make it a point of honour to pass Rugby on or before time and take the subsequent easier allowance as a bonus. I have before me details of

82

four typical runs on the 5.30 p.m. with loads, to Nuneaton, ranging between 390 and 425 tons. The drivers varied in the way they handled the train. One started very fast, and passed Bletchley in 48 min. 50 sec., others piled it on later, but the summary of the fastest times of these four journeys makes an interesting comparison with the sustained hard running of *George the Fifth* and *Wild Duck* on the two most celebrated runs.

and eventually reached Stafford a clear 5 min. early.

To study the uphill performances further, I have tabulated details of a number of journeys as between Watford Junction and Tring. These include the runs already discussed, and others of very fine quality (see foot of this page).

An examination of these twenty-one performances shows that while that of *Wild Duck* on that legendary occasion of 1911 was certainly in the 'top

Section					Miles	George the Fifth		Wild Duck		Fastest 5.30 p.m.		Engine on 5.30 p.m.
						m.	s.	m.	s.	m.	s.	
Willesden—Leighton	.	.	.	.	39.8	36	00	34	55	34	00	*Perseus*
Leighton—Weedon	.	.	.	.	29.5	25	30	26	00	26	25	*Landrail*
Weedon—Rugby	.	.	.	.	12.8	12	00	12	40	13	00	*Typhon*
Rugby—Polesworth	.	.	.	.	24.0	22	30	23	35	23	50	*Landrail*
Polesworth—Milford	.	.	.	.	23.0	20	15	20	55	21	15	*Partridge*

The times between Willesden Junction and Milford, 124.1 miles, total up to 116 min. 15 sec., 117 min. 55 sec., and 118 min. 30 sec. respectively, showing average speeds of 64.1, 63.2, and 62.8 m.p.h.; but where the drivers of the 5.30 p.m. engines were going relatively hard, as between Euston and Rugby, they were running fully up to the standards of the test trip and *Wild Duck*. Furthermore, engine No. 2494, *Perseus*, hauling a 390-ton train, made an exceptionally good start out to Willesden (passed in 9 min. 5 sec.), and was no less than 3 min. ahead of the test trip as early as Tring! Also, No. 1417, *Landrail*, hauling 400 tons, was within 10 sec. of *George the Fifth* at Bletchley,

seven', it was not an isolated phenomenon. It is, of course, the performance of No. 1294, *F. S. P. Wolferstan*, with the 435-ton load, when the average speed was 61.1 m.p.h., that stands in a class by itself, and it is fortunate that the recorder on this occasion, the late R. E. Charlewood, was one whose accuracy of note-taking can be accepted without question. The train was the 2 p.m. down 'Corridor' and Driver Jarvis was getting time in hand to offset a heavy relaying slack that was to come north of Bletchley.

The estimates of power output are made on the basis of the speeds over the last few miles of the ascent. Between Berkhamsted station and the sum-

L.N.W.R. 'GEORGE THE FIFTH' CLASS
PERFORMANCE BETWEEN WATFORD AND TRING: 14.2 MILES

Engine No.	Name								Load Tons gross	Time m. s.		Average speeds m.p.h.	Estimated e.d.h.p.
1725	*John Bateson*	.	.	.	.	.	.	.	350	15	20	55.7	789
2663	*George the Fifth*	.	.	.	.	.	.	.	360	15	15	55.9	857
1595	*Wild Duck*	.	.	.	.	.	.	.	370	15	30	55.0	809
1489	*Wolfhound*	.	.	.	.	.	.	.	380	14	40	58.1	900
2494	*Perseus*	.	.	.	.	.	.	.	390	14	30	58.7	920
1481	*Typhon*	.	.	.	.	.	.	.	395	15	35	54.7	885
1417	*Landrail*	.	.	.	.	.	.	.	400	14	35	58.4	945
5000	*Coronation*	.	.	.	.	.	.	.	400	14	45	57.8	965
1417	*Landrail*	.	.	.	.	.	.	.	400	14	50	57.4	965
2089	*Traveller*	.	.	.	.	.	.	.	400	16	03	53.0	845
2495	*Bassetthound*	.	.	.	.	.	.	.	400	15	56	53.4	845
1294	*F.S.P. Wolferstan*	.	.	.	.	.	.	.	410	15	20	55.5	910
1595	*Wild Duck*	.	.	.	.	.	.	.	410	14	45	57.8	985
1733	*Grouse*	.	.	.	.	.	.	.	415	14	35	58.4	1025
2279	*Henry Crosfield*	.	.	.	.	.	.	.	420	15	15	55.9	955
1713	*Partridge*	.	.	.	.	.	.	.	425	15	05	56.5	995
404	*Eclipse*	.	.	.	.	.	.	.	425	14	46	57.7	995
5000	*Coronation*	.	.	.	.	.	.	.	430	16	10	52.7	920
1294	*F.S.P. Wolferstan*	.	.	.	.	.	.	.	435	13	57	61.1	1170
1481	*Typhon*	.	.	.	.	.	.	.	440	16	30	51.6	935
2279	*Henry Crosfield*	.	.	.	.	.	.	.	445	15	50	53.8	1000

Engine No. 5000 'Coronation' at Crewe

10 a.m. ex-Holyhead at Britannia bridge: engine No. 1481 'Typhon'

mit at Milepost 31 the pace was usually quite steady, and so far as train resistance is concerned the present British Railways values in pounds per ton have been taken. With some rolling stock of the 1910-1914 period this assessment would give results that would be much too low; but the North Western main-line coaching stock of that period seems to have had a notably low rolling resistance, and the estimate of 857 equivalent drawbar horse-power for *George the Fifth* would seem to be in relatively close agreement with the indicated horse-power of around 1,100 recorded in the same locality. But even if the estimates of drawbar horsepower shown in the accompanying table are not strictly accurate in themselves, the relative values should be correct, and this shows that out of twenty-one recorded performances that of *Wild Duck* comes sixth in the order of power output.

On the up road, the 'Scotsman' leaving Crewe at 3.20 p.m. seems to have been a favourite train for the compilers of logs. Its minimum load was about 370 tons and with this, its schedule of 84 min. to Rugby and 92 min. forward to Euston constituted no problem. But very often it loaded much more heavily, and the two runs tabulated demanded some really hard work. The second one, indeed, with a make-up of no less than 62 axles, was 39 tons over the official load limit for the class. The first of the two runs was, strictly speaking, not made by a 'George the Fifth' at all but by one of the first 'Precursors' to be superheated. The engine concerned, No. 365, *Alchymist*, was rebuilt in May 1914; but with new cylinders, piston valves, and high-degree superheating these rebuilt engines conformed exactly to the 'George the Fifth' except in respect of the driving-wheel splashers. With a load of 435 tons, *Alchymist* made a fine start, attaining 47 m.p.h. at Betley Road, and then not falling below 40 m.p.h. on the 3 miles of 1 in 177 of Madeley bank. After that, the train was taken merrily along to reach Rugby in 81¾ min.

In studying the second of these two runs, how-

5.55 p.m. down Liverpool express, non-stop Euston to Edge Hill, near Kenton: engine No. 1733 'Grouse'

L.N.W.R. 3.20 p.m. CREWE—EUSTON

Engine No. Engine Name Load tons E/F			365 *Alchymist* 399/435		1489 *Wolfhound* 439/470	
Dist. miles		Sch. min.	Actual m. s.	Speeds m.p.h.	Actual m. s.	Speeds m.p.h.
0.0	CREWE . . .	0	0 00	—	0 00	—
4.8	Betley Road . . .		8 33	47	8 27	48
8.0	Madeley . . .		13 13	40	12 54	43
10.5	Whitmore . . .		16 47	—	16 17	—
14.7	Standon Bridge . .		21 07	—	20 30	—
19.2	Norton Bridge . .		25 19	—	24 40	—
21.2	Great Bridgeford . .		27 07	69	26 28	72½
24.5	STAFFORD . .	29	29 57	42	29 13	42
28.6	Milford . . .		34 57	—	34 08	—
30.9	Colwich . . .		37 18	—	36 29	—
33.8	Rugeley . . .	39	39 59	65	39 14	64½
37.1	Armitage . . .		43 06	—	42 20	—
41.8	Lichfield . . .		47 45	—	47 00	—
48.1	TAMWORTH . .	53	53 14	72½	52 32	72½
55.8	Atherstone . . .		60 50	—	60 10	—
61.0	NUNEATON . .	67	66 18	—	65 29	—
64.6	Bulkington . . .		70 23	51	69 36	50
70.0	Brinklow . . .		75 53	67	75 16	64½
75.5	RUGBY . . .	84	81 50		81 25	
7.3	Welton . . .		10 57	49*	11 36	45*
12.9	Weedon . . .		15 57	72½	16 40	69
19.8	Blisworth . . .		22 14	—	22 59	—
—			—		p.w.s.	
22.7	Roade . . .	26	25 08	59	26 00	56½
27.8	Castlethorpe . .		29 46	72½	30 52	69
30.2	Wolverton . . .		31 49	—	33 15	—
—			sigs.		sigs.	
35.9	BLETCHLEY . .	40	37 39	—	39 10	—
42.4	Leighton . . .		44 31	—	46 02	—
46.5	Cheddington . .		48 55	—	50 40	—
50.9	Tring . . .	58	54 09	47	56 06	49
54.6	Berkhamsted . .		58 02	—	60 09	—
58.1	Boxmoor . . .		61 11	—	63 24	—
61.6	Kings Langley . .		64 13	75	66 32	70½
65.1	WATFORD JUNCT. .	72	67 10	—	69 38	—
69.3	Hatch End . .		70 07	—	73 30	—
71.2	Harrow . . .		72 30	—	75 18	—
74.5	Wembley . . .		75 20	74	78 10	72½
77.2	WILLESDEN JUNCT. .	84	sigs.		80 32	
—			sigs.		—	
82.6	EUSTON . . .	92	87 11		87 28	

*attained speed at Kilsby Tunnel

ever, one naturally asks what a modern engineman in the final steam days would have said if given an engine of 'George the Fifth' proportions to work a 470-ton train without assistance! But back in the days just before World War I, the driver and fireman of *Wolfhound* set about things with such a vengeance that they beat the time of *Alchymist* to Whitmore by a clear half-minute. Such a minimum speed as 43 m.p.h. up Madeley bank was astonishing even by 'George the Fifth' standards; and having established this ascendancy over *Alchymist*, the mighty *Wolfhound* kept the lead throughout to Rugby, with an average speed of slightly over 60 m.p.h. over the 41.4 miles from Milford to Brinklow.

There was some equally fine running on both trips between Rugby and Euston. Both engines were driven most vigorously up the 1 in 366 gradient to the north end of Kilsby Tunnel, and the attained speeds of 49 and 45 m.p.h. in this distance of 4 miles were remarkable in themselves. No less noteworthy are the times of 16½ and 17 min. over the 15 adverse miles from Bletchley to Tring, both following after signal checks on the northern side of Bletchley. In the case of *Wolfhound*, the minimum speed of 49 m.p.h. was sustained for several miles. The downhill running was brisk but characteristic of most of the work of the 'George the Fifths'. The engines could run fast enough when occasion demanded it; but for the most part the uphill work was so good as to obviate

One of the earliest of the 'Precursors', as rebuilt with superheater boiler and piston valves: No. 1419 'Tamerlane'

any need for really high speed downhill. These two runs, with actual running times of 169 min. 1 sec. and 168 min. 53 sec., inclusive of several checks on each run, were truly splendid pieces of locomotive performance.

To show what the 'Georges' could do when really given their heads downhill, I have tabulated a short run from Bletchley to Willesden, with No. 89, *John Mayall*, hauling a load of 385 tons. From a dead start at Bletchley the 15 miles up to Tring were covered in 18 min. 42 sec., and then the 19.9 miles from Berkhamsted to Wembley were reeled off at an average speed of 74 m.p.h., with a maximum of 82 m.p.h. at King's Langley.

In their early days the 'George the Fifth' class engines did not work very frequently on the two-hour Birmingham expresses. The loads were mostly moderate, and the 'Precursors' could handle them quite comfortably. The morning business express from Euston, however, used to load up to over 300 tons on Monday mornings and, on a booking of 92 min. for the 88.6 miles from Willesden to Coventry, the 'Georges' had plenty of scope to display their prowess. This train used to slip a coach at Blisworth, for Northampton, and with a load of 350 tons behind the tender, engine No. 1725, *John Bateson*, covered the 26.3 miles up to Tring in 30 min. 43 sec., and the ensuing 43.6 miles on to Welton in 39 min. 44 sec. The time to Rugby, 77.2 miles, was 77 min. 21 sec., and Coventry was reached in $89\frac{3}{4}$ min. The load from

L.N.W.R. BLETCHLEY—WILLESDEN JNCT.
Load: 54 axles, 385 tons full
Engine: 4-4-0 No. 89 *John Mayall*

Dist miles		Actual m. s.	Av. speed m.p.h.
0.0	BLETCHLEY . .	0 00	—
6.5	Leighton Buzzard .	9 26	41.3
10.6	Cheddington . .	13 49	56.1
15.0	Tring . . .	18 42	54.0
18.7	Berkhamsted . .	22 23	60.2
22.2	Boxmoor . . .	25 19	71.6
25.7	Kings Langley . .	28 07	75.0
29.2	WATFORD JUNCT. .	30 46	79.3
30.7	Bushey . . .	31 56	77.2
33.4	Hatch End . . .	34 18	68.7
35.3	Harrow . . .	35 48	76.0
38.6	Wembley . . .	38 32	72.3
41.3	WILLESDEN JUNCT.	41 44	—

Engine No. Load to BL/COV (tons)		1725 350/320	896 350/320
Dist. miles		Actual m. s.	Actual m s.
0.0	Willesden Junct. .	0 00	0 00
6.0	Harrow . . .	8 42	8 43
12.1	Watford Junct. . .	15 23	15 13
26.3	Tring . . .	30 43	30 37
41.3	Bletchley . . .	43 48	43 48
50.4	Castlethorpe . .	50 49	50 51
57.4	Blisworth . . .	59 04	59 05
77.2	Rugby . . .	77 21	77 31
88.6	Coventry . . .	89 44	89 53

The down Irish Mail near Rhyl, hauled by superheated 'Precursor' No. 106 'Druid'

Blisworth was 320 tons. The correspondence between this run and of another on the same train, with engine No. 896, *George Whale,* would almost suggest the work of the same driver.

In days before World War I, there were several trains running non-stop between Euston and Birmingham, and on one of these, in the up direction, engine No. 2507, *Miles MacInnes,* worked a 315-ton load over the 112.9 miles from New Street to Euston in 117 min. 51 sec. But on this trip the 104.8 miles to Wembley had been covered in 104 min. 54 sec., inclusive of a bad signal check at Berkhamsted. Allowing for this, and for checks inward from Wembley, the net time was only 111¼ min., showing a net average speed of 61 m.p.h. throughout. Even so, the load conveyed did not require such hard work as on the Liverpool, Manchester and Scottish expresses, and it was not until the two-hour Birmingham expresses had been restored after the end of the war that 'George the Fifth' performance on them rose to its greatest heights. This work is referred to in a later chapter of this book.

In contemporary railway literature there is no doubt, however, that the early work of the 'George the Fifth' class engines created the most profound impression in the running of the Scotch expresses, north of Crewe. On the Southern Division at the time it was a case of improving upon a very sound

and satisfactory position; and although a modern assessment shows that improvement to have been well-nigh phenomenal, in the years 1911-1913, apart from certain isolated achievements like that of *Wild Duck,* it seems to have been taken as the natural course of development to be expected from Crewe products. But in the north, even the most staunch supporters of the 'Experiments' could hardly claim that the situation was satisfactory. Much good work was being done; but there was still a good deal of piloting, and there were more than merely isolated cases of losing time. Then the 'Georges' were put on to trains like the 10 a.m. and 2 p.m. from Euston, with their corresponding return trips, and the change was profound. 4—4—0s took the place of 4—6—0s, and immediately did vastly better. There is no doubt it was the success of the 'Georges' on the mountain section that did more than anything else to tarnish the reputation of the 'Experiments'.

A run on the Glasgow portion of the 10 a.m. from Euston with engine No. 2155, *W. C. Brocklehurst,* is impressive as much in the complete contrast it affords to 'Experiment' performance as in the intrinsic merit of the work itself. In Chapter 5, I detailed a run with the non-superheater 4—6—0 No. 887, *Fortuna,* with a 310-ton train, on which Carnforth was passed 8¼ min. early. Then almost the entire gain was lost in the ascent to Shap. The

Up two-hour Birmingham express:
engine No. 1059 'Lord Loch'

Excursion to the south coast, near Rugby:
engine No. 1504 'Boarhound'

31.4 miles from Carnforth to Summit took 46 min. 55 sec. against 39 min. schedule. By contrast, the superheater 4—4—0 engine, *W. C. Brocklehurst,* hauling 340 tons, took 84½ min. to pass Carnforth, but then only 41 min. 5 sec. to Shap Summit—passing the latter point 1½ min. early. An abbreviated log of this fine run is given herewith:

L.N.W.R. 1.12 p.m. CREWE—CARLISLE
Load: 48 axles, 340 tons full
Engine: 4—4—0 No. 2155 *W. C. Brocklehurst*

Dist. miles		Sch. min.	Actual m. s.	Av. speed m.p.h.
0.0	CREWE . .	0	0 00	—
4.8	Minshull Vernon		8 00	36.0
—			p.w.s.	
18.8	Preston Brook .		22 15	59.6
24.0	WARRINGTON .	27	27 05	64.6
31.0	Golborne . .		34 45	54.8
35.8	WIGAN . .	40	39 30	60.7
41.6	Coppull . .		46 40	48.6
50.9	PRESTON .	58	56 05	59.3
71.9	LANCASTER .	81	79 00	57.7
78.2	CARNFORTH .	88	84 30	68.8
85.5	Milnthorpe .		91 40	61.2
91.0	Oxenholme .	101	98 50	46.1
98.1	Grayrigg . .		110 35	36.7
104.1	Tebay . .	117	117 00	56.1
109.6	*Shap Summit* .	127	125 35	38.5
123.1	PENRITH .	141	138 45	61.2
141.0	CARLISLE .	159	155 10	65.5

The attack on the mountain section was made much more vigorously than on the 'Experiment' run, although time was lost on the very sharp point-to-point allowance from Carnforth to Oxenholme. The minimum speed on Grayrigg bank was 33¼ m.p.h. and a most exceptional effort was made up Shap itself. Speed had not fallen below 30 m.p.h. by the time the train was in sight of Summit; but then the engine suddenly slipped, and before this could be checked speed had fallen to 22½ m.p.h. Nevertheless, the time of only 8 min. 35 sec. from

Tebay to Summit was then a truly record one for an unassisted engine hauling 340 tons.

Such a tonnage as 340 would have been regarded as a maximum rather than an average load for the Glasgow portion of the 10 a.m. from Euston. Loads of 230 to 250 tons were much more usual, and it was, rather, on the 2 p.m. from Euston that the greater opportunities came for the prowess of the 'George the Fifth' class to be displayed between Crewe and Carlisle. The usual load of the latter train was about 400 tons gross from Crewe to Preston, and about 330 or 340 tons northward. The absolute minimum north of Preston was the 7-coach set of the special 12-wheeled stock representing about 305 tons gross; but it was rare not to have at least one additional coach. In deference to its weight, the 2 p.m. was allowed 42 min. in which to climb the 31.4 miles from Carnforth to Shap Summit. The 39-minute allowance of the 10 a.m.

Down Irish Mail passing Rhyl: engine No. 896
'George Whale'

was planned for the minimum load of 6 coaches— about 200 tons gross, and was very rarely kept even with the superheater engines, if more than one or two coaches were added to the train. On the 2 p.m., however, timekeeping from point to point was immaculate, and a study of 'George the Fifth' working in the years just before World War I reveals some of the most interesting and fascinating aspects of the performance of these engines. From the records that have been preserved, it would seem that the maximum loads taken unassisted by the inside-cylinder superheater engines was one of 54 axles, that is three 8-wheelers in addition to the basic 7-coach 12-wheeled set. With the method of reckoning loads at that time, this would be counted as 'equal to 18½', or about 370 tons tare.

It is worth analysing what the timetable required with this train. The vertical rise between Carnforth and Shap Summit is 885 ft., and the booked average speed was 44.8 m.p.h. One could also assume that the initial speed would be about 65 m.p.h., and the final speed about 25 m.p.h. With the minimum load of 305 tons, the equivalent drawbar horsepower necessary would have averaged 745 from Carnforth to Summit, while with the maximum load of 390 tons it would have been about 915. In actual running, speeds were usually between 30 and 32 m.p.h. sustained on the final reaches of Grayrigg bank, and these would require outputs of about 1,000 e.d.h.p.

It is interesting to see how this schedule worked out in actual practice, and to the details of five runs

L.N.W.R. CARNFORTH-SHAP SUMMIT

Engine 4–4–0 No. Engine Name		2498 *Cyprus*	2155 *W.C. Brockle- hurst*	2663 *George the Fifth*	2242 *Meteor*	1662 *Deer- hound*	1631 *Race- horse*	1188 *Penmaen- mawr*
Load tons gross behind tender		280	340	345	360	370	390	390
Dist. point to point		m. s.	m. s.	m. s.	m. s.	m. s.	m. s.	m. s.
7.3	Carnforth—Milnthorpe	6 42	7 00	7 00	7 00	13 54	7 27	7 00
5.5	Milnthorpe—Oxenholme	5 56	7 10	6 20	6 05		6 59	6 20
7.1	Oxenholme—Grayrigg	10 30	11 45	11 05	11 00	11 20	12 08	11 15
6.0	Grayrigg—Tebay	6 04	6 25	6 40	7 05	5 44	6 48	6 35
5.5	Tebay—Summit	10 12	8 35	10 00	10 50	8 46	8 54	10 35
31.4	Total	39 24	40 55	41 05	42 00	39 44	42 16	41 45
Minimum speeds m.p.h. (a) Grayrigg (b) Shap Summit		38 14*	33¼ 22½*	32¾ 22½	31¼ 19½	32 27¾	32 25	33 19
Approx. D.H.P. at Grayrigg Summit		920	910	905	890	940	990	1030

*Speed reduced by slipping near Summit

Glasgow portion of 10 a.m. ex-Euston, diverted from main line and approaching Northampton: engine No. 643 'Sirocco'

on the 2 p.m. from Euston I have added those of two runs on the 10 a.m. Except for a fractional excess of 16 sec. on one trip with a maximum load, every engine climbed from Carnforth to Shap Summit in 42 min. or less; but perhaps the most remarkable performance was that of *Deerhound* which, with a load of 370 tons, averaged 47.3 m.p.h. throughout, including a rather astonishing 8 min. 46 sec. from Tebay to Summit. In this case the average drawbar horsepower throughout the climb was about 950. The maximum individual output of power in this collection of runs appears to be that of *Penmaenmawr*, in breasting Grayrigg summit at 33 m.p.h. with a 390-ton train—approximately 1,030 e.d.h.p.

As in the case of the ascents from Willesden to Tring discussed earlier in this chapter, so also from Carnforth to Shap there is one run that overshadows all the rest. Direct comparison with the runs on the 10 a.m. and 2 p.m. 'Scotsman' cannot be made, as in this particular instance the train was one making an intermediate stop at Oxenholme. This run is set out in a separate table herewith.

The load was no more than moderate, amounting only to 265 tons, but the speed of ascent was astonishing; over the 15.5 miles from milepost 22 to milepost 37½ the average speed was over *fifty miles per hour*—50.3 m.p.h. to be exact! The average gradient is 1 in 157, and the average d.p.h. involved was about 920, but in comparison with other runs this engine ran rather easily from Grayrigg to Tebay, and the average power output is lower than the exceptional efforts on the Grayrigg and Shap

Miles				m.	s.	Average speed m.p.h.
0.0	OXENHOLME		dep	0	00	—
0.9	Milepost	20		2	47	—
1.9	,,	21		4	28	35.7
2.9	,,	22		5	55	41.4
3.9	,,	23		7	13	46.2
4.9	,,	24		8	29	47.3
5.9	,,	25		9	46	46.7
6.9	,,	26		11	10	42.9
7.1	Grayrigg			11	23	—
8.8	Low Gill			13	21	51.9
10.9	Milepost	30		15	21	63.0
11.9	,,	31		16	15	66.7
12.9	,,	32		17	10	65.4
13.1	Tebay			17	17	—
13.9	Milepost	33		18	08	62.0
14.9	,,	34		19	07	61.0
15.9	,,	35		20	22	48.0
16.9	,,	36		21	52	40.0
17.9	,,	37		23	26	38.3
18.4	,,	37½		24	23	31.6
18.6	Shap Summit		pass	24	46	—

L.N.W.R. OXENHOLME—SHAP SUMMIT
Load: 265 tons gross
Engine: Superheater 4-4-0 No. 2062 *Sunbeam*

inclines would lead one to expect. On Grayrigg bank, the equivalent drawbar horsepower was at least 1,070. It is particularly interesting that the engine concerned was one of the earliest of the 'Precursors' to be rebuilt with piston valves and superheater, and thus made equal in every respect to the 'George the Fifth' class.

Quite apart from the actual power outputs developed, these were wonderful performances for

One of the first 'Precursors' to be superheated with piston valves: No. 2062 'Sunbeam', rebuilt February 1913

4—4—0 locomotives weighing no more than 59 tons, though two of the runs did point to the inherent weakness in the design for such herculean tasks. From the table of performances on page 89 it will be seen that on two out of the seven runs the locomotives were affected by serious slipping on the 1 in 75 gradient of the Shap incline. So, brilliant though their work could be in the North, the 'George the Fifths' were taken off the Carlisle run as soon as sufficient superheater 4—6—0s were available. The 'Prince of Wales' class, which is dealt with in the next chapter, did not entirely supersede the 'Georges', and it was rather the four-cylinder 4—6—0s of the 'Claughton' class, with 59 tons of adhesion weight, that eventually became the regular engines on the heaviest expresses north of Crewe.

Nevertheless, the 'George the Fifth' have a special place in the eventful history of express train operation over Shap. In relation to the total engine weight, there have never been more competent locomotives on the line, and it is interesting to compare them with their successors. On the basis of engine weight, with a 59-ton engine hauling a paying load of 390 tons, the following loads represent the equivalent in the case of later classes:

Engine Class	Engine weight tons	Equivalent load tons
'Claughton' .	77	510
'Royal Scot' .	84	555
'Duchess' .	104	685

In ordinary working—the duty in which the 'Georges' so distinguished themselves—the maximum I have known with a 'Claughton' is 440 tons, with a 'Scot' 510 tons, and with a 'Duchess' 585 tons. Thus the demands made upon the 'Georges' were exceptionally severe. But their very success on the Scotch expresses emphasises the difference in their performance characteristics as compared with those of the 'Experiments'. Had they not been exceptionally reliable in their steaming, one would have found drivers going hard from Crewe to Carnforth, and then taking them more gently up the main ascent. As it was, they went about things in just the opposite way—flogging their engines from Carnforth up to Shap Summit and maintaining the strenuous point-to-point times. With the greatest respect to the fine engines that have worked over the route in later years, we have never since seen such performances over Shap as those of the 'Georges'.

There were times, indeed, when the virtually impossible was attempted. One evening in September 1913, when the down 'Corridor' was loaded to no less than eight twelve-wheelers, and three eight-wheelers, 419 tons tare and about 445 tons full, no pilot was evidently available and engine No. 845, *Saddleback*, took this huge train out of Preston unassisted. That a tremendous fight against odds was made goes almost without saying, when one writes of L.N.W.R. express running in those days. To Carnforth, passed in 30 min. 31 sec., indeed no more than seconds had been lost on this tough schedule. The rise to milepost 9½, including 2½ miles at 1 in 134, was cleared at a minimum of 45 m.p.h., and an all-out attack was made on the Grayrigg bank with speed worked up to no less than 67 m.p.h. at Milnthorpe. Then, in the worst possible place, there came a signal check at Oxenholme. A lesser pair than the two stalwarts on the footplate of *Saddleback* that day would have stopped and taken a pilot there and then; but the signals cleared in time to avoid a dead stand, and so they opened out again, and blasted their way up the Grayrigg bank.

The average speed between Oxenholme and Grayrigg was 30 m.p.h. and the minimum sustained

Engine No. 1573 'Dunrobin', carrying special train number 824

Engine No. 2081 'New Zealand'

on the final 2 miles at 1 in 106, 25 m.p.h. With such a load as 445 tons this was a magnificent effort, showing a very high equivalent drawbar horsepower, at this speed, of 900. The corresponding pull probably gives a better impression of the terrific effort this little engine was making, for it works out at 13,500 lb., or 67 per cent. of the nominal tractive effort. There was no shortage of steam after this, for a very rapid recovery of speed followed on the level stretch to Tebay, and although the train was slowing down on passing the latter station the time over the preceding 4.3 miles from Low Gill had been only 4 min. 36 sec. So the 53.1 miles from Preston to Tebay had been covered in 67 min. 8 sec. It is true that this showed a loss of 5 min. on schedule; but of this quite 2 min. could be debited to the check at Oxenholme. Rear-end banking assistance was taken up the Shap incline, and naturally with the stop, lasting 1 min. 24 sec., and the restart more time was lost, passing Shap Summit in 82 min. 7 sec. from Preston. But some fast running downhill from Penrith would have regained at least 2 min. had there not been a dead stand for signals outside Carlisle. All in all, however, the total time from Preston was 116 min., instead of the 104 min. schedule.

The last 'George the Fifth' to be built: No. 2370 'Dovedale', completed at Crewe July 1916, in wartime unlined black

CHAPTER 8

THE 'PRINCE OF WALES' CLASS

By the spring of 1911, the success of the 'George the Fifth' class was so evident in every way that an order for 40 more was placed with Crewe Works and the first of this new batch, No. 956, *Dachshund*, was completed in April. Construction continued throughout the summer, and an average of rather more than one new 'George' a week was turned out between April and the beginning of October. In the meantime, Bowen-Cooke had the Crewe drawing office very busy with the design of his large new 4—6—0 locomotive, which in time materialised as the *Sir Gilbert Claughton*. News that these engines were on order was published in *The Locomotive Magazine* for June 1911. For an order to be placed on the Works, the design would obviously have to have been in an advanced state; but it is now well known that Bowen-Cooke was not able to build the 'Claughtons' as he had originally planned them. Although, by placing all four cylinders in line and driving on to one axle, the reciprocating parts were completely balanced and there was no 'hammer blow' at all at any speed, the civil engineer would not accept the increased dead load on the coupled wheels, and the engines had to be fitted with a smaller boiler than was originally planned.

While this design modification was being carried out, and approval for the revised weight diagram obtained, work on the engines was of course held up, and arrangements were made for the large batch of 'George the Fifths' then going through the shops to be followed immediately by some super-heated 'Experiments'. Whether these engines were originally projected as part of the general plan of motive power development on the L.N.W.R., or whether they were inserted quickly as a stop-gap, because of the delay in production of the 'Claughtons', it is not possible to say now; but the fact remains that only ten of them were built at first and multiplication of them did not begin until

October 1913, by which time yet another large batch of 'George the Fifths' had been completed at Crewe. Be that as it may, there was less difference externally between the superheated and non-superheated 'Experiments' than between the 'Precursors' and the 'George the Fifths'. In the case of the 4—6—0s, the only difference was in the extended smokebox.

The first of the new engines was named *Prince of Wales,* and by that name the class eventually became one of the best known and most widely used of any originating at Crewe (in L.N.W.R. days). But before anything had been published about the possibility of a superheated version of the 'Experiments' there had been some ambiguity over the use of the name 'Prince of Wales'. In 1911, great was the patriotic interest in all the pomp and ceremony associated with the Coronation of King George V and Queen Mary, and the very appropriate selection of the 'George the Fifth' class 4—4—0, No. 1800, the 5,000th engine to be completed at Crewe, as the Coronation engine gave immense satisfaction throughout the length and breadth of the L.N.W.R.

The Locomotive Magazine, always very well informed, gave the news in its issue of June 1911, together with a photograph of No. 1800 in plain black, unlined and unnamed, standing at the north end of Crewe station. But the news was amplified by the statement that the engine would be named 'Prince of Wales', and would bear in addition the word 'CORONATION', and a crown over the splasher. At the same time, confirmation of this impending move could be inferred by the renaming of the 'Experiment' class 4—6—0 No. 1676, which had previously borne the name 'Prince of Wales', as *Shakespeare.* The name 'Prince of Wales', on No. 1676, had been inherited from a 'Lady of the Lake' 2—2—2, No. 291: an engine of tragic memories since its involvement in the terrible accident to the

The first superheater 4-6-0, No. 819 'Prince of Wales', photographed in grey

day Irish Mail at Abergele in 1868. Actually, of course, the new 4—4—0, No. 1800, never carried the double inscription, and the July issue of *The Locomotive Magazine* gave the first news of the impending construction of the superheater 4—6—0s.

The new *Prince of Wales* of the L.N.W.R., engine No. 819, was completed at Crewe in October 1911 and, unlike all the preceding new engine classes dealt with in this book, was one of a production batch. There was evidently no question of a prototype. The advantages to be derived from superheating had been demonstrated in no uncertain style on the 'George the Fifth' class, and ten of the new 4—6—0 engines were built straight off

the drawing-board, so to speak. Few famous locomotive classes can have made their appearance with less ceremony or publicity. *The Locomotive Magazine* of December 1911 gave their names and numbers, but it was not until August of the following year that the same journal first published a photograph of one of them! I think this rather modest beginning can be traced firstly to the fact that the 'Experiments', in popular opinion, were somewhat under a cloud following the unfortunate interchange trial with the Great Western Railway in the previous year. Second, the *début* of the 'George the Fifth' class had been so brilliant that the introduction of the 'Prince of Wales' class would be regarded as a mere matter of course, if

10 a.m. ex-Edinburgh, conveying through carriages for Euston, Birmingham, Liverpool and Manchester, and passing Tebay. Engine No. 819 'Prince of Wales'

not even an anti-climax. Furthermore, the interest of locomotive enthusiasts had been whetted by news of the 4-cylinder 4—6—0s under construction at Crewe, and the completion of the first super-heated 'Experiment' was just 'by the way', as it were. In his review of locomotive constructional activities in 1911, in the January 1912 issue of *The Railway Magazine*, Cecil J. Allen did not even mention the 'Prince of Wales' class.

Turning now to the technical details of these splendid engines, an immediate point of contrast to the 'George the Fifth' was the use of bogie wheels 3 ft. 9 in. diameter, as in the 'Experiments'. It was found possible to fit 8 in. diameter piston valves above the cylinders, and to mount the latter at an inclination of 1 in 16, as in the 'Experiments'. The Joy valve gear was indirect, through rocking levers as in the 'Georges', and the valve events were very similar. As originally built the 'Prince of Wales' valve gear had the following basic dimensions:

Travel of valve in full gear	$5\frac{3}{8}$ in.
Lap	$1\frac{1}{4}$ in.
Lead (inside)	$\frac{1}{8}$ in.
Exhaust clearance	$\frac{1}{16}$ in.

The front end was generally similar to that of the 'George the Fifths', but while the external appearance was very neat and compact, the setting of the chimney ahead of the centre-line of the bogie gave, from certain angles, a squashed-up look, which was absent in the 'Experiments'. The boiler was subject to some very slight modifications in heating surfaces from time to time; but the original drawing shows the following particulars of heating surfaces:

152 tubes $2\frac{1}{8}$ in. ext. dia. 13ft. long	969·9 sq. ft.
24 ,, 5 in. ,, ,, ,, ,,	405·9 sq. ft.
Firebox	135·8 sq. ft.
Total heating surface of boiler	1511·6 sq. ft.
24 sets of superheater tubes, $1\frac{1}{8}$ in. internal diameter	304·4 sq. ft
Total heating surface	1816·0 sq. ft·
Grate area	25·0 sq. ft·

In all other aspects, the 'Prince of Wales' class was a repetition of the 'Experiment', and required the quite distinct technique in firing which, by that time, had been satisfactorily mastered.

The names of the new engines were a sign of the times on the L.N.W.R. By the autumn of 1911 all the 'Lady of the Lake' class 2—2—2s had been scrapped, and the slaughter of the Webb 3-cylinder compounds was almost complete. The 160 names from these engines had nearly all been absorbed in the 'Precursor' and the 'Experiment' classes, and the only passenger engine names becoming available for perpetuation were those from the occasional 'Jumbos' that were being scrapped—probably be-

cause their frames were failing. There were not nearly enough old names becoming available for the flood of new express passenger locomotives emerging from Crewe Works and, with the exception of the first engine, the 'Prince of Wales' class, like most of the 'George the Fifth' class of 1911, had entirely new names, and very attractive ones, too! The first ten engines of the class were:

No.	Name
819	*Prince of Wales*
1388	*Andromeda*
1452	*Bonaventure*
1454	*Coquette*
1537	*Enchantress*
1691	*Pathfinder*
1704	*Conqueror*
1721	*Defiance*
2021	*Wolverine*
2359	*Hermione*

They went into service as unobtrusively as they first appeared. As far as I can trace, all ten were originally stationed at Crewe North, and worked mostly on the Carlisle road. Runs with *Prince of Wales*, *Andromeda*, *Bonaventure* and *Defiance* showed consistently good work, though rather lacking in that brilliance which had made the 'George the Fifth' class 'hit the headlines' some months earlier. But it was evident from the start that the

Euston—Glasgow express near Carnforth: engine No. 1388 'Andromeda'

American special leaving Euston: engine No. 2359 'Hermione'

The 2 p.m. 'Corridor' leaving Euston, with 'Precursor' No. 811 'Express', pilot to Willesden only, and superheater 4-6-0 No. 979 'W. M. Thackeray'

'Experiment' style of running was not being perpetuated. The superheater 4—6—0s climbed the banks of the fell country with a vigour and competence that made very fast downhill running unnecessary. Both north and south of Crewe, however, their load limits were the same as the 'George the Fifths'. With six-coupled wheels, they were not quite such a prey to slipping as the four-coupled engines in bad weather.

In view of the strictures imposed by the civil engineer on the design of the 'Claughtons', on the score of axle loading, it is interesting to look at the details of weight distribution and the 'dynamic augment' of that weight in its likely effect upon the track and underline bridges. As designed, the dead weights on the four axles of a 'George the Fifth', from front to rear, were: 10.9, 10.9, 19.1, and 19.15 tons; on the 'Prince of Wales' class the weights were: $9\frac{3}{4}$, $9\frac{3}{4}$, $18\frac{1}{4}$, and $13\frac{1}{4}$ tons. One can appreciate that, on dead weight alone, this distribution would have been far more attractive to the civil engineer than the actual figures that he accepted

for the 'Claughtons'—let alone what Bowen-Cooke originally proposed. The actual 'Claughton' figures were: $9\frac{3}{8}$, $9\frac{3}{8}$, $19\frac{3}{4}$, $19\frac{3}{4}$, $19\frac{1}{2}$ tons. In retrospect, it is ironical to reflect that both the 'George the Fifth' and 'Prince of Wales' classes had a far worse effect on the track than the 'Claughtons'.

It was standard Crewe practice with all the inside-cylindered express locomotives to balance the reciprocating parts in one pair of driving wheels, instead of distributing the balancing between two pairs in the case of the 'Georges', and three pairs on the 'Prince of Wales' class. The result was a tremendous hammerblow from one pair of wheels and nothing from the rest. This practice was brought to light shortly after the grouping, when the researches of the Bridge Stress Committee led to an examination of the balancing of a great variety of British locomotives. A 'George the Fifth' and a 'Prince of Wales' were put through their paces over a number of different bridges, including the famous viaduct over the Mersey at Runcorn. The results confirmed the theoretical examination of the details

HAMMER—BLOW AT 6 REV. PER SEC.

Engine Class	Total Weight (tons)	Max. axle load (tons)	Max. hammer blow (tons)	Total engine hammer-blow (tons)	Max. combined load per axle (tons)
'George V'	59.85	19.15	14.1	9.7	33.2
'Prince of Wales' . . .	66.25	18.25	11.4	8.8	29.7
'Claughton'	77	19.75	Nil	Nil	19.75

96

of their balancing, and it is certainly interesting to compare them with those of the much larger and heavier 'Claughton', opposite, at 6 rev. per sec.: In view of the restriction put upon the maximum axle-load of the 'Claughton', despite the careful and cogent arguments put forward concerning the perfection of the balancing, it might seem strange that the Crewe drawing office, and Bowen-Cooke himself, should have been content with so crudely balanced an engine as the 'Prince of Wales'. Quite apart from its damaging effect upon the track, it would undoubtedly contribute to rough and uncomfortable riding. But I can well imagine it was scarcely given a thought. The 'Experiments' were balanced in the same way, and no one had complained, so why change?

Some examples of the early work of the 'Prince of Wales' class are given in the accompanying table, relating particularly to the climb from Carnforth to Shap Summit. In this table, *Defiance* and *Bonaventure* were on the Glasgow portion of the 10 a.m. from Euston, and *Prince of Wales* was on the 2 p.m. Of these three engines, *Bonaventure* to some extent repeated the tactics used by the drivers of the 'Experiments': running hard to Carnforth, getting time in hand, and then taking things easily on the bank. On the other hand, *Defiance,* albeit with a lighter load, did exactly the reverse, and made an exceedingly fine climb of the Grayrigg bank. The heavy load of the 2 p.m., and the existence of the Preston stop, precluded any great variation in the

L.N.W.R. CARNFORTH-SHAP SUMMIT 'PRINCE OF WALES' CLASS LOCOMOTIVES

Engine No.		1721		1452		819	
Engine Name		Defiance		Bona-venture		Prince of Wales	
Load, tons gross behind tender		270		325		330	
dist. pt. to pt.		m.	s.	m.	s.	m.	s.
7.3	Carnforth—Milnthorpe	7	20	7	25	7	25
5.5	Milnthorpe—Oxenholme	6	00	7	05	6	45
7.1	Oxenholme—Grayrigg	9	15	13	40*	11	30
6.0	Grayrigg—Tebay	6	30	6	50	6	25
5.5	Tebay—Summit	8	10	9	20	8	25
31.4 Total		37	15	44	20	40	30
Minimum speeds m.p.h.							
(a) Grayrigg		39½		27½*		36	
(b) Shap Summit		30		25		28½	

*Low minimum speed due to slipping near summit of Grayrigg bank.

tactics used in working that difficult train; and the driver of *Prince of Wales* kept very closely to the point-to-point times. Although there is less data on which to form an opinion, it must be admitted that in their *début* on the Crewe-Carlisle road the

Fleetwood boat express climbing Camden bank: engine No. 2198 'John Ruskin'

'Princes' had to take second place to the 'George the Fifths'.

The usefulness of a stud of superheated 'Experiments'—as these engines were frequently called in their early days—was nevertheless beyond question, and a batch of 30 new engines of the class was completed at Crewe between October 1913 and March 1914, as follows:

Locomotive			Date built
362	Robert Southey	. .	October 1913
892	Charles Wolfe	. .	,,
1081	John Keats	. .	,,
1089	Sidney Smith	. .	,,
1134	Victor Hugo	. .	,,
2040	Oliver Goldsmith	.	November 1913
2075	Robert Burns	.	,,
2198	John Ruskin	.	,,
2205	Thomas Moore	.	,,
2213	Charles Kingsley	.	,,
321	Henry W. Longfellow	.	,,
479	Thomas B. Macaulay	.	December 1913
951	Bulwer Lytton	.	,,
1679	Lord Byron	.	,,
2249	Thomas Campbell	.	,,
2283	Robert L. Stevenson	.	,,
86	Mark Twain	.	January 1914
146	Lewis Carroll	.	,,
307	R. B. Sheridan	.	,,
637	Thomas Gray	.	,,
979	W. M. Thackeray	.	,,
1400	Felicia Hemans	.	,,
964	Bret Harte	.	February 1914
985	Sir W. S. Gilbert	.	,,
1321	William Cowper	.	,,
2152	Charles Lamb	.	,,
2293	Percy Bysshe Shelley	.	,,
2377	Edward Gibbon	.	,,
2443	Charles James Lever	.	March 1914
2520	G. P. Neele	.	,,

The last of this batch, No. 2520, was to have been *Francis Bacon,* and thus complete a group of thirty engines all named after poets and literary folk. But at the last minute there was a happy inspiration to name it *G. P. Neele*, after the famous Superinten-

dent of the Line who retired in 1895, and spent part of his retirement in writing a book of reminiscences which is one of the classics of railway literature. He lived until 1920, attaining the great age of 95 years.

While on the subject of engine names, may I digress for a moment to mention my particular affection for engine No. 2293 of this series? In the year 1921, I sat for the School Certificate Examination and the subject of the 'English Story' paper—read to us by the invigilator, and which we had to transcribe—was of an amusing tea-time meeting between Keats and Shelley. Christian names came into that story, and all but one boy in that examination room were puzzled by the mysterious name by which Keats addressed Shelley. All, with that same exception, spelt it 'Bish'! There was something in being an L.N.W.R. locomotive fan, even in those far-off days! It was somewhat ironical that in later years No. 2293, *Percy Bysshe Shelley,* was the very engine used in the tests by the Bridge Stress Committee; and far from emulating the light, airy touch of the poet after which it was named, the engine amply confirmed the murderous hammerblow effect on the track so characteristic of the 'Prince of Wales' class as a whole.

Another fifty engines of the class were put on order in 1915; and it was significant of the extent to which Crewe Works was then becoming engaged on special wartime tasks that, for the first time since the establishment of the Works, an order for new locomotives was placed with an outside manufacturer. Thirty of the new engines were built at Crewe and, simultaneously, the North British Locomotive Co. commenced delivery of an order for twenty. It was evidently a matter of some urgency, for to get the locomotives built in the specified time, the work had to be divided between the Hyde Park and Queens Park Works, thus anticipating by twelve years the procedure adopted in building the

Engine No. 2520 'G. P. Neele', in photographic grey

The West Coast 'Corridor' express, 2 p.m. ex-Euston, near Shilton: engine No. 1084 'Shark'

'Royal Scot' 4—6—0s for the L.M.S.R. These twenty 'Princes' built in Scotland in 1915-16 all had names that had formerly been borne by 2—4—0s of the 6 ft. and 6 ft. 6 in. series of 'Jumbos'. The first batch of Crewe-built engines completed in October-December 1915 had names of distinguished Allied war leaders and personalities. It was characteristic of North Western engine-naming practice that, among Emperors, Kings and Commanders-in-Chief, space should also have been found for the heroic Nurse Edith Cavell. These ten engines were:

27	*General Joffre*
88	*Czar of Russia*
122	*King of the Belgians*
160	*King of Serbia*
185	*King of Italy*
877	*Raymond Poincare*
1333	*Sir John French*
2275	*Edith Cavell*
2396	*Queen of the Belgians*
2408	*Admiral Jellicoe*

The second Crewe batch was named entirely from recently-scrapped 'Jumbos', but the third included some names of tragic memory. At that stage of the war there were few victories to celebrate, and the names of these engines were by way of a list of battle honours, and of noble ships lost in the fight against enemy submarines. The costly and abortive attempt to force the Dardenelles in 1915 had ended with the evacuation of the Gallipoli peninsula in December of that same year, and the new engines turned out at Crewe in the following March had a 'lest we forget' touch about some of their names:

95	*Gallipoli*
126	*Anzac*
833	*Suvla Bay*
849	*Arethusa*
1100	*Lusitania*
1324	*Falaba*
2092	*Arabic*
2276	*Persia*
2295	*Anglia*
2340	*Tara*

The remaining thirty were as below, and as tabulated on page 100.

No.	Name	Date
606	*Castor*	Jan. 1916
745	*Pluto*	,,
810	*Onyx*	,,
1084	*Shark*	,,
1346	*Trent*	,,
1352	*The Nile*	,,
1379	*Witch*	,,
1484	*Smeaton*	,,
2417	*Atlas*	Feb. 1916
2442	*Odin*	,,

By April 1916 ninety were at work, and they were rapidly becoming some of the best appreciated engines on the line. Everyone concerned with

99

'PRINCE OF WALES' 4–6–0s
Built by North British Locomotive Co. Ltd.

Hyde Park Works:					Queens Park Works:				
Eng. No.	Name			Maker's No.	Date	Eng. No.	Name			Maker's No.	Date

Eng. No.	Name	Maker's No.	Date	Eng. No.	Name	Maker's No.	Date
136	Minerva	21256	Oct. 1915	90	Kestrel	21266	Dec. 1915
173	Livingstone	7	,,	401	Zamiel	7	,,
257	Plynlimmon	8	Nov. 1915	525	Vulcan	8	,,
446	Pegasus	9	,,	610	Albion	9	,,
1749	Precedent	21260	,,	867	Condor	21270	Jan. 1916
2063	Hibernia	1	,,	1132	Scott	1	,,
2175	Loadstone	2	,,	1466	Sphinx	2	,,
2203	Falstaff	3	,,	1744	Petrel	3	,,
2300	Hotspur	4	Dec. 1915	2055	Milton	4	,,
2392	Caliban	5	,,	2339	Samson	5	,,

the working of traffic on railways like a 'general utility' locomotive, and this the 'Princes' certainly were. In main-line traffic their load rating was the same as that of the 'George the Fifths', but except in the highest class of express passenger traffic the 'Princes' were proving the better all-round job. In any case, for the heaviest duties there were thirty 'Claughtons' on the road by the end of 1916. Very soon after the end of the war Crewe was set to work on new locomotive construction. An order for sixty-five more 'Prince of Wales' class 4—6—0s was placed, and fifty-four of these were on the road by the end of 1919.

During the war, and to the great regret of most locomotive lovers, the L.N.W.R. had temporarily abandoned the naming of express engines, and twenty-seven out of a batch of thirty 'Claughtons' turned out in 1917 were finished in unlined black, unnamed, and had nothing more than the famous 'Britannia' crest on the splashers by way of adornment. Brass was in short supply, and anything that could be done to lessen the amount of work necessary on locomotives in those years was worth doing —or, rather, not doing! This unwelcome precedent was continued on the first post-war batch of new 'Prince of Wales' class 4—6—0s. For the most part, the new engines were kept looking very smart; but the absence of names, even more than the absence of familiar lining-out, made it a 'new look' all the same.

One of the Scottish-built 'Princes', No. 2175 'Loadstone', in 'photographic grey', outside Hyde Park Works, Glasgow

An unusual working. Engine No. 86 'Mark Twain', hauling a southbound goods on the Caledonian Railway, and passing Port Carlisle Junction

2.5 p.m. Manchester—Euston express on Castlethorpe troughs, hauled by unnamed 'Prince of Wales' 4-6-0 No. 395

101

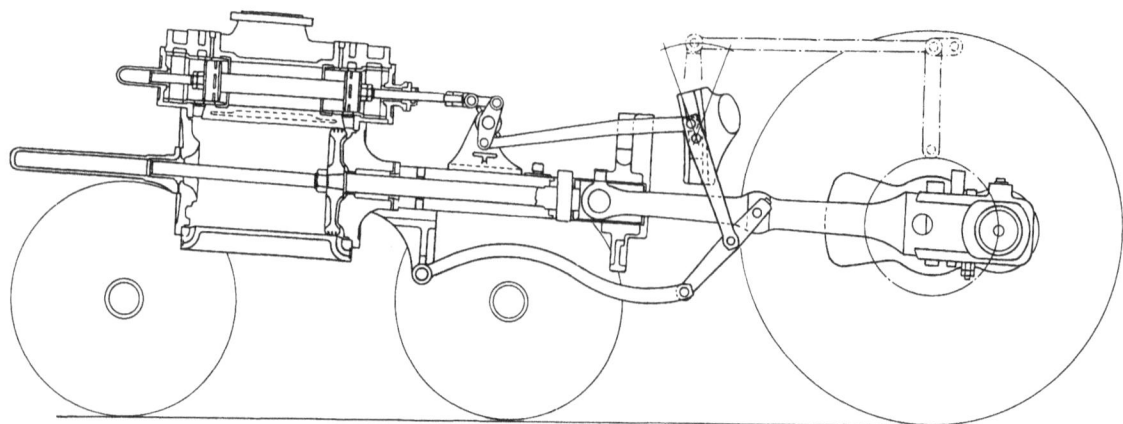

'Prince of Wales' class: diagram of 'indirect' Joy's valve gear

It was at this time that some investigations were made into the valve gear of the 'Prince of Wales' class engines. While these engines, like the 'George the Fifths', had indirect motion from the outset, the 4—6—2 superheater tank engines introduced in 1912 had the radius rod connected direct to the valve spindle instead of through a rocking lever, and attached to the motion link below, instead of above the sliding dies. This arrangement eliminated three pin-joints, but it could not be conveniently accommodated on the 'George the Fifths' and, presumably, when the design of the 'Prince of Wales' was originally prepared the 4—4—0 layout of valve gear was followed. The 'Princes' had never displayed the same brilliant performance characteristic of the 'George the Fifths', and it was pointed out that drivers were disinclined to use a wide regulator opening. One of the engines was indicated and it was found that the existing valve events gave excessive back pressure if one tried to work with a fairly wide regulator opening, and the gear well linked up. In 1920, an arrangement of direct

motion was fitted to one of the 'Poet' series, No. 479, *Thomas B. Macaulay*. The accompanying drawings show the respective layouts of the indirect and direct gear on the 'Prince of Wales' class. Since the first engines were built a change in setting of the indirect motion had been made; but although the new arrangement had the advantage of eliminating three pin-joints, it seemed, on balance, a retrograde move in that the valve travel in full gear was reduced from $5\frac{1}{8}$ in. to 4 9/16 in. The dimensions of the two layouts then were:

'PRINCE OF WALES' VALVE GEAR

		Indirect	Direct
Travel of valve, full gear in.	.	$5\frac{1}{8}$	$4\frac{9}{16}$
Lap of valve in.	.	$1\frac{1}{16}$	$1\frac{1}{16}$
Lead in.	.	$\frac{3}{16}$	$\frac{3}{16}$
Exhaust clearance in.	.	$\frac{1}{8}$	$\frac{1}{8}$
Diameter of valve in.	.	8	8

But a study of the actual valve readings of both arrangements shows that, although the port openings to steam were reduced in the full gear position in the new layout as compared with the old, a far better port opening was obtained at the ordinary working positions of the reverser. For example, at a nominal cut-off of 27 per cent. the indirect gear had provided port openings of only $\frac{1}{8}$ in. at the front end of the cylinder, and 3/16 in. at the back end. The corresponding dimensions for the direct motion were $\frac{1}{4}$ in. and $\frac{3}{8}$ in.—exactly double in each case. I have, nevertheless, heard from engineers with extensive footplate experience on these engines that the 'indirect' 'Princes' were stronger in hauling

Unnamed 'Prince' No. 1694

'PRINCE OF WALES' CLASS: VALVE READINGS
INDIRECT MOTION

Gear	Lead in.		Port opening in.		Cut-off %		Release %		Compression %		Travel of Valve in.
	F.	B.	F.	B.	F.	B.	F.	B.	F.	B.	
Full forward	$\frac{1}{16}$b	$\frac{1}{16}$b	$1\frac{5}{8}$b	$1\frac{9}{32}$	79	82	93	95	$93\frac{3}{4}$	$94\frac{1}{2}$	$5\frac{3}{32}$
49% ,,	$\frac{1}{64}$	$\frac{1}{16}$f	$1\frac{5}{32}$b	$\frac{3}{8}$f	52	46.5	82	81.5	85	84.5	3
27% ,,	0	$\frac{1}{16}$f	$\frac{5}{8}$f	$\frac{3}{16}$	31	24	71	66.5	72.5	75.5	$2\frac{7}{16}$
Full backward	$\frac{3}{8}$b	$\frac{5}{32}$b	$1\frac{1}{4}$	$1\frac{11}{16}$b	85	81.5	95.5	94.5	95.7	96.5	$5\frac{1}{16}$
56% ,,	$\frac{7}{16}$b	$\frac{1}{8}$	$\frac{7}{16}$b	$\frac{9}{16}$f	59.5	53	86	85	87.5	88.5	$3\frac{3}{8}$

DIRECT MOTION

Gear	Lead in.		Port opening in.		Cut-off %		Release %		Compression %		Travel of Valve in.
	F.	B.	F.	B.	F.	B.	F.	B.	F.	B.	
Full forward	$\frac{5}{32}$b	$\frac{3}{16}$b	$1\frac{1}{16}$	$1\frac{3}{8}$f	82	70.8	94.4	88.5	90.5	95.7	$4\frac{9}{16}$
47% ,,	$\frac{5}{32}$	$\frac{7}{32}$f	$\frac{7}{16}$b	$\frac{5}{8}$f	45	48.7	80.7	77.5	81.6	84.5	$3\frac{5}{16}$
26% ,,	$\frac{5}{32}$	$\frac{1}{4}$b	$\frac{1}{4}$b	$\frac{3}{8}$	23	29.5	65	66.3	71.2	70.8	$2\frac{1}{4}$
Full backward	$\frac{1}{4}$f	$\frac{7}{32}$b	$1\frac{5}{16}$	$1\frac{1}{4}$	74.8	75.6	90.5	92	93.3	93.1	$4\frac{1}{16}$
51% ,,	$\frac{5}{32}$b	$\frac{7}{32}$b	$\frac{9}{16}$	$\frac{5}{8}$b	51.5	50.8	81	81.4	84.4	83.9	$3\frac{5}{16}$
26% ,,	$\frac{5}{32}$b	$\frac{1}{4}$b	$\frac{1}{4}$	$1\frac{1}{32}$f	24.2	28.4	67.1	67.3	72	71.3	$2\frac{23}{32}$

a train than the 'direct'. With vivid recollections of what a rocking lever can do in the case of the Gresley conjugated gear towards causing over-running of the valve spindles, through 'slogger' developing in the pin-joints, these Crewe men have confided to me that they felt much the same was happening with the 'indirect' 'Princes', and that they were getting port openings far greater than the nominal values in consequence of the over-running. While this gave the engines more power, it was highly detrimental to their working in other ways. The full set of valve readings, taken from the Crewe drawings bearing Bowen-Cooke's signature, are given in the accompanying tables. In these tables, the letters 'b' and 'f' after certain dimensions indi-cate the engineers' parlance 'bare' and 'full' for readings a shade under or over the fractional dimensions quoted.

The results obtained from engine No. 479 were good enough for the direct motion layout to be adopted as a future standard, and it was specified for a further large order for ninety of these engines placed with Beardmore's in 1921. The running numbers of this batch, the last L.N.W.R. express passenger engines ever to be built, are given in the Appendix. They were delivered to Crewe from Dalmuir Works in 'shop grey', given the austerity plain black finish, and had their number plates fixed at Crewe itself. These post-war 'Princes' had a much duller and less glossy black than the

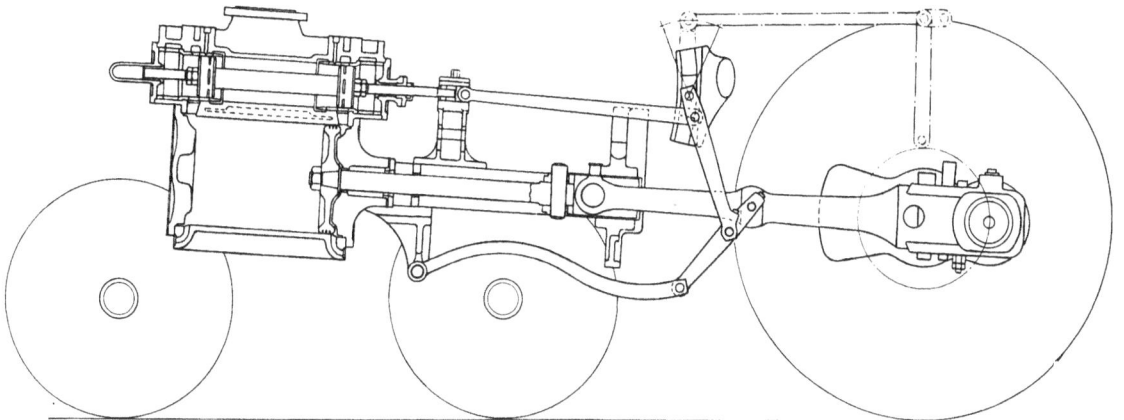

'Prince of Wales' class. Diagram of 'direct' Joy's valve gear

Up Irish Mail near Colwyn Bay, hauled by superheater 4-6-0 No. 522, then unnamed: later 'Stentor'

magnificent 'blackberry black' of earlier days, though some of the sheds, notably Preston, managed to work up quite a gloss on them as time went on. In those post-war years, when train services were still decelerated below the best pre-war standards, the new 'Princes' were used turn and turn about with 'Claughtons' on many of the best trains. In my photographing days at Grayrigg and Tebay, for example, one never knew if the Glasgow portion of the 10 a.m. from Euston would turn up hauled by a 'Prince' or a 'Claughton', and one of the new 'Princes' was frequently on the combined train between Euston and Crewe. None of the runs recorded during that period had any great distinction, though the working was for the most part very

smart and punctual. It was in the earliest post-war years, in competitive trials with other L.M.S.R. locomotives, that engines of the 'Prince of Wales' class rose to their greatest heights of performance.

Before leaving the pre-grouping era of the superheater 4—6—0s, mention must be made of the 'Experiment' class engine No. 1361, *Prospero*, which was rebuilt in 1915 as a 4-cylinder superheater locomotive to test out the Dendy-Marshall arrangement of cylinders and valves. The rebuilding is sometimes referred to as an experiment to try the Dendy-Marshall 'valve gear'. This is not correct. There was no such thing as a Dendy-Marshall valve gear; *Prospero* had the inventor's arrangement of cylinders and valves, and the steam

Manchester dining car express near Kenton: engines 88 'Czar of Russia', and 504 unnamed, but later named 'Canning'

'Experiment' class 4-6-0 No. 1361 'Prospero' as rebuilt with the Dendy Marshall arrangement of cylinders and valves

distribution was by means of the standard Joy valve gear, worked as usual off the inside connecting rods. The two accompanying diagrams explain the action, in its principles, as described in a paper read to the Institution of Locomotive Engineers in 1916 by the inventor.

The valves are combined and placed at the apex of a triangle, the base of which is formed by the line joining the centres of the cylinders. In the section shown, the system is drawn as if the valve were in between the cylinders, as indeed it could be were it not for outside considerations. The cylinders are arranged slightly *en echelon,* so that the front port of one is opposite the back port of the other, and they therefore take steam and exhaust together. This being so, it follows that the end ports are also opened and closed at exactly the same moment. The valve has to be of large diameter, as in the centre it has double duty to perform, and advantage is taken of this to connect up the exhaust spaces

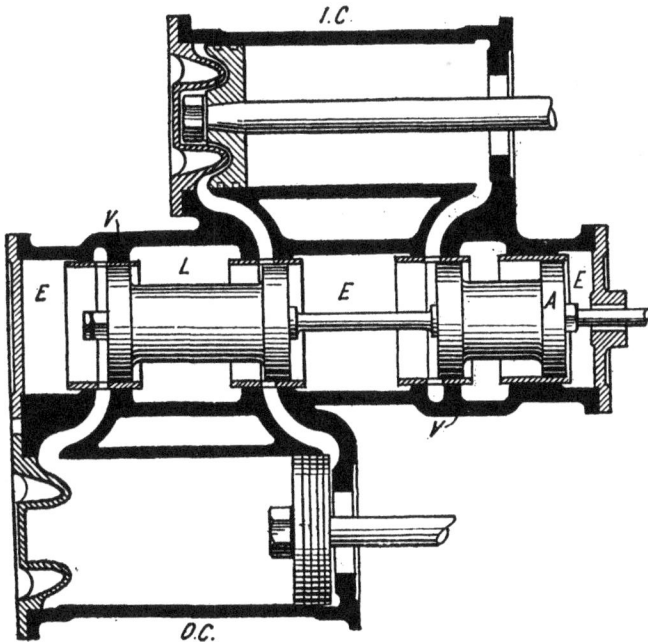

Diagram of cylinders and valves, Dendy Marshall system

105

Arrangement of cylinders and motion: engine No. 1361 'Prospero'

The down 'Corridor' near Farington, hauled by unnamed 'Prince' No. 1428

through the interior of it, thereby saving complicated passages in the casting. A triple valve would be sufficient to distribute the steam, as there are only three places where it passes to and from the cylinders; but in that case there would be an unbalanced force on the valve, owing to there being steam pressure at one end and exhaust at the other; hence, four elements are necessary to produce equilibrium, one being a dummy, which can be placed at either end. The steam has an easy path, because it passes through a semi-circular port adjacent to the cylinder instead of a circular one, half of which is on the opposite side of the valve, as occurs with an ordinary piston valve.

Prospero was fitted with four cylinders, 14 in. diameter by 26 in. stroke, and did some good work on the line. Of course, the war years did not constitute a very propitious time for experiments with new devices; but Bowen-Cooke was sufficiently interested to run some trials with the dynamometer car. The engine was put on to the up Fleetwood boat express, allowed 166 min. for the run of 152.7 miles from Crewe to Willesden. A load of about 430 tons gross was conveyed. The actual engine performance was very good, and many years later Dendy-Marshall himself quoted from a report dated 1920, as follows:

	49 standard 'Princes'	*Prospero*
Mileage between repairs in shops	46,666	58,365
Coal consumption over the above period average lb. per mile .	68.1	62.7

Down Irish Mail leaving the Britannia Tubular Bridge, with a 'Jumbo' piloting a 'Prince of Wales' 4-6-0

Down Scotch express approaching Rugby hauled by engine No. 2152 'Charles Lamb'

Up Irish Mail passing Colwyn Bay, with engine No. 2285

CHAPTER 9

TRIALS AND TRIBULATIONS

IN the railway amalgamations of 1922 and 1923, the London & North Western was affected more deeply than any other of the major companies. First, from January 1922, came the merger with the Lancashire & Yorkshire, in which Crewe became subservient to Horwich. Until it was actually imminent, such an event might have seemed unthinkable—that Crewe, above all locomotive centres, should ever have to play a secondary part to anyone. But once high policy had negotiated the merger of the two companies, the sequel in the locomotive department had become inevitable by the death in the autumn of 1920, at the early age of 62, of C. J. Bowen-Cooke. He was succeeded as Chief Mechanical Engineer by Hewitt Beames, another engineer of whom it was once said that to him Crewe and the L.N.W.R. were the very breath

H. P. M. Beames, Chief Mechanical Engineer, 1920-1

of life. But in 1920 he was still a relatively young man, while his counterpart on the Lancashire & Yorkshire Railway, George Hughes, was one of the veterans of the profession, and had indeed held the highest office at Horwich longer than Bowen-Cooke had been chief at Crewe. Hughes was still some years short of retiring age and, being in good health, the post naturally went to him on the enlarged London & North Western Railway. But a full year before the still greater amalgamation which produced the London Midland & Scottish Railway, the appointment of Hughes had the effect of bringing to a dead stop any further development of Crewe locomotive practice. The historic lineage that began with the work of Alexander Allan ended, so far as express motive power was concerned, with the completion of the last 'Claughton' at Crewe in 1921, and the delivery of the last 'Prince' from Beardmore's in April 1922.

During 1922, some trials were run between Crewe and Carlisle in which 'Princes' and 'Claughtons' were matched against Lancashire & Yorkshire Class '8' 4-cylinder 4—6—0s. No precise data was published as a result, but it was generally understood at the time that the Crewe engines had come off second best. Whatever happened in 1922, however, this was not the case in 1925 when a more extensive set of trials was carried out between Preston and Carlisle. The excellent work of the 'Prince', No. 90, *Kestrel*, will be discussed later. The 'trials' referred to in the heading to this chapter were engineering ones, but the 'tribulations' that came to affect the old L.N.W.R. from end to end of the line arose from the new administration set up in January 1923. This is no place in which to enlarge or gossip over the bitter antagonisms that grew up between Derby and Crewe, save to remark that the star of Crewe, which had begun to wane from the time of the L. & Y.R. amalgamation, was forced into positive eclipse from January 1923.

109

An unnamed 'Prince' No. 1351, fully lined out, alongside a Lancashire and Yorkshire 'Highflyer', No. 1418

Some of those interested in locomotive performance were ensnared into writing much conjectural nonsense as to why the North Western locomotives did not seem able to repeat their haulage feats of pre-grouping days, and their facile assumptions led to an impression that much of the earlier prestige of Crewe was ill-founded, and that reports of pre-war prowess could be regarded as so many fairy tales. The plain facts of certain outstanding runs, like those of *Wild Duck* and the early test performances of the 'Claughtons', were discounted as isolated achievements, incapable of repetition.

So far as the 'George the Fifth' class is concerned, earlier chapters of this book have shown how wrong these post-grouping assumptions were, while I have dealt several times elsewhere with the 'Claughton' saga. What is not generally realised, however, is the extent to which North Western engines underwent detailed modifications to make them conform to Derby ideas, and how these changes came to affect not only their maximum output but also their overall performance. But before these changes came into effect, Crewe had a splendid chance of showing what the 'Prince of Wales' class could do in maximum conditions of power output. Immediately after grouping, the locomotive stock of the L.M.S.R. was classified in the Midland style and this immediately produced the anomaly of placing the 'George the Fifths' in a lower power classification than the 'Princes'. On the North Western they had always been regarded as equal. Apart from this, it put the 'Georges' in a

lower power classification than the Midland compounds, and this in itself was enough to set the heather of Crewe on fire! As one North Western man, burning with indignation, said to me of the 'Georges': 'Class 3! Imagine a Johnson Belpaire [also Class 3] taking a 400-ton train up to Tring at a sustained 50 m.p.h.—I ask you!'

Among Class '4' engines on the L.M.S.R. in January 1923, there were 45 Midland compounds, 10 of the '999' simple 4—4—0s, and no fewer than 245 North Western 'Princes'. There were various Class '4' types in Scotland, including the 'Cardean' class 4—6—0s of the Caledonian; but none in sufficient numbers to warrant consideration as a future L.M.S.R. standard. No one also seems to have given a thought to the six ill-fated 'River' class 4—6—0s of the Highland—without much doubt the finest express passenger engines in Scotland, but largely ignored and relegated to goods traffic by their adopting parents, the Caledonian. So far as Class '4' motive power was concerned, the new administration was really faced with a clear-cut choice between Crewe and Derby; 245 'Princes' against 45 compounds or 10 of the '999' simples.

So there eventuated the historic series of dynamometer-car trials between Leeds and Carlisle, held between December 10, 1923 and January 17, 1924. In the choice of dates there was certainly to be no shirking of hard tasks. In the wild country traversed by the Settle & Carlisle line, the weather is never likely to be at its best around Christmas time, and the loads required to be hauled unassisted were

*A gathering of the 'Precursor' Family at Willesden shed, on Cup Final Day, including one 'Experiment',
two Superheater 'Precursors' and three 'Princes'*

unprecedented so far as the Midland was concerned. They were, of course, nothing out of the ordinary to North Western men accustomed to working over Shap. Indeed, on the basis of past achievement which Chapter 7 of this book emphasises, engines of the 'George the Fifth' class should have been able to do as well as, if not better than, the 'Princes'. Class '3' indeed!

In a previous volume in this series, *The Midland Compounds*, I have told what could be described as the Derby side of the story. From the Midland point of view, the stage management of those trials was superb. I am not suggesting that there was

anything but completely fair play for all the competitors; but had things been arranged differently I could well imagine it would have been difficult to persuade even the most expert of Midland drivers to take loads of 350 tons tare unassisted over Aisgill. So those responsible sent the North Western in to bat first. The 'Prince of Wales' 4—6—0 No. 388 showed, in no uncertain style, what could be done, and then the crew of the compound No. 1008 set out to go one better and, generally speaking, they succeeded. But the work of the L.N.W.R. engine No. 388 represents one of the best and most detailed studies of the performance of the 'Princes',

Up Irish Mail, on Castlethorpe troughs, 14-coach train behind 4-4-0 engine No. 2233 'Blackpool'

L.N.W.R. 4–6–0 engine No. 388   CARLISLE—LEEDS

	Load tons tare	305.6	302.6	305.6	352.6	354.6
Dist. Miles		Sch. min.	Actual m. s.	Actual m. s.	Actual m. s.	Actual m. s.	Actual m. s.
0.0	Carlisle	0	0 00	0 00	0 00	0 00	0 00
15.4	Lazonby	21	24 24	23 13	23 37	23 20	25 08
48.3	Aisgill	68	68 · 46	68 53	66 58	66 09	72 34
59.5	Blea Moor	80	81 12	81 24	79 36	78 17	85 15
— 113.0	Leeds	143	sigs. 141 51	sigs. 142 14	sigs. 143 28	sigs. 143 06	— 143 41

and it is fortunate that very complete details are available. For the opportunity of studying these in full I am indebted to Mr. A. E. Robson, Chief Mechanical and Electrical Engineer, London Midland Region, British Railways. Engine No. 388 was built at Crewe in 1919, and at the time of the trials she had been out of the shops six months since her last general repair. She had a piston and valve examination just before the trials, but I have not been able to ascertain whether she had direct motion by November 1923.

The trials were made on two of the regular day Scotch expresses, in each case running non-stop between Carlisle and Leeds. The Edinburgh trains were chosen in preference to the Glasgow; being normally of relatively light formation, they could be augmented as required to give the stipulated test loads of 300 and 350 tons tare, inclusive of the Horwich dynamometer car. Engine No. 388 was worked by a North Western driver normally stationed at Upperby shed, Carlisle; but for a period of five or six weeks prior to the tests he had been working regularly to Leeds, and was quite familiar with the road. In the ordinary way, Midland engines stationed at Durran Hill, Carlisle, were supplied with Tyneside coal; but for the purpose of these trials the competing engines had best

South Yorkshire 'hards', from Grimesthorpe Colliery, and so that the North Western man could familiarise himself with this beforehand it was supplied to engine No. 388 for regular workings during the week previous to the trials. The conditions were thus made as fair as possible for the L.N.W.R. engine, and according to the official report she steamed freely throughout, even in the heaviest conditions of working.

Detailed logs are available of only two out of her ten test journeys, one southbound with a 350-ton train, and one northbound with a 300-ton train. These logs were compiled by a very experienced recorder, and published in *The Railway Magazine* by Mr. Cecil J. Allen. But before discussing these, the details of the hill-climbing on all the ten runs are worthy of close study.

From these tables it will be seen that, except on the very last day, No. 388 kept very good time, though on the down journeys the 'long drag' from Settle Junction to Blea Moor took its toll with the 350-ton trains. Time was kept on two out of three runs with 300-ton loads, but with the 350-ton trains the time losses were 2½ and 3½ min. With these heavy trains the average speeds between Settle Junction and Blea Moor were much the same as those made by the Midland compound; but

L.N.W.R. 4–6–0 engine No. 388   LEEDS—CARLISLE

	Load tons tare	290.6	300.6	294.6	345.6	342.6
Dist. Miles		Sch. min.	Actual m. s.	Actual m. s.	Actual m. s.	Actual m. s.	Actual m. s.
0 0	Leeds	0	0 00	0 00	0 00	sigs. 0 00	stop 0 00
— 39 5	Settle Junction	51	51 29	52 29	51 09	52 31	60 31
53.5	Blea Moor	73	73 28	75 19	73 03	77 00	85 59
64.7	Aisgill	86	86 24	88 46	84 56	90 38	98 56
113.0	Carlisle	135	133 55	135 16	131 28	137 51	147 11

Manchester—Euston express on Castlethorpe troughs: engine No. 1749 'Precedent'

generally speaking, the Midland 4—4—0s, both simple and compound, passed Settle Junction at considerably higher speeds than the 'Prince', and their minimum speeds were lower. With the 350-ton trains, the comparative climbing speeds were:

Date	Engine No.	Load tons tare	Av. speed m.p.h.	Min. speed m.p.h.
13/12/23	L.N.W.R. 388	345.6	34.3	28.5
14/12/23	L.N.W.R. 388	342.6	33.0	26.2
18/12/23	M.R. 1008	343.6	33.1	26.0
15/1/24	M.R. 1008	342.6	33.3	25.0
3/1/24	M.R. 998	353.6	33.6	22.0
17/1/24	M.R. 998	344.6	32.6	19.5

From this table it will be seen that, on average, the 'Prince' did the best work of all, though on the southbound trips the compound had the advantage taking an average of the performance between Lazonby and Aisgill. A full log is available of the test run made by the 'Prince' on December 13, 1923, the first up run with a 350-ton load. The compound made generally faster times between Lazonby and Aisgill, but over the heaviest part of the climb, the 17.5 miles immediately south of Appleby, the 'Prince' once again held the advantage over one of the finest of the compound perform-

L.M.S.R. 12.10 p.m. CARLISLE—LEEDS

Load: 353 tons tare, 370 tons full
Engine: L.N.W.R. 4–6–0 No. 388

Dist. miles		Sch. min.	Actual m. s.	Speeds m.p.h.
0.0	CARLISLE . .	0	0 00	—
2.7	Scotby . .		6 04	32
—			—	41
8.4	*Low House Box* . .		15 36	34¾
13.5	*Summit* . .		21 32	47½
15.4	Lazonby . .	21	23 20	65
19.8	Langwathby . .		27 38	50¼
23.4	Culgaith . .		31 28	57
27.9	Long Marton . .		36 34	58
30.8	APPLEBY . .	39	39 52	47
33.2	Ormside . .		42 30	62½
36.5	*Top of 1 in 100* . .		46 53	36¾
38.3	Crosby Garrett . .		49 24	47
41.5	Kirkby Stephen . .		54 04	32½
44.8	*Mallerstang* . .		60 13	29¼
—			—	40
48.3	*Aisgill* . .	68	66 10	32¼
51.4	Hawes Junct. . .		69 47	62
59.5	*Blea Moor* . .	80	78 18	55½
73.5	*Settle Junct.* . .	93	91 14	69*
76.8	HELLIFIELD . .	97	94 49	—
—			—	64
86.8	SKIPTON . .	109	106 14	—
—			sigs.	14
102.1	Shipley (Bingley Junct.) .	129	128 30	—
—			—	66
113.0	LEEDS . .	143	143 36	—

*Maximum on descent

113

ances. Comparing the runs of December 13 and December 18, the times over the 17.5 miles from Appleby to Aisgill were 26 min. 18 sec. by the 'Prince' and 26 min. 44 sec. by the compound. The respective minimum speeds leaving Birkett Tunnel were $29\frac{1}{4}$ and 27 m.p.h., and at Aisgill summit $32\frac{1}{4}$ and $27\frac{1}{4}$ m.p.h. As usual, the Midland engine commenced the climb from a higher speed at Ormside viaduct, but the respective speeds show the extent of the North Western superiority on the backbreaking grind from Smardale viaduct, near Crosby Garrett, to Aisgill summit. The full log is shown in the table on page 113.

In a series of trials of this kind, the details of individual engine performance, however fascinating they may be to enthusiasts, do not count for much with those making an overall assessment, and while the 'Prince of Wales' class engine worked the trains satisfactorily enough, her coal consumption was higher than that of the compound. This important feature of the overall performance, in pounds per drawbar horsepower, is given for the complete series of trials, in company with the corresponding figures for the Midland compound:

trials was carried out on the same trains, and three other compounds were used at different times. Two of these compounds were of the new 6 ft. 9 in. series, and the third was a standard 7 ft. engine, No. 1023. On these later trials the coal consumption was not measured separately on the up and down runs, but taken for the complete round trip from Carlisle to Leeds and back; and the eight round trips gave very consistent results in terms of coal per drawbar horsepower hour, irrespective of the engines employed. The figures recorded were: 4.46, 4.39, 4.33, 4.45, 4.42, 4.68, and 4.43. The average for the entire set of trials was 4.45, against the North Western average a year earlier of 4.60. In the light of these later compound trials, the advantage over the 'Prince of Wales' engine was no more than slight—so slight, indeed, as to make it desirable to consider many factors other than coal consumption in assessing the two types.

In those early post-grouping years Crewe men felt that the dice was loaded against them in every facet of the mechanical engineering work of the line. Under Midland operating methods, the maximum unassisted load south of Carnforth was fixed at 360 tons, for both 'Princes' and 'Claughtons'

COAL CONSUMPTION: LEEDS—CARLISLE TRIALS

Date	Engine	Load tons tare	Coal lb./ d.h.p. hr.
10/12/23 Up	L.N.W. 388	$305\frac{1}{2}$	4.43
10/12/23 Dn	,,	$290\frac{1}{2}$	4.77
11/12/23 Up	,,	$302\frac{1}{2}$	4.52
11/12/23 Dn	,,	$300\frac{1}{2}$	4.62
12/12/23 Up	,,	$305\frac{1}{2}$	4.31
12/12/23 Dn	,,	$294\frac{1}{2}$	5.12
13/12/23 Up	,,	$352\frac{1}{2}$	4.31
13/12/23 Dn	,,	$345\frac{1}{2}$	4.97
14/12/23 Up	,,	$354\frac{1}{2}$	4.39
14/12/23 Dn	,,	$342\frac{1}{2}$	4.67
17/12/23 Up	M.R. 1008	$305\frac{1}{2}$	3.93
17/12/23 Dn	,,	$293\frac{1}{2}$	3.64
18/12/23 Up	,,	$354\frac{1}{2}$	3.83
18/12/23 Dn	,,	$343\frac{1}{2}$	3.73
19/12/23 Up	,,	$355\frac{1}{2}$	4.2
19/12/23 Dn	,,	$220\frac{1}{2}$	4.22
20/12/23 Up	,,	$309\frac{1}{2}$	4.02
20/12/23 Dn	,,	$225\frac{1}{2}$	4.5
31/12/23 Up	,,	$349\frac{1}{2}$	3.71
31/12/23 Dn	,,	$248\frac{1}{2}$	3.94
15/1/24 Up	,,	$352\frac{1}{2}$	3.7
15/1/24 Dn	,,	$342\frac{1}{2}$	3.9

Up semi-fast train leaving Lancaster; engine No. 525 'Vulcan'

A 'George the Fifth' No. 1623 'Nubian' piloting a 'Claughton' at Blisworth

The advantage in coal consumption lay clearly with the compound, though it was not generally realised at the time that this particular engine was putting up a somewhat exceptional performance. In November and December 1924 a further series of

L.N.W.R. ENGINE No. 388: 300-TON TRAINS: TEST RUNS CARLISLE AND LEEDS

Date	10 DEC., 1923		11 DEC., 1923		12 DEC., 1923	
Train	12.10 p.m.	4.7 p.m.	12.10 p.m.	4.7 p.m.	12.10 p.m.	4.7 p.m.
Weight of train (with dynamometer car) in tons	305.6	290.6	302.6	300.6	305.6	294.6
Train Miles	112.8	112.8	112.8	112.8	112.8	112.8
Ton Miles (excluding engine)	34472	32780	34133	33908	34472	33231
10% added for passengers and luggage	37551	35690	37178	36930	37551	36186
Running time in minutes	142.03	134.0	142.44	135.58	143.5	131.42
Time including stops in minutes	142.03	134.0	142.44	135.58	143.5	131.42
Average speed, m.p.h.	47.7	50.5	47.5	49.9	47.1	51.5
Maximum speed, m.p.h.	74.5	71.6	74.5	76.0	72.0	74.0
Minimum speed on bank—m.p.h.	29.0	33.8	30.5	29.0	30.5	30.0
Average drawbar pull—tons	2.28	2.125	2.3	2.03	2.275	2.05
Maximum drawbar pull on bank—tons	4.4	4.0	4.3	4.05	4.15	3.9
Average drawbar horsepower	616.5	609.0	615.5	580.0	606.0	605.5
Maximum drawbar horsepower	882.5	870.0	867.5	920.0	879.0	866.0
Maximum d.h.p. occurred at (miles from Leeds)	66.0	52.875	73.23	52.75	73.0	52.25
COAL— pounds per mile	47.2	45.0	47.1	43.5	45.2	47.7
„ pounds per d.h.p. hour	4.43	4.77	4.52	4.62	4.31	5.12
„ average rate of firing—tons per hour	1.004	1.012	0.999	0.97	0.952	1.097
„ per sq. ft. of grate area per hour (average)	89.9	90.8	89.5	86.9	85.3	98.3
„ maximum rate of firing—tons per hour	2.03	1.68	1.64	1.64	—	—
„ max. per sq. ft. of grate area per hour (lbs.)	182.0	151.0	147.0	147.0	No figures	
„ total time occupied in firing (min.)	26.62	26.53	24.27	23.12	quoted	
„ Ratio of firing time to total running time	0.187	0.196	0.17	0.17	—	—
WATER—Gallons per mile	31.2	28.5	27.7	29.6	28.5	28.3
„ pounds per d.h.p. hour	29.35	30.2	26.6	31.4	27.2	30.4
„ pounds per lb. of coal	6.62	6.325	5.89	6.81	6.3	5.93
OIL— Motion: pounds used per 100 miles					3.66	
„ Mech. lubricator pounds per 100 miles (av.)	Averages for three return				2.47	
„ Total. Pounds used per 100 miles (average)	trips				613	

L.N.W.R. ENGINE No. 388: 350-TON TRAINS: TEST RUNS CARLISLE AND LEEDS

Date	13 Dec., 1923		14 Dec., 1923	
Train	12.10 p.m.	4.7 p.m.	12.10 p.m.	4.7 p.m.
Weight of train (with dynamometer car) in tons	352.6	345.6	354.6	342.6
Train miles	112.8	112.8	112.8	112.8
Ton Miles (excluding engine)	39773	38984	39999	38645
10% added for passengers and luggage	43383	42514	43631	42142
Running times in minutes	143.15	137.93	143.6	144.22
Time including stops in minutes	143.15	137.93	143.6	147.23
Average speed, m.p.h.	47.25	49.1	47.1	46.9
Maximum speed, m.p.h.	69	74.4	75	72
Minimum speed on bank—m.p.h.	29.0	28.5	27.0	26.2
Average drawbar pull—tons	2.56	2.23	2.77	2.49
Maximum drawbar pull on bank—tons	5.0	4.5	5.2	5.15
Average drawbar horsepower	690	631	742	666
Maximum drawbar horsepower	965	836	951	921
Maximum d.h.p. occurred at (miles from Leeds)	68.25	45.75	72.0	45.5
COAL— pounds per mile	49.5	53.9	54.5	56.5
„ pounds per d.h.p. hour	4.31	4.965	4.39	4.67
„ average rate of firing—tons per hour	1.044	1.118	1.148	1.159
„ per sq. ft. of grate area per hr (average)	93.6	105.8	102.8	103.8
„ maximum rate of firing—tons per hour	1.770	1.830	—	—
„ max. per sq. ft. of grate are per hour (lbs.)	158.0	164.0	—	—
„ total time occupied in firing (min.)	25.1	26.2	—	—
„ Ratio of firing time to total running time	0.175	0.190		
WATER—Gallons per mile	32.3	31.8	35.1	32.2
„ pounds per d.h.p. hour	28.13	29.35	28.25	26.67
„ pounds per lb. of coal	6.53	5.91	6.43	5.71
OIL— Motion: pounds used per 100 miles	3.66			
„ Mech. lubricator pounds per 100 miles (average)	2.47	Averages for 2 return trips		
„ Total. Pounds used per 100 miles (average)	6.13			

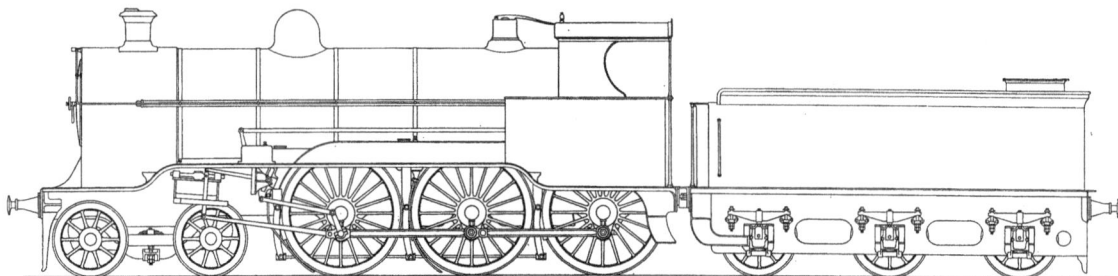

'Prince of Wales' class 4-6-0 with Walschaerts valve gear

alike, and a vast amount of double-heading immediately became necessary. The administrative upheaval following the merger with the Lancashire & Yorkshire, coming at a time when things had barely recovered from all the difficulties of war conditions, had led to a deterioration in standards of maintenance, and several serious failures of connecting rods occurred through fracture at the point of attachment of the jack link. No such trouble had been experienced with locomotives fitted with the Joy valve gear in days before World War I, when 'Precursors', 'Experiments' and 'George the Fifths' alike were being worked to the limit of their endurance for months on end. Although there was much good running in the early 1920s, the tasks performed were not as hard as those in the years prior to 1916. After several mishaps with Joy valve engines, there was one most alarming failure on a 'Prince' while descending Madeley bank at high speed, and it was felt that something had to be done to counteract this new trend of failures.

Hewitt Beames, from being Chief Mechanical Engineer of the L.N.W.R. was, from 1922, in the position of being little more than a divisional officer; but he was devoted to Crewe and the spirit of the old North Western, and two developments of the post-amalgamation era were due largely to him. In November 1922, a design was worked out for an outside Walschaerts gear for the 'Prince of Wales' class engines, while still retaining inside cylinders and valves. This enabled a plain connecting rod to be used, instead of the previous standard type with a hole for the jack link connection. This was first applied to one of the 'Poet' series, No. 964, *Bret Harte*, and very curious the engine looked.

At one time, it was thought there would be wholesale conversions to the new arrangement of valve gear, both on the 'Prince of Wales' and 'George the Fifth' classes, but actually only four engines were altered, and these not very rapidly.

The conversions to outside Walschaerts gear were:

964	*Bret Harte*
2340	*Tara*
867	*Condor*
56	unnamed

I have never seen details of any outstanding work with them—in fact, the only log of their running I have ever known of was one of my own, on the West of England night mail from Shrewsbury to Crewe in 1928. The train was divided and *Bret Harte,* then L.M.S.R. No. 5632, had a load of only 255 tons. The running was adequate, but quite indistinguished in comparison with the best standards of the 'Prince of Wales' class. At the time of the British Empire Exhibition at Wembley, in 1924, Beardmore's built for the exhibition a new engine similar to the Crewe rebuilds but having a Belpaire firebox. This engine was numbered 5845, and for the period of the exhibition carried the name *Prince of Wales*.

In 1923, under the direction of Hewitt Beames, proposals were prepared at Crewe for a range of new boilers for L.N.W.R. locomotives, having Belpaire fireboxes and being completely interchangeable with the older type. The drawing for the 'Prince of Wales' class is dated October 6, and that for the 'George the Fifth', October 19. These were duly authorised and replacement boilers for both classes were afterwards built to the new designs. Complete interchangeability thereafter became the watchword, and many engines of both classes had periods with Belpaire fireboxes, only to emerge after their next general overhaul with the round-topped firebox. The very last 'Prince of Wales' 4—6—0 to remain in service went to the scrapyard in 1949 with a round-topped firebox. At the same time, the use of 'Pop' safety valves became general, following their introduction on the first post-war batch of 'Claughtons', in 1919. The principal dimensions of the new boilers with Belpaire fireboxes are compared with those of the original design in the accompanying table:

BOILERS
Heating surfaces in sq. ft.

Engine class	'George the Fifth'		'Prince of Wales'	
	Original*	Belpaire	Original*	Belpaire
Small tubes	942.14	862	969.9	907
Superheater flues . .	380.44	380	405.9	401
Firebox . .	165.75	164.5	135.8	140
Total H.S. of boiler . .	1488.33	1406.5	1511.6	1448
Superheater elements .	285.67	284.5	304.4	304.4
Total H.S. .	1774.0	1691.0	1816.0	1752.4
Grate area .	22.4	22.4	25.0	26.0

* as running in 1923

There were, thus, slight reductions in heating surfaces, but not such as to exert any appreciable influence on performance. One notable change, however, was the increase in grate area on the 'Prince of Wales' class from 25 to 26 sq. ft.

After the grouping, Crewe Works was required to build many locomotives of alien design, and although new standards were introduced to cover details of construction that differed considerably from previous practice, in one respect the old traditions of Crewe persisted to the very end of the steam era; that respect was the quality of boiler-making. Not many years ago, Sir William Stanier was asked what were his strongest impressions of the diverse stud of locomotives for which he assumed responsibility when he became Chief Mechanical Engineer of the L.M.S.R. He mentioned the Crewe boiler shop, and particularly the boilers of the 'Prince of Wales' and 'George the Fifth' engines which, he said, had a very fine record of performance. Although the original 'Crewe-look' of the engines became somewhat changed, with Belpaire fireboxes and 'Pop' safety valves, none of the express passenger engines, so far as I know, received the Stanier-type chimney that was fitted to many of the 'Super-D' 0—8—0 goods engines.

A major alteration in detail affected the engines of all the classes described in this book during the 1920s; and although it came to exert a very serious influence on performance it was a change of which very few people outside L.M.S.R. locomotive circles were aware. Doubtless by order of the new régime, the centre bearings on the driving axles were removed. At first, the bushes were machined clear; but at a later period the support castings were removed altogether. This, of course, had the effect of reducing the maximum capacity of the locomotives themselves. If drivers attempted to flail their engines along in the style of 'old Crewe', the increased bearing pressures set up in the journals carried in the main frames became excessive

'Prince of Wales' class 4-6-0 No. 964 'Bret Harte', rebuilt with outside Walschaerts valve gear

117

and over-heating occurred. It was not surprising, therefore, that in L.M.S.R. days 'Georges' and 'Princes' could not repeat their pre-grouping feats of haulage. From 1927 onwards, when the 'Royal Scots' were introduced and the 'Claughtons' stepped down to 'second line' duties in many areas, the 'Georges' and 'Princes' were not normally required to do such heavy work as previously. The removal of the centre bearing was probably justified as a means of reducing maintenance costs, but it was equally the cause of the de-rating of the engines as load-haulers.

A number of engines of all the inside-cylinder L.N.W.R. express passenger classes had the width of their cabs cut down to enable them to work on the Midland Division, but in actual fact very few were transferred or did any regular work there. For a time, non-superheater 'Precursors' became the regular passenger motive power on the former Furness Railway, and they certainly livened up the running on the faster trains. At a later date, a number of 'Princes' worked over the line, in some cases continuing, without change, from Carlisle to Carnforth *via* Whitehaven and Barrow. Generally speaking, however, the engines with which I am here concerned made no impression beyond their own line in post-grouping days, and although the 246 locomotives of the 'Prince of Wales' class were to put in many years of useful service all over the Western Division of the L.M.S.R., it was more in the guise of second-line general-utility 'hacks' than as a group with a definite niche of their own. It was rather sad for Crewe men, seeing how narrowly the victory had been won in 1923-4, to witness the fame achieved by their great rivals in the 'No. 4 class' power category—the Midland compounds.

Up Irish Mail leaving Britannia Tubular Bridge. Non-superheater 'Precursor' No. 675 'Adjutant' piloting an unnamed 'Prince' No. 2073

CHAPTER 10

POST-GROUPING PERFORMANCE

THE prowess of the Midland compounds in the early years of the grouping was a constant thorn in the side of Crewe, and while those in higher authority might have received news of their successes in Scotland, the rank and file came up against the 'Crimson Ramblers', as they were nick-named, in real earnest in the working of the two-hour Birmingham expresses. Pre-war timings had been restored in the autumn of 1921, but with the difference that nearly all trains included an intermediate stop within the overall time of two hours. Some called at Coventry, others at Willesden, and although I believe there was originally an intention to limit the load of these trains to 200 tons, the 'George the Fifth' class engines immediately struck such splendid form that it was not long before the traffic department began piling on the tonnage, and loads of 300 tons and more became common on the more popular services. When the tonnage system of reckoning train loads was first introduced, superseding the old method of specifying so many 'coaches', the load for 'Georges' and 'Princes' on two-hour Birmingham non-stops was laid down as

350 tons. In post-war years, loads almost as great were, for a time, taken on a train like the 9.10 a.m. down, which called intermediately at Willesden.

It was when the 'Georges' were at the very zenith of their post-war achievements that high authority, in its wisdom, decided to put Midland compounds on to the job. To say that the fat was in the fire would be an understatement! To illustrate the kind of performance that was jettisoned, I have tabulated on page 120 three runs on the 9.21 a.m. from Willesden Junction to Birmingham, on all of which some fine work was done. The first of these, with engine No. 7, *Titan*, carried a light load for the North Western; but if one compares 190 tons with the weight and nominal tractive effort of a superheater 'Precursor', and then reflects upon the tonnage and locomotive power of some of our more recent flyers, the feat of covering the first 50 miles of the journey in a shade over 45 min. can be seen as quite outstanding. It was the product of a vigorous climb to Tring, and of some very fast running afterwards. From Castlethorpe onwards, the train was so well ahead of time that a much

*A 'George the Fifth' No. 956 'Bulldog',
still black, hauling a semi-fast with
coaches in Midland red*

*A 'Prince' No. 5751 (formerly No. 1549),
in Midland red livery, on up Aberdeen
express near Kenton*

L.M.S.R. WILLESDEN—BIRMINGHAM

Run No.			1		2		3	
Engine No.			7		238		282	
Engine Name			*Titan*		*F. W. Webb*		*Alaric*	
Load, tons E/F			180/190		270/290		295/320	
Dist. Miles		Sch. min.	Actual m. s.	Speeds m.p.h.	Actual m. s.	Speeds m.p.h.	Actual m. s.	Speeds m.p.h.
0.0	WILLESDEN . . .	0	0 00	—	0 00	—	0 00	—
2.7	Wembley . .		4 20	56½	5 15	—	5 00	—
6.0	Harrow . . .		7 50	60	9 25	49½	8 40	55½
7.9	Hatch End . . .		9 40	61	11 40	53	10 45	57½
12.1	WATFORD JUNCTION .	14	13 35	70½	16 10	62	14 50	69
15.6	King's Langley . .		16 45	66	19 45	58	18 10	—
19.1	Boxmoor . . .		19 55	65	23 20	60	21 45	58
22.6	Berkhamstead . .		23 10	62½	26 50	60	25 15	58
26.3	Tring . . .	29	26 50	61½	30 35	60	29 10	58
30.7	Cheddington . .		30 30	83½	34 25	80½	32 55	79
34.8	Leighton . . .		33 30	80½	37 30	—	36 15	71½
41.3	BLETCHLEY . .	43	38 25	79	42 35	—	41 50	70½
47.0	Wolverton . .		42 45	80½	47 05	77½	46 50	—
49.4	Castlethorpe . .		44 40	75	49 00	—	49 00	—
54.5	Roade . . .	55	49 50	52½	53 50	64½	54 25	53½
57.4	Blisworth . .	58	52 55	easy	56 20	72½	57 25	—
64.3	Weedon . . .		59 45	—	62 05	—	63 35	67
69.9	Welton . . .		65 25	—	67 05	64½	68 40	61½
—			sigs.	5	sigs.	—	sigs.	—
77.1	RUGBY . . .	77	75 00	—	75 00	—	82 30	—
					sig. stop		—	
83.7	Brandon . .		82 10	66	87 45	68	90 10	67
88.6	COVENTRY . .	88	86 35	—	92 10	—	94 40	—
92.1	Tile Hill . .		90 20	56½	95 35	60	98 20	55½
94.1	Berkswell . .		92 20	—	97 35	—	100 30	—
97.4	Hampton . .		95 20	74	100 30	75	103 35	71½
103.7	Stechford . .		100 40	—	105 45	68	109 15	—
105.6	Adderley Park .		102 35	—	107 35	—	111 05	65
			PWS		—		—	
107.5	BIRMINGHAM .	109	107 00		110 25		113 50	

		1	2	3
Net times min. . . .		102½	103½	106
Average speed, m.p.h. Watford—Tring . .		64.3	59.1	59.4
Tring—Castlethorpe .		77.7	75.2	69.9

more modest effort was needed. Judging from the records available, it seemed rare for this train to get a clear run through Rugby.

The second run, with a 290-ton train, had a curiously slow start; and speed had not exceeded 62 m.p.h. when Watford was passed. But then came some grand work with a sustained minimum of 60 m.p.h. up to Tring, and downhill running very little slower than that of *Titan*. The checks in the neighbourhood of Rugby cost at least 7 min. on this trip; but although Coventry was passed more than 4 min. late in consequence, 2½ min. was regained on the last stages into Birmingham. The last run, with the superheated 'Precursor' No. 282, *Alaric*, shows the kind of speed that was necessary for close point-to-point timekeeping; and with such a load as 320 tons it needed some hard work. This run was, indeed, very little inferior in quality to the standard of performance put up by the 'George

the Fifths' in their finest years. As will be seen from the table, *Alaric* sustained 58 m.p.h. up to Tring, touched 79 m.p.h. on the north descent, and was comfortably inside 'even time' when the usual delays came at Rugby. They were particularly bad on this trip, and although some fine running was made in conclusion, the arrival in Birmingham was 4¾ min. late.

One of the most important events in early grouping days, so far as L.N.W.R. locomotives were concerned, was the series of trials carried out in May 1925 between Preston and Carlisle with engines of the former Lancashire & Yorkshire, London & North Western, and Midland Railways, and supplemented a year later by some exactly similar tests with a Caledonian '60' class 4—6—0. One had, therefore, a set of comparative runs with the dynamometer car on special trains with the following classes of locomotive:

120

A 'Prince' in the new livery: No. 5834 (formerly No. 53)

L.N.W.R. 'Prince of Wales' 4—6—0
L.N.W.R. 'Claughton' 4—6—0
L.M.S.R. New Standard 6 ft. 9 in. compound
L.& Y.R. Class '8' 4—6—0
C.R. Pickersgill '60' class 4—6—0

The Class '4' engines were tested with trains of 300 and 350 tons, while the Class '5' 4—6—0s—'Claughton' and L. & Y. '8'—were tested with 350 and 400-ton trains. One had, therefore, the interesting experience of studying dynamometer car results from all five engines with 350-ton trains, and results from the three smaller engines with 300-ton trains.

The post-grouping controversies within the L.M.S.R. management were at their height in 1925. There was a very strong movement to re-cast all the main-line services on the Midland pattern, with strict limitations of load; and certain authorities pressed their claim that nothing larger than a Midland compound was needed for all express work. The trials in May 1925 were, therefore, in the nature of a challenge—'Midland compounds *versus* the Rest'. In this book, one is not so concerned with the railway political background as with the data it provided relative to the performance of the 'Prince of Wales' class, and the merits and demerits of that performance in comparison with that of

other well-known locomotives which were then grouped in L.M.S.R. ownership. It is particularly interesting to compare the working of the 'Prince' and the 'Claughton' on the same duty and with the same load; furthermore, the return test working from Preston to Carlisle was made on a schedule that corresponded very closely to that of the old 'Corridor' of pre-1914 days, which has always been regarded as something of a yardstick in L.N.W.R. locomotive performance on the Northern Division. Purely for the record, it is a pity that a 'George the Fifth' was not included in the 1925 trials over Shap; but I have already lamented enough in this chapter over the denigration of these splendid engines under L.M.S.R. management, and in any case the North Western was in one respect favoured in having two engines engaged in the trials.

The 'Prince of Wales' class was represented by engine No. 90, *Kestrel*, by then renumbered 5660. She had run only 6,529 miles since her last general overhaul and was in first-class condition throughout the trials. Although needing to be worked hard on the banks with the 350-ton train, she steamed consistently well and maintained water level in the boiler without any difficulty. The trials were made on special trains of empty stock, and in the southward direction they were booked to pass Shap

121

Engine No. 5273 'Jason', in red, climbing Camden bank

Birmingham—Peterborough express entering Rugby: engine No. 5300 'Hydra'

Summit, 31.4 miles from Carlisle, in 50 min. After that the schedule was relatively easy, with an allowance of 64 min. for the remaining 58.7 miles to Preston. Northbound, the test trains were given a time of 103 min. from Preston to Carlisle, with 1 min. less than the old pre-war 'Corridor', to passing Shap Summit. So far as the present theme

300-ton TEST TRAINS

Railway	Engine	Coal consumption	
		lb. per mile	lb. per d.h.p. hr.
L.N.W.R.	'Prince of Wales' .	40.1	5.1
C.R.	Pickersgill 4–6–0 .	48.7	5.18
L.M.S.R.	Standard Compound .	38.1	4.29

is concerned, interest is centred upon the working of *Kestrel*. The southbound runs can be fairly quickly dismissed. The engine made faster time from Carlisle to Shap Summit with the 350-ton train than with 300 tons. The respective passing times were 48 min. 7 sec. and 47 min. 33 sec., with minimum speeds between Clifton and Shap station

of 35 and 33 m.p.h. These may be compared with a run of No. 1388, *Andromeda*, when new, hauling a gross load of 375 tons, during which Shap Summit was passed in 47 min. 5 sec. from Carlisle, and the minimum speed above Clifton was 36 m.p.h.

The return working was a much more severe test, and the official report fortunately gives complete details. The accompanying logs therefore include not only the times made and the speeds, but

350-ton TEST TRAINS

Railway	Engine	Coal consumption	
		lb. per mile	lb. per d.h.p. hr.
L.N.W.R.	'Prince of Wales' .	48.3	5.05
C.R.	Pickersgill 4–6–0 .	51.6	4.73
L.M.S.R.	Standard Compound .	43.4	4.25
L.Y.R.	Class '8' 4–6–0 . .	51.3	5.13
L.N.W.R.	'Claughton' .	42.4	4.75

full particulars of the engine working. In connection with the latter, a regulator position of 0.5 indicates half-open, and so on, while a water level of 0.5 would indicate the water was halfway down in the gauge glass. The details of these performances show

Up Sunny South Special passing Lichfield, with engine No. 5834 ('Prince of Wales' class)

Up Irish Mail approaching Lichfield, hauled by a red 'Prince' No. 5838, with tender from 'Precursor' No. 5290

every evidence of a locomotive well on top of its job, and it is interesting to see that for the fast running on level track the valves were well linked up. It is rather unfortunate that the figures of coal consumption were taken for the complete round from Carlisle to Preston and back, rather than separately for the southbound and northbound runs. To a large extent also, the method of timing trains was left to the discretion of the individual drivers. In comparison with the actual coal used, the basic consumptions in pounds per drawbar horsepower hour are a little difficult to reconcile. But here, nevertheless, are the actual figures as set down in the report.

There was no loss of time to engine on any of the test journeys, though some drivers ran harder than was necessary to do the job. Although the comparisons cannot be carried to extremes owing to the variable quantities inherent in road tests of this nature, certain broad deductions can be made. With 300-ton trains the 'Prince' used little more coal than the compound to do the job, though when related to the actual work done on the drawbar of the train the performance was not so good as that of engine No. 388 in the Leeds-Carlisle trials of 1923. With the 350-ton train, the 'Prince' was not as economical as the 'Claughton' in doing the job. The latter engine seems to have been most skilfully

L.M.S.R. DYNAMOMETER-CAR TEST RUNS
4-6-0 Locomotive No. 5660 *Kestrel*

Load tons tare		Sch. min.	299.3		345.9	
Dist. Miles			Actual m. s.	Average Speeds m.p.h.	Actual m. s.	Average Speeds m.p.h.
0.0	PRESTON	0	0 00		0 00	
1.3	Oxheys Box	3	3 48		3 47	
—			sigs.		sigs.	
21.0	LANCASTER	23	24 56		23 44	
27.3	CARNFORTH	29	31 15	59.9	31 12	50.5
40.1	Oxenholme	43	45 19	54.6	46 25	50.5
47.2	Grayrigg	55	56 11	39.2	58 00	40.3
53.2	Tebay	61	62 41	55.3	64 41	53.8
58.7	Shap Summit	71	71 14	38.3	73 11	38.8
90.1	CARLISLE	103	102 43	59.7	103 33	62.3
	Net times min.		100¾		101½	

Time: Carnforth—Summit	42	39 59		41 59	

Engine Working:			Reg.	Cut-off %	Reg.	Cut-off %
	Scorton		0.2	24	0.5	28
	Carnforth		0.7	25	Full	32
	Milnthorpe		0.7	30	Full	35
	Oxenholme		0.7	32	Full	35
	Grayrigg		0.8	38	0.6	44
	Tebay		0.8	30	0.7	34
	Milepost 36		Full	45	Full	52
	Summit		Full	48	0.7	52

Boiler Performance:			B.P. p.s.i.	Water level	B.P. p.s.i.	Water level
	Scorton		168	0.9	166	0.9
	Carnforth		175	0.9	170	0.9
	Oxenholme		175	0.9	175	0.9
	Grayrigg		162	0.8	178	0.8
	Tebay		175	0.8	170	0.8
	Milepost 66		168	0.8	175	0.8
	Summit		166	0.5	164	0.5

Min. speed on Shap, m.p.h.		27		26½	
Max. drawbar pull		4.3 tons		4.7 tons	
Corresponding speed, m.p.h.		27		26½	
Max. speed to Carlisle, m.p.h.		74		74	

Non-superheater 'Precursor' No. 5273 'Jason' in the first version of the new livery as applied to L.N.W.R. locomotives (formerly No. 2064)

The famous 'Coronation' engine of 1911, in L.M.S.R. unlined black, but still retaining the original brass bands on the boiler

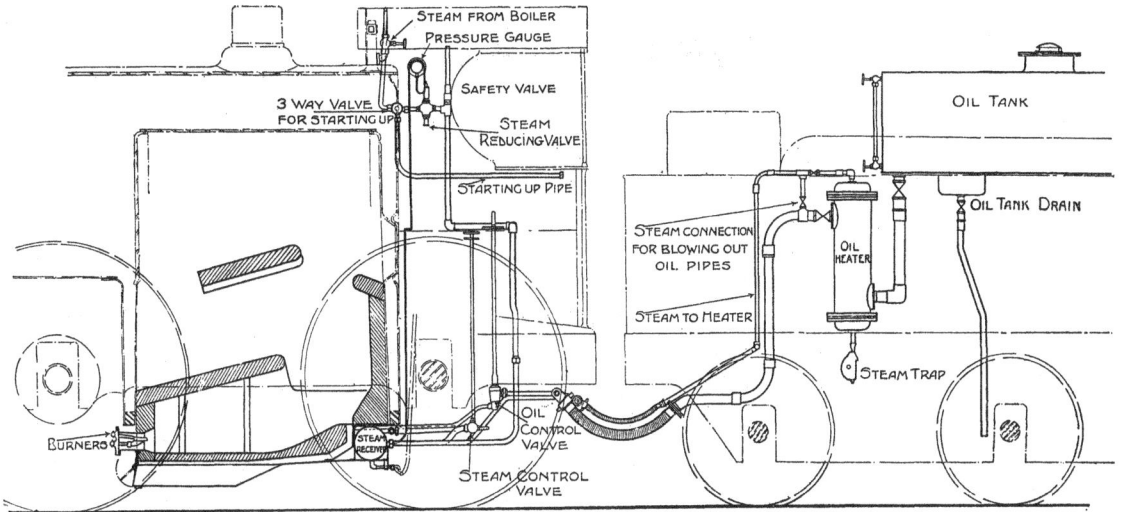

Diagram of oil-burning apparatus applied to engine No. 2585 'Watt'

handled and used less coal than the compound. Nevertheless, the basic consumptions of both 'Prince' and 'Claughton' were higher than that of the compound, and on these figures alone the preference of the L.M.S.R. authorities for the famous Derby design was amply justified.

During the prolonged coal strike of 1926, which followed the General Strike in May of that year, a number of locomotives were equipped for oil burning and the system followed that tried experimentally in 1920 by the L.N.W.R. on engine No. 2585, *Watt*, of the non-superheated 'Precursor' class. The Scarab system was used. This had its origin in Mesopotamia in World War I, when difficulties connected with fuel for military needs had represented a practically insurmountable barrier. It had since been adapted to various classes of boilers and other uses, including that of oil burning in locomotive fireboxes. The Scarab burner belongs to that class of burner in which the oil is atomised by a jet of air or steam. The general arrangement drawing reproduced shows the disposition of the burners and of the oil and steam supply pipes, as applied to engine No. 2585. The burners were placed at the front end of the firebox, a special 'ashpan' being arranged below the foundation ring. The flame was projected towards the rear end of the firebox and thence deflected towards the tube plate.

Three burners were installed and so connected to the oil and steam supply that the centre burner, the two outside burners, or all three burners could be used. Originally, it was intended that with full load the three burners would be operating, but after some preliminary runs had been made it was found that best results were obtained with the centre burner only, and this burner was accordingly provided with a nozzle capable of dealing with up to 160 gallons of oil per hour.

A certain quantity of air was admitted through the burner casings themselves. Additional air entered through a damper placed below the firebox and was heated by its contact with the hot surfaces of the 'ashpan' exposed to the flame. A considerable proportion of air passed to the burner by a passage provided immediately underneath the nozzle; a further amount entered the furnace through a number of small holes in the firebrick false bottom of the 'ashpan' a few feet in front of the burner nozzle. The remainder of this air supply was allowed to pass into the furnace close to the back plate of the firebox and, having been highly heated on its way, was admitted to the furnace to provide the necessary oxygen to complete combustion of the highly-atomised oil.

Steam for the oil burners for atomisation was taken from the steam mounting on the top of the boiler to a reducing valve set to deliver steam at 15 lb. pressure, which was conveyed to a receiver placed longitudinally in a space provided at the back of the 'ashpan'. A safety valve was provided

125

The first oil-burner. 'Precursor' No. 2585 'Watt' as fitted with the Scarab system in 1920

on the low pressure side of the pipe line, and steam was conveyed from the receiver by pipe lines to the burners, through regulating valves operated from the footplate. A connection for starting up the engine from cold by means of an auxiliary supply of air or steam was fitted in the cab. This connection was also fitted with a pipe, leading from the blower ring in the smokebox, for creating a draught when starting up.

During the 1926 coal strike, a total of 49 engines of the 'Prince of Wales' class was fitted up for oil burning, and the engines concerned are duly noted

The first oil-burner, No. 2585 'Watt', climbing Camden bank

126

in the case history of the class given in the appendix to this book. The record is complicated by the fact that, in 1926, many engines of the class were still carrying their L.N.W.R. numbers, and so as to give the contemporary picture here, in its proper sequence, the list is set out opposite:

OIL-FIRED 'PRINCE OF WALES' CLASS
Engines carrying L.N.W.R. numbers

56		1123	
86	Mark Twain	1452	Bonaventure
142		1620	
146	Lewis Carroll	1679	Lord Byron
241		1732	
242		2075	Robert Burns
246		2195	
252		2198	John Ruskin
362	Robert Southey	2213	Charles Kingsley
388		2249	Thomas Campbell
433		2359	Hermione
849	Arethusa	2392	Caliban

From the above, it will be seen that two engines, *Arethusa* and *Bonaventure,* appear in both lists. The explanation may have been that they were repaired and repainted during the period when they were oil-fired, and that during this time in their history they carried both their L.N.W.R. and L.M.S.R. numbers successively.

In actual performance on the road, as measured in minutes against miles, there was little to distinguish between the work of oil-fired and coal-fired engines of the 'Prince of Wales' class. At one time I travelled fairly frequently in the Euston through carriage conveyed on the 9.15 a.m. train from Barrow. This was attached to the 8.25 a.m. from

OIL-FIRED 'PRINCE OF WALES' CLASS
Engines carrying L.M.S.R. numbers

5600	Prince of Wales	5671	Arethusa
5602	Bonaventure	5696	
5607	Defiance	5702	
5608	Wolverine	5703	
5628	R. B. Sheridan	5712	
5630	W. M. Thackeray	5731	
5638	Charles James Lever	5741	
5641	Czar of Russia	5750	Marathon
5645	Raymond Poincaré	5774	
5651	Pluto	5791	
5655	Smeaton	5829	
5661	Gallipoli	5841	
5666	Plynlimmon	—	

Carlisle at Carnforth and, with a heavy train and several intermediate stops, it made quite a hard run from Carnforth to Crewe. I have tabulated on page 128 two runs with 'Prince of Wales' class engines clocked on this duty, one coal-fired and one oil-fired. The earlier run was an extremely competent performance with the unnamed engine No. 198. Except between Preston and Wigan, where

The last engine of the 'Precursor' family to be built. The 'Prince of Wales' class 4-6-0 No. 5845 built by Beardmore's in 1924, with outside Walschaerts gear, for exhibition at the British Empire Exhibition, Wembley. The name 'Prince of Wales' was transferred temporarily from No. 819

L.M.S.R. 10.28 a.m. CARNFORTH—CREWE

Date			4/8/26		16/1/24	
Engine: No. ('Prince')			241		198	
Fuel:			oil		coal	
Load tons E/F:			346/375*		396/425	
Dist. Miles		Sch. min.	Actual m. s.	Speeds m.p.h.	Actual m. s.	Speeds m.p.h.
0.0	CARNFORTH		0 00	—	0 00	—
3.2	Hest Bank		5 45	50	5 45	51
—			sigs.			
6.3	LANCASTER	10	10 55		9 45	
1.0	*Lancaster Junction*		3 15		3 10	
4.3	Galgate		7 50	55	7 55	54
8.3	Scorton		11 50	62½	11 50	61
11.5	Garstang		14 50	64½	15 00	62
16.2	Barton		19 20	57½	19 35	—
19.7	*Oxheys Box*		23 00		23 00	64 (max.)
—			sigs.		—	
21.0	PRESTON	26	26 10		25 15	
2.3	Farington		4 50	—	4 35	—
5.5	*Euxton Junction*		9 25	44	9 10	45
6.7	Balshaw Lane		10 55	54	10 45	53
9.3	Coppull		14 15	39	14 10	37
11.8	Standish		17 30	55	17 40	54 (max.)
—			sigs.		sigs.	
15.1	WIGAN	21	22 25		23 15	
4.8	Golborne		7 20		7 40	
8.3	*Winwick Junction*		10 45	62½	11 20	
—			sigs.			
11.8	WARRINGTON	17	16 00		15 15	
2.8	Moore		6 15	54	4 55†	58
7.9	*Weaver Junction*		11 50	49	10 25	50
12.2	Hartford		16 20	61½	14 50	61
—			sigs.			63
16.3	Winsford		21 15		19 05	—
19.2	Minshull Vernon		25 35	55	21 50	57
—			sigs.		sigs.	
24.0	CREWE	29	32 45		27 00	

*Load 321/350 tons from Warrington
†Banked to Acton Grange Junction

there was a bad signal check, things were comfortably in hand with this heavy load of 425 tons. Both trains were banked up the 1 in 98 from Lancaster to the old junction, and No. 198 had the advantage over the oil-fired engine by being banked from Warrington up to the Ship Canal viaduct. This run was typical of the tough jobs set to the 'Princes' at that time. The oil-fired engine also did well and, except in the immediate start out of Preston, where No. 198 was driven very hard, had the advantage of the lighter load. These were, nevertheless, heavy trains to set before a relatively small 4—6—0 locomotive, which even at the time of its first introduction in 1911 was really no more than an intermediate type.

An excellent example of the ordinary work of the 'Prince of Wales' class engines during the immediate post-war period is provided by a run I clocked on the up Aberdeen express, then due to arrive at Euston at 7.30 p.m. Engine No. 433 worked the train from Carlisle to Crewe, and my own record, from the Whitehaven-Euston through coach, began when we were attached to the train at Preston. For a moderate-powered engine, some hard work was involved with this heavy train from Preston up to Coppull summit. In view of compari-

Engine No. 1472 'Moorhen', as fitted experimentally with the Weir feed-water heater

L.M.S.R. CREWE—PRESTON

Load: 52 axles: 369 tons tare, 395 tons full
Engine: 'Prince of Wales' 4-6-0 No. 433

Dist. Miles		Actual m. s.	Speeds m.p.h.
0.0	PRESTON. . .	0 00	—
2.3	Farington . . .	4 20	—
5.5	*Euston Junct.* . .	9 35	36.6
6.7	Balshaw Lane . .	11 15	43.2
9.3	Coppull . . .	14 35	46.9
11.8	Standish . . .	18 05	42.9
15.1	WIGAN . . .	21 20	61.0
19.9	Golborne . . .	26 20	57.6
23.4	*Winwick Junct.* . .	29 30	66.4
26.9	WARRINGTON .	33 10	57.3
29.7	Moore . . .	36 35	49.3
34.8	*Weaver Junct.* . .	42 20	53.2
39.1	Hartford . . .	47 05	54.3
46.1	Minshull Vernon .	54 00	60.8
50.9	CREWE . . .	60 05	—

An unnamed 'Prince' No. 5826, coupled to a 'Royal Scot' at Camden sheds

sons that were then being made between L.N.W.R. and L.Y.R. locomotives it was interesting that on my next two runs with this same train we were hauled by the Class '8' Hughes 4-cylinder 4—6—0s and did very poorly. On the first, with a 350-ton load and one moderate check, we took 67¼ min. to reach Crewe, and on the second, with 415 tons, we took 16¾ min. to pass Coppull, against 14 min. 35 sec. by the stalwart little 'Prince of Wales' No.

433. Once over the summit, the latter engine was taken along in great style. There were no checks in the Wigan-Warrington area, and although this was before my stop-watching days, it is clear from the times that a maximum speed of around 70 m.p.h. was touched at Winwick Junction. Best of all, however, was the work on the gradually rising length from Weaver Junction to Crewe, giving a time of only 17¾ min., pass to stop, for this distance of 15.1 miles. This run was made in April 1924.

A route over which both 'Georges' and 'Princes' continued to have opportunities for showing their quality for some years after grouping was that

'Moorhen', as L.M.S.R. No. 5371, passing Berkhamsted on an up Manchester express

129

J

L.M.S.R. 1.10 p.m. CREWE—SHREWSBURY

Run No.		1		2		3		4	
Engine No.		5282		5635		5281		2275*	
Engine Name		Champion		Charles Lamb		Erebus		Edith Cavell	
Engine Type		4-4-0		4-6-0		4-4-0		4-6-0	
Load tons E/F		342/370		382/410		393/425		405/435	
Dist. Miles		Actual m. s.	Speeds m.p.h.	Actual m. s.	Speeds m.p.h.	Actual m. s.	Speeds m.p.h.	Actual m. s.	Speeds m.p.h.
0.0	CREWE . .	0 00	—	0 00	—	0 00	—	0 00	—
								sig. stop	
2.9	Willaston . .	5 50	47½	6 50	—	6 45	45	9 25	—
4.5	Nantwich . .	7 50	57	9 00	55½	8 45	57½	12 15	47½
8.9	Wrenbury . .	14 05	39/45	15 15	41/46	15 15	36/43½	20 40	31½/36
12.0	Milepost 12 .	19 40	28	20 40	27½	22 35	21½	26 50	27
13.8	WHITCHURCH .	22 00	52½	23 05	47½	25 00	50½	29 20	—
18.7	Prees . .	27 15	65	28 25	68	30 25	67	34 20	70½
22.0	Wem . . .	30 35	52½	31 40	58½	33 35	60	37 20	63½
25.5	Yorton . .	35 10	40	35 45	49	37 45	45	41 05	54
28.1	Hadnall . .	38 15	56/47	38 35	60/49	40 40	58½/47½	43 50	62½/50
		—	66	—	62	p.w.s.	67	—	65
32.7	SHREWSBURY .	44 25	—	45 10	—	46 40	—	49 40	—
	Net times min. .	44½		45¼		46¼		43½	

*Original numbering

between Shrewsbury and Crewe; and if the length of run was relatively short there were, nevertheless, some good loads to be hauled, and some stiff gradients to be climbed. I have tabulated details of four runs which I clocked personally between 1926 and 1929 on the 1.10 p.m. ex-Crewe, which carried through portions from Liverpool and Manchester to Plymouth. In this direction of running the principal difficulty, other than the awkward, sharply curved start out of Crewe, is the bank from Nant-

An unnamed 'Prince' working a northbound special past Barrs Court Junction, Hereford

wich to milepost 12, which is inclined at 1 in 97-184 to milepost 8; then there is a brief descent, at 1 in 384, followed by 3½ miles at 1 in 230-110-107-115.

The first two runs in this table were unchecked. The superheated 'Precursor' No. 5282, *Champion*, got away smartly, touching 57 m.p.h. at Nantwich, and not falling below 28 m.p.h. at the summit. By contrast, the 4—6—0 No. 5635, *Charles Lamb*, made a very slow start, but then climbed well. On the third run another 4—4—0, *Erebus*, hauling a heavy load of 425 tons, slightly bettered the 'Prince' out to Nantwich, but then made rather heavy weather of the bank, falling to 21½ m.p.h. at the summit. From there onwards the gradients are falling gently to Prees, level on to Wem, and then undulating with sharp rises near Yorton and Hadnall. From the last-mentioned station there is a steep descent into Shrewsbury; but although the alignment is good one rarely notes maximum speeds much in excess of 60 m.p.h.

Champion ran easily after Whitchurch and finished just inside the schedule time of 45 min. *Charles Lamb* was more brisk, and with a maximum speed of 68 m.p.h. and nothing less than 49 past Yorton, recovered the effect of the slow start and arrived practically on time. *Erebus*, which had fallen well behind the two preceding engines through the poor climb from Wrenbury, ran well to Hadnall; but a slight permanent way check in the approach to Shrewsbury caused a loss of ½ min. This was, however, the only case of time to be

One of the 'Princes' with outside Walschaerts gear, No. 5672 'Condor', at New Street, Birmingham (formerly No. 867)

booked against an L.N.W.R. engine that I have noted on this train, and with such a load as 425 tons it was no discreditable performance.

The last run, clocked in 1926, was the finest of them all. More than three years after grouping, this engine was still carrying her old number and still looking very smart in the old colours, fully lined out. We were making a splendid start out of Crewe when adverse signals compelled a dead stand, and in consequence of this, in re-accelerating we were doing no more than $47\frac{1}{2}$ m.p.h. at Nantwich. In the circumstances, the climb to milepost 12 was very fine, with a load of 435 tons. Then the driver really went for it, and his subsequent speeds were much the fastest of any in the table. By comparison with the other runs, it would seem that the signal check cost a full 6 min., and the net time of $43\frac{1}{2}$ min. represented a run in the finest traditions of the old L.N.W.R. It is appropriate to recall this run at a time when the 50th anniversary of her death brings to mind particularly the heroic English nurse after whom this engine was named.

From 1926 onwards, a number of locomotives of the 'Precursor' family were at work on the Furness line, and in course of travelling to and from my home at Barrow I noted some interesting work. Some heavy gradients are involved in crossing the Barrow isthmus, and on the up journey the ascent to Lindal begins just before Furness Abbey, and

includes nearly 4 miles at 1 in 97-103. I have tabulated two runs on expresses calling only at Ulverston, between Barrow and Carnforth. The schedule times on these two sections were 18 and

L.M.S.R. BARROW—CARNFORTH

Engine No.		2580	145
,, Name		*Problem*	—
,, Class		'Precursor'	'Prince of Wales'
Load tons E/F		168/190	208/225
Dist. miles		Actual m. s.	Actual m. s.
0.0	BARROW . .	0 00	0 00
1.7	Roose .	3 50	4 05
3.5	Furness Abbey .	6 45	6 45
5.1	Dalton .	9 50	9 30
6.8	Lindal .	13 35	12 40
9.9	ULVERSTON .	18 20	17 55
1.8	*Plumpton Junct.* .	2 45	2 55
6.0	Cark .	7 35	8 00
8.4	Kents Bank .	10 25	10 55
10.2	Grange-over-Sands .	12 35	13 05
—		—	sig. stop
13.4	Arnside .	16 20	21 30
15.8	Silverdale .	19 10	27 05
19.0	CARNFORTH .	24 05	33 00
Speeds m.p.h.			
Roose (max.) . .		39	$41\frac{1}{2}$
Lindal (min.) . .		$25\frac{1}{2}$	30
Max. to Silverdale . .		53	$52\frac{1}{2}$

L.M.S.R. CARNFORTH—BARROW
4.45 a.m. Down Mail

Load: 238 tons tare, 250 tons full
Engine: 4—4—0 No. 5208 *Messenger*

Dist. Miles				Actual m. s.	Speeds m.p.h.
0.0	CARNFORTH .	.		0 00	—
3.2	Silverdale .	.		6 10	47½
5.6	Arnside .	.		9 20	54½
8.8	Grange-over-Sands	.		12 45	56
10.6	Kents Bank	.		14 40	56
13.0	Cark	.		17 15	56
17.2	*Plumpton Junct.* .	.		21 35	58½
19.0	ULVERSTON .	.		23 45	—
1.0	*Milepost 20*	.		2 40	—
2.0	*Milepost 21*	.		5 05	23½
3.1	Lindal	.		7 30	32
4.8	Dalton	.		9 30	60
6.4	Furness Abbey	.		11 10	62
—				—	53 (slack)
8.2	Roose	.		13 00	58½
				sigs.	
9.9	BARROW	.		16 55	—

29 min. The latter, with a fine downhill start to the Leven viaduct and easy gradients afterwards, presented no difficulty; but the non-superheater 'Precursor' No. 2580, *Problem*, barely kept time to Ulverston, falling to a minimum of 25½ m.p.h. on the bank. On the other hand, the 'Prince', No. 145, did excellently, with a minimum speed of 30 m.p.h. on this winding, difficult incline.

On the down road, I tried the early morning mail several times in the course of overnight journeys from London, chiefly to see what could be made of the fast timing of 24 min. start to stop from Carnforth to Ulverston. We had Midland 0—6—0s: a non-superheated Midland Class '2' 4—4—0, and an occasional 'Precursor'; and generally when the engine was not losing time there were checks. Then one morning a non-superheater 'Precursor', No. 5208, *Messenger*, was on the job, and the result is tabulated herewith. We raced round the curves along the seashore at 56 to 58 m.p.h., and just kept time to Ulverston. Then came the real thrill. The ascent out of Ulverston is at 1 in 79 off the platform end, easing to 1 in 107 after a mile. Here speed rose, by hard work, to 23½ m.p.h., but it was the subsequent descent that was like nothing I had experienced before. We usually came down that steep winding descent through Dalton and Furness Abbey with the brakes frequently applied, and occasionally touching 50 m.p.h. To come tearing down it at over sixty was certainly an exciting start to the day!

From the introduction of the 'Royal Scots' in 1927, the 'Princes' began to disappear from main-

line work. A more regularised system of engine allocation appointed selected batches of 'Claughtons' to duties for which the 'Scots' were not available, and the rather indiscriminate use of locomotives that had followed the grouping came to an end. It so happened, however, that in the early 1930s I was to witness at first-hand a great deal of the performance of all the classes that have featured in this book, and their work became a matter of live daily concern to me. After a long period living in 'digs' in Central London, I became a season-ticket holder between Watford and Euston, and my journeys by the 8.53 a.m. up non-stop, and the 6.15 p.m. down, non-stop to Bushey, provided a fascinating daily interest in going to and from work. Both trains were worked by engines from Bletchley shed, and until the year 1935 it was most exceptional to have anything except ex-L.N.W.R. engines on those trains. On the 6.15 p.m. down, we used to get non-superheater as well as superheater engines; but the 8.53 a.m. up, with its smart timing of 21 min. for the 17.5 miles from Watford Junction to Euston, was exclusively a superheater job. This latter train was worked by Bletchley men on Mondays, Wednesdays and Fridays, and by Rugby men on Tuesdays and Thursdays. I must admit that the running honours, with the same engines, were

*A 'Prince' with Walschaerts gear, No. 2340
'Tara', piloting a 'Claughton' past
Edge Hill sheds, Liverpool*

*Glasgow—Euston express leaving Carlisle;
unnamed 'Prince' No. 5815*

132

Up intermediate express, Rugby to Euston, on Bushey troughs, hauled by a superheater 'Precursor'
No. 5241 'Napoleon' (formerly No. 1311)

heavily on the side of Bletchley! On the 6.15 p.m. down, I have only three records of a 'Prince' being used; but we had 'Precursors', 'Experiments' and 'George the Fifths' to our hearts' content.

I must admit that the 'Experiments' did not show up too well. Among my old logs I have notes of running with *President, Buffalo, Sarmatian, City of Edinburgh, John Penn, Herefordshire* and *Sisyphus* and although they used to start vigorously enough up Camden bank with our usual load of 215 tons,

it was rare to find one of them making any good speed after Willesden. I have set down in the accompanying table the fastest I have had with each type of engine on this particular train.

The fastest individual start up Camden bank was made by an 'Experiment', No. 5458, *City of Edinburgh*; but the 'Prince' No. 5771 on the run tabulated left her standing after South Hampstead.

By far the most interesting work was performed on the up train. I remember telling an L.M.S. man

L.M.S.R. 6.15 p.m. EUSTON—BUSHEY
Load: 7 coaches (non-corridor) 215 tons gross

Run No. Engine No. Engine Name Class		1 5237 *Pearl* 'Precursor'	2 5537 *Herefordshire* 'Experiment'	3 5244 *Tubal* 'George V'	4 5771 — 'Prince'
Dist. Miles		Actual m. s.	Actual m. s.	Actual m. s.	Actual m. s.
0.0	EUSTON	0 00	0 00	0 00	0 00
1.0	Milepost 1	3 25	4 00	3 25	2 52
2.4	South Hampstead	5 55	6 30	5 55	5 10
5.4	WILLESDEN	9 40	10 10	9 35	8 40
8.1	Wembley	12 32	13 08	12 25	11 27
11.4	Harrow	16 22	17 05	16 00	15 00
13.3	Hatch End	18 42	19 20	18 05	17 02
14.8	Carpenders Park	20 32	21 10	19 45	18 37
16.0	Bushey	22 15	23 00	21 30	20 20
Average speed Willesden—Carpenders Park, m.p.h.		51.8	51.3	55.5	56.7

In the final L.M.S. style, with an additional '2' prefixing the number; engine No. 25304 'Greyhound', in unlined black (formerly No. 302)

of my acquaintance about some of these runs, and he rather brushed their merit to one side with the comment: 'Oh, but it's all downhill!' Actually, of course, in the 15.1 miles from Watford Junction to South Hampstead there are only 7½ miles downhill at 1 in 335; the rest is level. In appraising the work of the Crewe superheater engines on the 8.53 a.m. up, one should note the vigour of the starts and the continuation of the speed from Brent Junction to South Hampstead, as well as the high maximum speeds attained in the neighbourhood of Wembley. I first began to use this train in September 1932, and in my old notebooks I have records of 52 runs with ex-L.N.W.R. express locomotives, and on 30 of these the 15.1 miles from Watford start to passing South Hampstead were covered in 16 min. or less. Another 14 gave passing times of between 16 and 16½ min. A total of 27 different engines were

L.M.S.R. 8.53 a.m. WATFORD—EUSTON

4-4-0 LOCOMOTIVES

Run No.		1	2	3	4	5	6
Engine No.		5246	5245	5246	5244	5313	5246
Engine Name		*Adjutant*	*Antaeus*	*Adjutant*	*Tubal*	*Etna*	*Adjutant*
Load, tons gross		285	285	285	285	285	305
Dist. miles		Actual m. s.	Actual m. s.	Actual m. s.	Actual m. s.	Actual m. s.	Actual m. s.
0.0	WATFORD	0 00	0 00	0 00	0 00	0 00	0 00
1.5	Bushey	3 10	3 07	3 05	3 03	3 10	3 02
2.7	Carpenders Park . . .	4 42	4 37	4 40	4 32	4 43	4 30
4.2	Hatch End	6 22	6 15	6 22	6 02	6 25	6 02
6.1	Harrow	8 05	8 02	8 08	7 50	8 12	7 45
9.4	Wembley	10 43	10 43	10 48	10 35	10 57	10 21
10.5	*Brent Junction* . . .	11 34	—	11 38	11 27	—	—
12.1	WILLESDEN . . .	12 48	12 51	12 52	12 45	13 05	12 30
15.1	South Hampstead . .	15 17	15 27	15 22	15 25	15 33	15 20
		sigs.	—	sigs.	—	sigs.	—
17.5	EUSTON	20 15	19 55	20 05	19 30	20 00	20 00
Average speed		m.p.h.	m.p.h.	m.p.h.	m.p.h.	m.p.h.	m.p.h.
	Harrow—South Hampstead . .	75	72.8	74.5	71.2	73.5	71.2
Max. speed	. . . .	79	75½	80½	74½	76½	79

A 'Prince' in the final style: engine No. 25673 'Lusitania', formerly No. 1100.
One of the last to survive, scrapped January 1949

involved, 8 'Prince of Wales', 17 superheater 'Precursors', with piston valves, and 2 'George the Fifths' proper.

In the case of the 4—4—0s, I have picked out for tabulation the six fastest runs, and of these all except one were made with the minimum load of 285 tons gross behind the tender. Again, note should be taken of the vigour of the starts, after which a speed of 50 m.p.h. was usually attained by Carpenders Park, before the 1 in 335 descent was commenced. The maximum speeds clocked up at Brent Junction are spectacular enough, but the average speeds sustained over 9 miles out of this 17.5-mile journey are perhaps even more impressive. We used to get this kind of running, with very little variation, day after day with the Bletchley

L.M.S.R. 8.53 a.m. WATFORD—EUSTON
4–6–0 LOCOMOTIVES

Run No.		1	2	3	4	5	6
Engine No.		5727	5680	5681	5828	5828	5828
Engine Name		—	*Loadstone*	*Falstaff*	—	—	—
Load, tons gross		285	285	285	315	325	345
Dist. Miles		Actual m. s.	Actual m. s.	Actual m. s.	Actual m. s.	Actual m. s.	Actual m. s.
0.0	WATFORD	0 00	0 00	0 00	0 00	0 00	0 00
1.5	Bushey	3 06	3 03	3 10	3 10	3 00	3 07
2.7	Carpenders Park	4 33	4 33	4 33	4 40	4 32	4 37
4.2	Hatch End	6 07	6 09	6 24	6 16	6 10	6 17
6.1	Harrow	7 48	7 54	8 10	7 59	7 55	8 05
9.4	Wembley	10 28	10 40	10 54	10 39	10 42	10 52
10.5	*Brent Junction*	—	11 31	11 45	11 29	11 33	11 45
12.1	WILLESDEN	12 35	12 48	13 00	12 43	12 52	13 07
15.1	South Hampstead	15 10	15 16	15 28	15 14	15 28	15 47
17.5	EUSTON	19 35	19 33	19 47	p.w.s. 20 32	19 40	20 00
Average speed Harrow—South Hampstead . .		m.p.h. 73.4	m.p.h. 73.4	m.p.h. 74	m.p.h. 74.5	m.p.h. 71.5	m.p.h. 70.1
Max. speed		76½	76½	77½	79	75	72½

men. The Rugby drivers usually eased their engines through Willesden, and an example of this is to be seen on Run No. 6. As far as Wembley, this was the fastest of the whole series, despite the load of 305 tons; but the driver eased to $62\frac{1}{2}$ m.p.h. through Willesden. Curiously enough, the star men in the Bletchley link all had names commencing with 'B'—Barden, Bates, Bowler and Brewer— and with any of these drivers one could be sure of an immaculate display, whatever engines they had. I always remember one week in March 1933 when Bowler had the train, with *Antaeus* on Monday, *Tubal* on Wednesday, and *Candidate* on Friday. The variations in his passing times were no greater than 3 sec. at Harrow, 6 sec. at Willesden, and 9 sec. at South Hampstead! Among the 4—4—0s, engine No. 5246, *Adjutant*, was undoubtedly the favourite, and what a flyer she was!

Taken all round, however, there was little to choose between the 4—4—0s and the 4—6—0s. With regard to the latter, the runs tabulated were not all my fastest, because I have included two in which the loads were 325 and 345 tons. The last-named was another of Driver Bowler's performances, and despite 60 tons extra load, the start was barely distinguishable from the usual 285-ton efforts. The heaviest load I noted with a 4—4—0 engine was 335 tons, with *Antaeus*. We passed South Hampstead in 16 min. 28 sec. but were checked outside Euston, and for once failed to keep the 21-min. schedule. I had another run with *Falstaff* that involved the fastest-ever start out of Watford, and a time of 11 min. 10 sec. to Brent Junction. But, unfortunately, it was a Rugby day and, true to type, the driver eased right down before passing through Willesden, otherwise we could have passed South Hampstead in less than 15 min. This latter feat I never succeeded in doing until the new '23XX' class 2—6—4 tanks replaced the 'Precursor' tanks, on the Saturday working.

The weekday 8.53 a.m. certainly sounded the swan-song of the Crewe inside-cylinder express engines. My most lasting impression of those daily journeys is of the relative ease and quietness with which the engines did the job. True, we had a good healthy bark from the exhaust as they were getting away, but by the time Carpenders Park was passed they had lapsed into relative silence. Engines like *Adjutant*, *Antaeus* and *Tubal*, among the 4—4—0s, were obviously in first-class condition, while the 'Prince of Wales' 4—6—0s—particularly the unnamed engine No. 5828—were as good Class '4' units as any to be found on the L.M.S.R. system at that time. But by the year 1933 the sands were beginning to run out for all the Crewe express passenger engines, and it is time now for a final appraisal of the breed as a whole, to try and establish their true place in history.

A flashback to their finest years: a superheater 'Precursor', No. 301 'Leviathan', on the northbound Sunny South Special near Kenton

136

CHAPTER 11

A FINAL APPRAISAL

IN the foregoing chapters I have described, as dispassionately as I can, the rise, the zenith and the decline of the great family of 571 Crewe express passenger locomotives, which originated with the *Precursor* of 1904 and ended with Walschaerts valve-geared *Prince of Wales* of 1924. In this monograph, it has been my aim to set down their achievements, factually; and having done so, to try and ascribe to them their true place in the history of the British railway steam locomotive. This is not an easy thing to do with any of the old North Western engines. Mergers, take-overs and amalgamations of any kind are rarely accomplished without some strife between the personnel principally involved, and the formation of the London Midland & Scottish Railway was not carried out with a superabundance of tact and goodwill on the part of those who grasped the reins of higher management. There was much antagonism at lower levels, which resulted in the creation of a deep-seated feud between Crewe and Derby.

Supporters of one side or the other were naturally given to excesses of partisanship in extolling one engine design or denouncing its rival on the other side, and in this technical 'slanging match' it was inevitable, at the time, that Crewe should get the worst of it. High authority, for perfectly sound reasons, preferred the products of Derby; but unfortunately certain onlookers, possessed of facile pens, rushed into print in praise of the new order, at the same time going out of their way to discredit those who had come off second best. The fury of Crewe partisans was understandable; they slung mud for mud, and it took all the sagacity of the

The last 'Prince' to be built, as running in her final L.M.S. days: engine No. 25845 with outside Walschaerts gear

The scrapping of 'Coronation' begins, in June 1940

second generation of L.M.S.R. management to begin the welding together of the once rival interests, and the replacement of North Western and Midland traditions by a new L.M.S. tradition. Even today, I still meet men who get distinctly hot under the collar in support of Crewe or of Derby; but by and large the old fires have died down, and one can now look at the saga of 'Precursors', 'Experiments', 'Georges' and 'Princes' in more distant perspective.

It is interesting to try and recapture something of the atmosphere that prevailed in the early days of Bowen-Cooke's régime. The new chief, like his predecessor, had been a running man rather than a designer or a workshop expert, and he would have been keenly aware of the splendid spirit that was traditional of the L.N.W.R. footplate men. Even in the most difficult days of the Webb compound era, there still prevailed an intense feeling of pride in the job, and time was lost by engine only when it was literally impossible to do any better. It was only natural that such men took to the Whale 'Precursors' as ducks to water, and quickly established new traditions of hard running with a high standard of punctuality. So it fell to Bowen-Cooke to add those touches of finesse and higher thermal efficiency to the hard-slogging 'Precursors' and

'Experiments', as manifested in the 'George the Fifth' and 'Prince of Wales' classes. In the hands of men who were brought up to drive hard and to fire hard, the results were little short of phenomenal. Nowhere else in Great Britain could one see engines worked so hard or so efficiently as between Euston and Crewe. On schedules requiring average speeds of 54 to 55 m.p.h., the rostered load for a 'George' was 400 tons. In the period from 1910 to 1914, loads of 400 tons were quite rare, except on the North Western. The Great Eastern and the Great Western worked trains of this magnitude at summer holiday peak periods; but on the Great Eastern the schedules were not so fast, and the crack West of England trains of the G.W.R. were by that time always worked by the Churchward 4—6—0s. On the basis of power output per ton of engine weight, the work of the 'George the Fifth' class 4—4—0s in the years 1911-15 was unquestionably the finest to be seen in Great Britain.

Nevertheless, in retrospect, could one apply to the general locomotive policy of the L.N.W.R. a paraphrase of the famous comment upon the Charge of the Light Brigade at Balaclava: 'It was magnificent, but it was not good railway working'? Taken by and large, it has generally been traditional to treat British locomotives fairly gently.

'Experiment' class 4-6-0 No. 5484 'William Cawkwell', with Belpaire firebox (formerly No. 2269)

There have always been drivers who would flail their mounts unmercifully in attempts to meet cases of overload, or late running; but the policy of most locomotive superintendents has been to provide engines capable of meeting requirements at economical rates of steaming—no one more so in this respect than Churchward on the Great Western. In those spacious days, most British railways could rely upon ample supplies of first-class coal, and on most railways locomotive boilers and fireboxes were smaller than those of their Continental and American contemporaries. The difference between the London & North Western and other railways was that, on so many top link duties locomotives were worked far more nearly to their limit, and for far longer spells, than anywhere else. Although 'Georges' and 'Princes' had two points of weakness in their mechanical design, which led to deterioration in standards of performance as mileage mounted up between successive visits to Crewe for general overhaul, there is no doubt that the engines themselves stood up to the heavy and continuous demands made upon them; and on that ground alone the policy of Crewe was amply justified.

What was applicable to the years 1911-15 was not necessarily the right course to adopt in the years after World War I, and it is by what happened subsequently that the earlier brilliant period is sometimes judged. The two factors that particularly prejudiced the work of the superheater engines were the weakness of the frame design, and the Schmidt patent piston rings. The former led to a roughness at speed that could well have been intolerable to a lesser breed of drivers and firemen, while wear of the rings led to a serious leakage of steam past the piston valves, and consequently to a greatly increased coal consumption. But a criticism of policy, rather than of detailed design, centred

An 'Experiment' No. 5520 'Sisyphus' on westbound goods at Sandy on the Cambridge line

An unnamed 'Prince' No. 25722, entering Euston with an up stopping train

upon the post-war decision to build large numbers of new locomotives to pre-war designs, when large-scale replacement of stock immediately after the war became a matter of managerial policy. It was then that the North Western became the victim of its own wealth, its great resources and of the pre-war prestige of its locomotive department.

With the resources of Crewe Works at his command, Bowen-Cooke had been able to make an outstanding contribution towards the production of weapons of war and munitions. Many special devices and machinery had been designed and built in record time, so much so that there had been no time for considering any developments in locomotive design. During the war, there had been no need for any such development; there were plenty of 'Georges', 'Princes' and 'Claughtons' to work the traffic. In general, there was no need for any special allocation of engine power. 'Georges' and 'Princes' which had taken 400-ton loads on the fastest pre-war schedules could readily tackle 450-500 tons on the greatly decelerated schedules in force from January 1917 onwards, and, except on the day Anglo-Scottish expresses, 'Georges', 'Princes' and 'Claughtons' were pooled for almost indiscriminate use on the main line.

Engine No. 25631 'Felicia Hemans';
formerly No. 1400

Outside valve gear 'Prince' No. 25672,
formerly 'Condor'

When the end of the war came and the demand for special tasks of munition production ceased, Bowen-Cooke was anxious enough to get back to locomotive work, and some steps towards new development were taken. But when the management decided to order, at short notice, large quantities of new locomotives for general service, there was nothing for it but to perpetuate the 'Prince of Wales' class, as it stood, for general utility work, and the 'Claughtons' for heavy main-line express duty. Apart from the change to direct motion on the last 90 'Princes', and an alteration to the grates of the 'Claughtons', post-war locomotive construction for the L.N.W.R. was thus entirely to designs dating back to 1911 and 1913.

Other British railways, whose workshop facilities had not allowed of munition making on so vast a scale as Crewe, had been able to devote some time to thoughts of post-war locomotive development, and the result of this was the appearance, in 1918-20, of some notable new designs. Equally it can be said that the locomotive practice of these companies, as well as their performance on the road, had been far inferior to that of Crewe in pre-war years. But although the circumstances that led up to it are clear enough, the fact remains that in the last years of the pre-grouping era the London & North Western Railway was relying entirely upon locomotives of pre-war design, and that by the time of the amalgamation with the Lancashire & Yorkshire Railway no steps had been taken towards any new development. Of course, the situation at Crewe was complicated by the death of Bowen-Cooke in the autumn of 1920, and his successor, Hewitt Beames, had little time to take stock of the situation before he became subordinate to the chief mechanical engineer of the former Lancashire & Yorkshire Railway.

It is interesting to speculate as to what would have happened had it not been for Bowen-Cooke's untimely death. Although George Hughes of the L. & Y. had been in office as Chief Mechanical Engineer longer than Bowen-Cooke, it is hard to imagine that he would have been preferred at the time of the merger of the L. & N.W.R. and the L. & Y.R. in 1921. Had he remained in harness, it is unlikely that Bowen-Cooke would have been content to rest upon his pre-war laurels, but whether he, who had had so much experience in the running of compound locomotives, would have been tempted to venture back to them is another matter. Had he become C.M.E. of the L.M.S.R. the developments at Crewe would most likely have been concerned mainly with the larger engines, but one thing is certain—there would have been plenty

The last L.N.W.R. 4-4-0 No. 25297 'Sirocco'; formerly No. 643. Built November 1904; superheated February 1915; scrapped October 1949

of interchange trial running. Having engineered the various locomotive exchanges in which North Western engines were engaged in 1909, there is little doubt that he would have set his 'George the Fifths' against the Midland compounds. With selected units and keen enginemen, such an exchange would have been a very close-run thing. On the heaviest gradients the honours would have been with the compounds, but the Crewe engines would have had all the advantages on the faster stretches, particularly when it came to climbing moderate gradients at high speed.

Despite this, however, the 'George the Fifths'— and the 'Prince of Wales' class, too, for that matter —were rapidly becoming obsolete in the 1920s. The weakness arising from their design of piston valves could have been overcome, as, indeed, was done on the 'Claughtons'. The trouble caused by the relative flimsiness of their frames could have been countered by careful and vigilant maintenance,

The last of the 'Princes'; 4-6-0 No. 25752 scrapped October 1949 (formerly No. 1557)

The last line-up: 'Sirocco', the large-boilered 'Claughton' No. 6004, and 'Prince' No. 25752, at Crewe, October 1949

albeit at the expense of heavy repair charges. But the centre bearing on the driving axle was asking a little too much of the maintenance methods of post-grouping days. There was no doubt justification for taking that bearing out, but it immediately reduced the maximum capacity of the locomotives. Thus it can be truly said that at the heights of their achievements on the road the 'Georges' and 'Princes' were period pieces, and with the passing of the years their period, too, passed and their work became but a shadow of what it had been.

Certainly there were many 'Georges' and 'Princes'—and among the former I include the 'Precursors' rebuilt with superheater boiler and piston valves—capable of excellent work in the 1930s. This work was, nevertheless, qualified by the age of the locomotives, and the duties involved. The running of the Bletchley engines on the outer-London residential trains provided an outstanding example, but such work could not be compared to what the same engines had been doing twenty years earlier. Thus, in the post-grouping era, neither the 'Georges' nor the 'Princes' had a place of any prominence, and both classes were completely outshone by the Midland compounds. To assess their place in history, one cannot proceed far beyond the life of the London & North Western Railway. If

the general performance of the superheated members of the 'Precursor' family is reviewed in the light of years 1910 to 1922—and in particular the period from 1911 to 1916—even the most critical of appraisals cannot fail to be enthusiastic to the last degree.

The question then arises from studying data such as that included in Chapter 7 of this book: 'Can the achievements of a mere six years place a locomotive family among the immortals?' Their great predecessors, the 6 ft. and 6 ft. 6 in. 'Jumbos', achieved fame as much by their longevity as by the 'David *versus* Goliath' traditions of their work on the road. Their greatest contemporaries on other railways—the Great Northern 'Atlantics' and the Midland compounds—far outlasted them in first-class duty. But in any assessment of the position of the 'Georges' and 'Princes' in history, one must take into account the deeply-involved railway politics of early L.M.S. days, and one arrives back at the point of trying to conjecture how Crewe would have coped with the economic conditions of the post-war era if allowed to go its own way, as of old, without any extraneous managerial interference.

The assessment must, therefore, be based upon the years 1911 to 1916, and the standards then set up that were largely, though briefly, restored after

World War I by the 'Georges' and the 'superheated Precursors' on the Birmingham trains, and by the 'Princes' in the dynamometer-car trials in the north after grouping. Cecil J. Allen, writing in *The Railway Magazine* of 1919, described the 'George the Fifth' class 4—4—0s as 'incomparable'. In the light of their achievements up to that time incomparable they certainly were among 4—4—0 locomotives the world over. One could almost add 'among four-coupled engines' so far as Great Britain was concerned; for at that time no 'Atlantic' had surpassed their maximum achievements of the years 1911-16. In later years, of course, the performance of the Great Northern 'Atlantics' rose at times to almost celestial heights. But if the pre-eminence of the 'George the Fifths' was no more than transitory it was very real while it lasted, and those six years of outstanding achievement place them in a very honoured niche in locomotive history the world over.

Farewell to one of Crewe's most famous engines, June 1940

CHAPTER 12

CASE HISTORIES

THE 'PRECURSOR' CLASS

L.N.W.R. No.	Date Built	L.M.S. No.	Date Superheated		Date Scrapped
			Slide Valves	Piston Valves	
513	3/04	5278	2/13	1/15	7/36
1395	3/04	5291	—	9/14	7/37
1419	3/04	5285	—	11/13	3/36
2023	4/04	5187	—	3/24	3/36
2164	4/04	5277	—	1/13	8/46
2	6/04	5308	—	8/20	11/36
7	6/04	5276	—	1/13	11/35
412	6/04	5188	—	3/23	4/40
510	6/04	5189	—	—	8/33
659	6/04	5296	—	1/15	5/36
639	10/04	5190	—	—	9/28
648	10/04	5191	—	—	1/28
685	10/04	5192	—	—	4/32
60	10/04	5298	—	4/15	11/38
106	10/04	5294	—	12/14	5/37
301	11/04	5289	—	6/14	5/36
305	11/04	5307	—	6/20	3/37
643*	11/04	5297	—	3/15	10/49
1102	11/04	5193	—	—	9/31
1117	11/04	5194	—	—	11/31
310	12/04	5290	—	6/14	11/36
333	12/04	5284	—	10/13	9/36
515	12/04	5282	—	9/13	12/39
622	12/04	5195†	—	—	12/27
638	12/04	5196	—	—	4/33
303	1/05	5305	1/19	9/28	2/36
645	1/05	5197	—	—	11/30
806	1/05	5318	—	1/23	10/35
1120	1/05	5310	—	10/21	8/39
1137	1/05	5299	—	4/15	9/36
323	2/05	5303	6/17	1/23	11/36
1104	2/05	5199	—	—	12/30
1111	3/05	5200	—	—	10/34
1431	3/05	5201	—	—	12/30
2064	3/05	5273	5/18	Saturated 7/29	8/31
—	—	—	—	—	—
40	3/05	5198	—	—	11/30
520	3/05	5202	—	—	1/34
1469	3/05	5288	—	4/14	3/37
1737	3/05	5316	—	10/22	8/36
2031	3/05	5203	—	—	12/31
365	4/05	5287	—	5/14	6/37
1115	4/05	5205	—	—	2/28
1545	4/05	5206	—	—	5/32

THE 'PRECURSOR' CLASS—*continued*

L.N.W.R. No.	Date Built	L.M.S. No.	Date Superheated		Date Scrapped
			Slide Valves	Piston Vavels	
1573	4/05	5286	—	5/14	9/37
2061	4/05	5207	—	3/25	8/36
184	5/05	5204	—	—	9/31
366	5/05	5292	—	11/14	4/45
519	5/05	5208	—	—	12/31
1430	5/05	5210	—	—	10/31
2120	5/05	5209†	—	—	10/27
113	7/05	5211	—	12/24	10/36
300	7/05	5301	—	1/17	11/35
302	7/05	5304	7/17	7/22	1/47
315	7/05	5212	—	4/23	12/36
688	7/05	5274	6/18	3/23	11/35
1509	8/05	5214	—	—	3/28
1617	8/05	5300	—	5/15	7/40
1723	8/05	5295	—	12/14	12/36
2062	8/05	5279	—	2/13	8/39
2257	8/05	5215	—	—	5/33
311	9/05	5213	—	—	12/33
374	9/05	5317	—	12/22	6/36
811	9/05	5311	—	11/21	3/41
911	9/05	5216	—	3/24	2/36
1114	9/05	5217	—	—	2/33
1116	9/05	5218	—	4/23	5/36
1510	9/05	5219	—	—	12/30
1784	10/05	5220	—	—	12/31
2166	10/05	5280	—	2/13	12/35
2202	10/05	5221	—	—	12/30
117	10/05	5222	—	—	9/33
1301	10/05	5225	—	8/25	12/36
1363	10/65	5272	—	5/18	12/39
127	11/05	5223	—	3/23	12/36
229	11/05	5224†	—	—	11/27
1396	11/05	5226	—	—	12/30
1439	11/05	5275	6/18	Saturated	2/33
—	—	—	—	4/30	—
2007	11/05	—	—	—	10/27
2012	11/05	5228	—	—	11/31
2115	11/05	5229	—	—	4/32
2576	12/05	5230	—	—	9/33
2577	12/05	5313	—	2/22	2/36
2578	12/05	5309	—	8/20	8/36
2579	12/05	5231	—	2/25	2/36
2580	12/05	5232	—	—	12/31
2581	12/05	5233	—	—	8/34
2582	12/05	5234	—	—	12/28
2583	1/06	5235	—	—	4/35
2584	1/06	5312	—	1/22	12/35
2585	1/06	5236	—	—	12/33
723	2/06	5239	—	7/23	1/36
837	2/06	5240	—	—	10/33
1312	2/06	5242	—	—	11/30
1387	3/06	5306	9/19	5/26	2/36
1642	3/06	5243	—	5/24	12/35
234	3/06	5237	—	—	2/32
526	3/06	5238	—	—	12/28
1311	3/06	5241	—	4/23	2/36
2017	3/06	5244	—	10/26	12/35
2513	3/06	5293	—	11/14	6/39
282	4/06	5314	—	4/22	12/35
561	4/06	5245	—	12/24	3/41
675	4/06	5246	—	6/26	2/36
772	4/06	5247†	—	—	10/27
804	4/06	5248	—	3/23	11/35
988	4/06	5249	—	—	6/33
990	4/06	5319	—	1/23	12/40
1433	4/06	5250	—	3/25	2/36

K

THE L.N.W.R. 'PRECURSOR' FAMILY

THE 'PRECURSOR' CLASS—*continued*

L.N.W.R. No.	Date Built	L.M.S. No.	Date Superheated		Date Scrapped
			Slide Valves	Piston Valves	
1650	5/06	5251†	—	—	2/28
1787	5/06	5252	—	—	12/30
1	6/07	5253	—	—	11/30
218	6/07	5254	—	—	8/33
419	6/07	5255	—	—	12/30
469	7/07	5270	5/18	—	5/36
564	6/07	5281	—	9/13	10/36
665	6/07	5256†	—	—	10/27
276	7/07	5261	—	—	11/27
754	7/07	5262	—	—	12/30
802	7/07	5271	5/18	Saturated 6/30	12/31
—	—	—	—	—	—
1011	7/07	5257	—	—	1/33
1364	7/07	5258	—	—	12/30
2053	7/07	5259	—	—	3/34
2181	7/07	5260	—	—	12/33
807	8/07	5263	—	—	12/33
976	8/07	5264	—	—	12/28
1297	8/07	5265	—	—	11/31
1309	8/07	5302	5/17	11/22	6/37
1516	8/07	5266	—	—	11/31
2011	8/07	5283	—	9/13	3/36
2051	8/07	5315	—	6/22	9/36

*Engine 643 *Sirocco* (L.M.S. No. 5297) was the last Crewe express passenger 4-4-0 to be scrapped.
†L.M.S.R. number allotted, but not carried.
Names: Engine 412, originally *Alfred Paget* became *Marquis* in 11/04.
Engine 1363, originally *Cornwall* became *Brindley* in 5/11.
Engine 2583, originally *Teutonic*, became *The Tsar* in 11/14, and *Moonstone* in 12/15.
Engines, which had their names removed were: 811 in 9/36; 1120 in 9/36; 2584 in 7/33.
Engines 2576 and 2577 were built as 1307 and 2287 respectively, but were renumbered in 1/06.

THE 'EXPERIMENT' CLASS

L.N.W.R. No.	Date Built	L.M.S. No.	Date Scrapped	Notes
66	4/05	5450	7/31	
306	6/05	5451	12/30	
353	6/05	5452	12/30	
372	6/05	5453	10/28	
507	6/05	5454	9/32	
565	1/06	5455†	6/25	
893	1/06	5456	8/35	
1074	1/06	5457	10/34	
1357	1/06	5458	12/33	
1669	1/06	5464	12/30	
165	2/06	5459	12/30	
828	2/06	5460	10/34	
978	2/06	5461	5/34	
1405	2/06	5462	11/34	
1575	2/06	5463	10/28	
1986	9/06	5465†	10/25	
1987	9/06	5466	11/34	
1988	9/06	5467	8/28	
1989	10/06	5468	12/29	
1990	10/06	5469	3/32	
1991	10/06	5470	2/28	
1992	10/06	5471	12/33	
1993	10/06	5472	12/33	Superd. 12/26
1994	10/06	5473	8/35	
1995	10/06	5481†	9/25	

THE 'EXPERIMENT' CLASS—*continued*

L.N.W.R. No.	Date Built	L.M.S. No.	Date Scrapped	Notes
61	11/06	5474	12/33	
222	11/06	5475	7/35	
291	11/06	5476	12/31	
667	11/06	5477	12/33	
1304	11/06	5478	8/31	
1676	11/06	5479	11/34	
1709	11/06	—	3/28	
2027	11/06	5482	10/31	
2052	12/06	5483	12/30	
2269	12/06	5484	8/31	
496	9/07	5485	7/30	
830	9/07	5486†	7/25	
902	9/07	5487	10/34	
937	9/07	5488	3/34	
1014	9/07	5489	3/28	
1135	9/07	5491	6/34	
2112	9/07	5490	12/30	
1361	10/07	5554	6/33	4 cyl. superd. 6/15
1526	10/07	5492	11/28	
2161	10/07	5493†	8/25	
322	12/08	5494	6/29	
884	12/08	5495	12/30	
887	1/09	5496	3/32	
1020	1/09	5497	11/34	
1483	1/09	5498	12/33	
1490	1/09	5499	12/33	
1553	1/09	5500	12/31	
1571	1/09	5501	1/28	
2076	1/09	5502	10/34	
2116	1/09	5503†	7/25	
2621	2/09	5504	11/34	
2622	2/09	5505	4/28	
2623	2/09	5506	3/34	
2624	2/09	5507†	2/28	Superd. 2/26
2625	2/09	5508	8/35	
2626	2/09	5509	5/35	
2627	2/09	5510	5/28	
2628	2/09	5511	7/35	
2629	3/09	5512	2/28	
2630	3/09	5513	3/32	
1406	4/09	5514	8/35	
1413	4/09	5515†	9/25	
1477	5/09	5516	4/28	
1498	5/09	5517†	9/25	
1566	5/09	5518	12/33	
1603	5/09	5519	12/30	
1649	5/09	5520	9/32	
1661	5/09	5521	6/28	
1781	5/09	5522	5/30	
2022	5/09	5523	4/34	
2637	6/09	5524	2/32	
2638	6/09	5525	6/34	
2639	6/09	5526	4/34	
2640	6/09	5527†	9/26	
2641	6/09	5528	8/35	
2642	6/09	5529	12/33	
2643	6/09	5530†	10/27	
2644	6/09	5531	8/34	
2645	7/09	5532	10/34	
2646	7/09	—	8/28	
1412	11/09	5534	2/32	
1418	11/09	5535	12/31	
1420	11/09	5536	12/33	
1455	11/09	5537	12/33	
1611	11/09	5538†	9/25	
1616	11/09	5539	3/34	
1624	11/09	5545	12/33	
1652	11/09	5546	12/33	

THE L.N.W.R. 'PRECURSOR' FAMILY

THE 'EXPERIMENT' CLASS—*continued*

L.N.W.R. No.	Date Built	L.M.S. No.	Date Scrapped	Notes
1689	12/09	5547	3/32	
1703	12/09	5548	3/34	
71	12/09	5540	4/28	
275	12/09	5541	8/28	
677	12/09	5542	12/33	
1002	12/09	5543	12/30	
1534	12/09	5544†	9/25	
1471	1/10	5549	3/32	
1561	1/10	5550	8/28	
1618	1/10	5551	3/34	
1621	1/10	5552	6/35	
1658	1/10	5553	12/31	

†L.M.S.R. number allotted but not carried.

Renaming:
Engine 372 *Germanic* renamed *Belgic* 10/14.
Engine 1676 *Prince of Wales* renamed *Shakespeare* 7/11.
Engine 1989 Name removed 12/28.

'QUEEN MARY' CLASS

L.N.W.R. No.	Date Built	Converted to Geo. V	L.M.S. No.	Date Scrapped
2664	7/10	6/13	5329	3/36
238	10/10	9/14	5336	3/36
896	10/10	1/14	5332	2/36
1195	10/10	9/14	5337	7/36
1550	10/10	9/13	5330	9/36
1559	10/10	1/14	5333	3/36
2151	10/10	4/14	5334	11/37
2271	10/10	11/13	5331	11/38
2507	10/10	6/14	5335	11/35
2512	11/10	10/14	5338	11/35

'GEORGE THE FIFTH' CLASS

L.N.W.R. No.	Date Built	L.M.S. No.	Date Scrapped
2663	7/10	5320	2/36
1059	11/10	5321	2/48
1294	11/10	5322	12/38
1583	11/10	5323	9/39
1725	11/10	5324	11/38
2155	11/10	5326	5/37
2025	12/10	5325	12/36
228	1/11	5327	2/36
445	1/11	5328	11/35
2168	1/11	5339	4/37
956*	4/11	5340	11/35
1489	4/11	5341	3/36
1504	4/11	5342	11/35
1513	5/11	5343	4/36
1532	5/11	5344	1/37
1628	5/11	5345	12/36
1662	5/11	5346	2/36
1706	5/11	5347	2/41

'GEORGE THE FIFTH' CLASS—*continued*

L.N.W.R. No.	Date Built	L.M.S. No.	Date Scrapped
1792	5/11	5353	6/36
2495	5/11	5357	1/39
1800	6/11	5348	6/40
502	6/11	5349	7/36
868	6/11	5350	5/48
882	6/11	5351	2/36
1218	6/11	5352	11/35
2081	6/11	5354	1/36
2212	6/11	5355	7/36
2291	6/11	5356	10/41
2177	7/11	5358	11/36
2498	7/11	5359	12/36
361	7/11	5360	9/37
888	7/11	5361	11/35
1360	7/11	5362	3/39
1394	8/11	5363	2/36
1623	8/11	5364	11/36
1631	8/11	5365	4/37
1644	8/11	5366	11/36
2089	8/11	5367	12/36
2220	8/11	5374	11/38
2494	8/11	5368	11/36
1371	9/11	5369	9/36
1417	9/11	5370	12/36
1472	9/11	5371	9/39
1595	9/11	5372	12/36
1681	9/11	5373	5/48
1713	9/11	5375	12/35
1730	10/11	5376	1/48
1733	10/11	5377	7/37
1777	10/11	5378	6/37
1799	10/11	5379	8/36
82	1/13	5380	2/37
752	2/13	5381	11/35
1138	2/13	5385	8/36
2124	2/13	5382	6/37
2154	2/13	5387	2/37
2282	2/13	5388	4/36
89	3/13	5383	5/36
132	3/13	5384	2/36
681	3/13	5390	11/35
845	3/13	5391	2/36
1193	3/13	5386	1/36
2279	3/13	5395	2/37
404	4/13	5389	6/37
1188	4/13	5392	10/41
1481	4/13	5396	9/36
1680*	4/13	5393	12/41
2086	4/13	5394	7/36
2197	4/13	5397	12/35
2242	5/13	5398	9/36
2428*	5/13	5399	7/36
363	5/15	5400	11/35
789	5/15	5401	2/36
984	5/15	5402	6/36
104	6/15	5403	11/35
226	6/15	5404	2/36
1086	6/15	5405	1/36
2153	6/15	5406	5/37
2233	6/15	5407	4/37
2106	7/15	5408	11/35
2370*	7/15	5409	5/37

*Changes of name.
  956 renamed *Bulldog* in Dec. 1915.
  1680 ordered as *Plynlimmon*, but renamed *Loyalty* in honour of Royal Visit to Crewe in April 1913.
  2428 ordered as *Caliban*, but renamed *Lord Stalbridge* after the former L.N.W.R. Chairman.
  2370 ordered as *Ashbourne*, but actually named *Dovedale*.

THE L.N.W.R. 'PRECURSOR' FAMILY

'PRINCE OF WALES' CLASS

L.N.W.R. No.	Date Built	Works	L.M.S. No.	Date Scrapped	Remarks
819	10/11	Crewe	5600	/33	O/F
1388	10/11	,,	5601	3/35	
1452	11/11	,,	5602	6/37	O/F
1454	11/11	,,	5603	8/35	
1537	11/11	,,	5604	10/34	
1691	11/11	,,	5605	11/34	
1704	11/11	,,	5606	/33	
1721	11/11	,,	5607	12/34	O/F
2021	12/11	,,	5608	2/35	O/F
2359	12/11	,,	5609	/33	O/F
362	10/13	,,	5610	/33	O/F
892	10/13	,,	5611	6/35	
1081	10/13	,,	5612	1/36	
1089	10/13	,,	5613	2/35	
1134	10/13	,,	5614	12/34	
2040	11/13	,,	5615	3/35	
2075	11/13	,,	5616	11/34	O/F
2198	11/13	,,	5620	3/36	O/F
2205	11/13	,,	5621	9/34	
2213	11/13	,,	5622	12/33	O/F
321	11/13	,,	5617	1/35	
479	12/13	,,	5618	2/35	
951	12/13	,,	5619	8/34	
1679	12/13	,,	5623	5/35	O/F
2249	12/13	,,	5624	3/37	O/F
2283	12/13	,,	5625	12/36	
86	1/14	,,	5626	5/36	O/F
146	1/14	,,	5627	7/36	
307	1/14	,,	5628	11/34	O/F
637	1/14	,,	5629	12/34	
979	1/14	,,	5630	10/34	O/F
1400	1/14	,,	5631	6/36	
964	2/14	,,	5632	/33	
985	2/14	,,	5633	8/35	
1321	2/14	,,	5634	11/34	
2152	2/14	,,	5635	3/34	
2293	2/14	,,	5636	1/35	
2377	2/14	,,	5637	12/36	
2443	3/14	,,	5638	4/36	O/F
2520	3/14	,,	5639	/33	
27	10/15	,,	5640	2/37	
88	10/15	,,	5641	9/36	O/F
122	11/15	,,	5642	3/36	
160	11/15	,,	5643	10/34	
185	11/15	,,	5644	3/36	
877	11/15	,,	5645	6/36	O/F
1333	11/15	,,	5646	12/34	
2275	11/15	,,	5647	1/35	
2396	12/15	,,	5648	10/48	
2408	12/15	,,	5649	/33	
136	10/15	N.B.L. Co. Ltd. Hyde Park	5663	1/35	
173	10/15	,,	5664	2/35	
257	11/15	,,	5666	10/34	O/F
446	11/15	,,	5668	8/35	
1749	11/15	,,	5677	1/35	
2063	11/15	,,	5679	5/35	
2175	11/15	,,	5680	5/37	
2203	11/15	,,	5681	5/35	
2300	12/15	,,	5687	10/34	
2392	12/15	,,	5689	9/36	O/F
90	12/15	N.B.L. Co. Ltd. Queens Park	5660	8/36	
401	12/15	,,	5667	11/34	
525	12/15	,,	5669	4/37	
610	12/15	,,	5670	10/35	
867	1/16	,,	5672	12/36	
1132	1/16	,,	5674	2/36	

150

'PRINCE OF WALES' CLASS—*continued*

L.N.W.R. No.	Date Built	Works	L.M.S. No.	Date Scrapped	Remarks
		N.B.L. Co. Ltd.			
1466	1/16	Queens Park	5675	8/36	
1744	1/16	,,	5676	4/35	
2055	1/16	,,	5678	4/35	
2339	1/16	,,	5682	6/35	
606	1/16	Crewe	5650	4/36	
745	1/16	,,	5651	7/34	O/F
810	1/16	,,	5652	/33	
1084	1/16	,,	5656	8/38	
1346	1/16	,,	5657	4/36	
1352	1/16	,,	5653	10/35	
1379	1/16	,,	5654	3/35	
1484	1/16	,,	5655	12/34	O/F
2417	2/16	,,	5658	10/35	
2442	2/16	,,	5659	3/35	
95	3/16	,,	5661	2/35	O/F
126	3/16	,,	5662	8/36	
233	3/16	,,	5665	4/36	
849	3/16	,,	5671	12/36	O/F
1100	3/16	,,	5673	1/49	
1324	4/16	,,	5683	1/46	
2092	4/16	,,	5684	4/36	
2276	4/16	,,	5685	8/36	
2295	4/16	,,	5686	11/34	
2340	4/16	,,	5688	/33	
28	1/19	,,	5690	11/34	
263	1/19	,,	5691	9/36	
295	1/19	,,	5692	7/37	
391	1/19	,,	5693	5/37	
740	1/19	,,	5694	11/47	
805	1/19	,,	5695	11/34	
863	1/19	,,	5696	12/34	O/F
940	1/19	,,	5697	7/36	
1196	2/19	,,	5698	1/36	
1546	2/19	,,	5699	11/35	
621	2/19	,,	5700	3/36	
707	2/19	,,	5701	4/35	
1373	2/19	,,	5702	5/36	O/F
1453	3/19	,,	5703	9/34	O/F
1584	3/19	,,	5704	9/36	
57	3/19	,,	5705	3/35	
504	3/19	,,	5706	12/36	
974	3/19	,,	5707	4/35	
1673	3/19	,,	5708	8/36	
2184	3/19	,,	5709	12/34	
33	4/19	,,	5710	4/35	
388	4/19	,,	5711	4/35	O/F
1123	4/19	,,	5712	4/37	O/F
1215	4/19	,,	5713	7/35	
1351	4/19	,,	5714	5/35	
1437	5/19	,,	5715	2/35	
1670	5/19	,,	5716	8/35	
1732	5/19	,,	5717	6/36	O/F
2073	5/19	,,	5718	6/36	O/F
2285	5/19	,,	5719	11/34	
444	5/19	,,	5720	11/35	
497	6/19	,,	5721	7/36	
501	6/19	,,	5722	3/48	
522	6/19	,,	5723	1/36	
601	6/19	,,	5724	6/35	
783	6/19	,,	5725	12/45	
924	6/19	,,	5727	5/35	
1125	7/19	,,	5728	1/36	
1290	7/19	,,	5729	2/35	
1307	7/19	,,	5730	12/36	
56	7/19	,,	5726	7/36	O/F
67	7/19	,,	5731	8/35	O/F
635	8/19	,,	5732	11/38	
686	8/19	,,	5733	8/35	

'PRINCE OF WALES' CLASS—*continued*

L.N.W.R. No.	Date Built	Works	L.M.S. No.	Date Scrapped	Remarks
812	8/19	Crewe	5734	7/35	
969	8/19	,,	5735	10/34	
1325	8/19	,,	5736	6/35	
1341	8/19	,,	5737	2/36	
1355	9/19	,,	5738	5/35	
1620	9/19	,,	5739	3/36	O/F
35	9/19	,,	5740	12/35	
487	9/19	,,	5742	3/35	
1178	9/19	,,	5743	10/34	
395	9/19	,,	5741	1/36	O/F
889	10/19	,,	5744	3/36	
1113	10/19	,,	5745	12/34	
1408	10/19	,,	5746	2/36	
1422	10/19	,,	5747	4/36	
1478	10/19	,,	5748	9/36	
1535	10/19	,,	5749	1/46	
1542	11/19	,,	5750	3/36	O/F
1549	11/19	,,	5751	7/44	
1557*	11/19	,,	5752	5/49	
1694	11/19	,,	5753	2/36	
2516	11/19	,,	5754	5/35	
120	6/21	Beardmore	5755	11/34	
123	8/21	,,	5756	12/38	
125	8/21	,,	5757	9/36	
129	8/21	,,	5758	11/34	
135	8/21	,,	5759	7/35	
140	8/21	,,	5760	10/34	
141	8/21	,,	5761	12/34	
142	8/21	,,	5762	4/36	O/F
145	8/21	,,	5763	8/39	
148	8/21	,,	5764	6/36	
224	8/21	,,	5765	12/34	
227	8/21	,,	5766	8/35	
232	9/21	,,	5767	5/37	
237	9/21	,,	5768	4/37	
239	9/21	,,	5769	1/36	
240	9/21	,,	5770	4/35	
241	9/21	,,	5771	3/36	O/F
242	9/21	,,	5772	3/36	O/F
243	9/21	,,	5773	5/37	
244	9/21	,,	5774	10/34	O/F
246	10/21	,,	5775	11/47	O/F
247	10/21	,,	5776	2/36	
248	10/21	,,	5777	3/37	
249	10/21	,,	5778	9/34	
251	10/21	,,	5779	5/37	
252	10/21	,,	5780	5/37	O/F
258	10/21	,,	5781	3/36	
259	10/21	,,	5782	12/34	
261	10/21	,,	5783	12/34	
266	10/21	,,	5784	8/36	
267	10/21	,,	5785	5/36	
268	10/21	,,	5786	12/34	
269	11/21	,,	5787	5/48	
270	11/21	,,	5788	4/37	
272	11/21	,,	5789	3/34	
273	11/21	,,	5790	9/36	
274	11/21	,,	5791	12/47	O/F
394	10/21	,,	5792	5/37	
277	11/21	,,	5793	5/35	
281	11/21	,,	5794	12/36	
284	1/22	,,	5795	1/36	
292	11/21	,,	5796	7/36	
293	11/21	,,	5797	6/47	
296	11/21	,,	5798	6/45	
313	11/21	,,	5799	7/35	
324	11/21	,,	5800	4/37	
325	12/21	,,	5801	3/36	

'PRINCE OF WALES' CLASS—*continued*

L.N.W.R. No.	Date Built	Works	L.M.S. No.	Date Scrapped	Remarks
331	12/21	Beardmore	5802	3/47	
355	12/21	,,	5803	3/36	
357	12/21	,,	5804	2/46	
359	12/21	,,	5805	6/45	
435	12/21	,,	5806	10/34	
436	12/21	,,	5807	11/34	
438	12/21	,,	5808	4/35	
440	12/21	,,	5809	11/34	
442	12/21	,,	5810	6/35	
443	12/21	,,	5811	1/35	
452	12/21	,,	5812	12/36	
483	12/21	,,	5813	5/36	
489	12/21	,,	5814	2/35	
490	12/21	,,	5815	7/35	
492	1/22	,,	5816	4/36	
17	2/22	,,	5817	3/36	
153	2/22	,,	5818	8/46	
198	2/22	,,	5819	2/37	
354	2/22	,,	5820	4/36	
491	1/22	,,	5821	3/37	
493	1/22	,,	5822	3/36	
518	1/22	,,	5823	3/36	
551	2/22	,,	5824	11/34	
554	2/22	,,	5825	12/36	
549	1/22	,,	5826	2/36	
557	2/22	,,	5827	3/48	
558	2/22	,,	5828	11/36	
778	3/22	,,	5829	1/37	O/F
1099	3/22	,,	5830	8/36	
1179	3/22	,,	5831	5/35	
1316	3/22	,,	5832	9/36	
1339	3/22	,,	5833	5/37	
53	3/22	,,	5834	9/36	
197	3/22	,,	5835	3/35	
433	4/22	,,	5836	3/36	O/F
614	4/22	,,	5837	3/35	
1083	4/22	,,	5838	5/35	
1320	4/22	,,	5839	1/37	
1349	3/22	,,	5840	1/36	
1323	4/22	,,	5841	9/47	O/F
1344	4/22	,,	5842	6/36	
1742	4/22	,,	5843	8/36	
2043	4/22	,,	5844	9/36	
—	2/24	,,	5845	11/47	

★The last *Prince of Wales* to remain in service
O/F at one time oil fired.
†Built new with Walschaerts valve gear.
     Names of engines 867, 2339 and 2417 removed in 7/33.
     Name of engine 849 removed in 9/36.

CHRONOLOGY

May	1903	George Whale became Chief Mechanical Engineer
March	1904	First 'Precursor' built
March	1904	Successful dynamometer car run, engine 513
April	1905	First 'Experiment' built
August	1907	Last 'Precursor' built
March	1909	C. J. Bowen-Cooke appointed Chief Mechanical Engineer
June	1909	Interchange trials: *Albatross* and *Marquis* versus Great Northern 'Atlantics'
June	1909	Interchange trials: *Titan* versus L.B.S.C. 4—4—2 tank No. 23
June	1909	Interchange trials: 'Experiments' versus Caledonian 'Cardean' class 4—6—0
January	1910	Last 'Experiment' built
July	1910	First 'George the Fifth' built
July	1910	Successful dynamometer car run, engine 2663
August	1910	Interchange trials: 'Experiments' versus Great Western non-superheater 'Star' 4—6—0s
October	1910	Interchange trials: *Redgauntlet* versus N.B.R. 'Atlantic'
June	1911	5,000th engine completed at Crewe, the *Coronation*
October	1911	First 'Prince of Wales' engine built
January	1913	First 'Precursor' rebuilt with superheater and piston valves
October	1915	First 'Prince of Wales' engines by North British Locomotive Company completed
July	1916	Last 'George the Fifth' built
September	1920	Engine No. 2585 *Watt* equipped for oil-burning
October	1920	Death of C. J. Bowen-Cooke
November	1920	H. P. M. Beames appointed Chief Mechanical Engineer
January	1922	Amalgamation of L. & Y.R. with L. & N.W.R.; George Hughes appointed Chief Mechanical Engineer, of enlarged L. & N.W.R.
April	1922	Last standard 'Prince of Wales' 4—6—0 completed by Beardmore and Co. Ltd.
November	1922	Outside Walschaert's valve gear fitted to 'Prince of Wales' 4—6—0 No. 964, *Bret Harte*
January	1923	L. & N.W.R. becomes part of the L.M.S.R. at grouping
December	1923	Dynamometer car test runs of engine No. 388 ('Prince of Wales' class) against M.R. Class '4' 4—4—0s
April	1924	Construction of engine No. 5845, with outside Walschaert's gear by Beardmore, for British Empire Exhibition at Wembley
May	1925	Dynamometer car trials, Preston and Carlisle, with engine No. 90 *Kestrel*
June	1925	First 'Experiment' scrapped
October	1927	First non-superheater 'Precursor' scrapped
January	1933	First 'George the Fifth' scrapped
December	1933	First 'Prince of Wales' scrapped
April	1935	Last non-superheater 'Precursor' scrapped (No. 2583, *Moonstone*)
August	1935	Last 'Experiment' scrapped
October	1949	Last 'George the Fifth' scrapped*
October	1949	Last 'Prince of Wales' scrapped

* Including 'Precursors' rebuilt with superheater boilers and piston valves

Aberdeen—Euston express on Tebay troughs, hauled by 4-6-0 No. 2249 'Thomas Campbell'

Up Liverpool express on Whitmore troughs; engine No. 412 'Marquis', superheated with piston valves

ACKNOWLEDGEMENTS

The author and publishers wish to express their thanks to the following for permission to use illustrations:

The Locomotive Publishing Co. Ltd.: p.22, 23, 24 centre, 26, 30, 39, 82, 86, 87, 91 right, 101 upper, 121, 124 top, 126 top, 126 bottom, 129 top.

Real Photographs Co. Ltd.: p.24 bottom, 35, 47 top, 67, 71, 78 top, 80, 88 bottom, 102 left, 104 top, 107 top, 108 bottom, 111 top, 114 top, 122 top left, 136, 154 top and bottom.

Locomotive and General Railway Photographs: p.28, 31 left, 31 right, 45 top, 46, 58, 65, 68 top left, 75 bottom, 88 top right, 99, 108 upper, 122 bottom left, 122 bottom right, 132 left, 139 bottom left, 139 bottom right, 140.

The Railway Magazine: p.20 left, 12 right, 33, 59 right, 95 top.

Kenneth H. Leech, Esq. for the following taken by the late C. Laundy: p.36 top, 42, 61 left, 61 right, 68 top right, 73 top, 76, 88 top left.

Leslie J. Thompson, Esq.: p.45 bottom, 84 top right, 89, 101 left, 111 bottom, 113, 114 left, 118.

Eric Mason, Esq.: p.43 top, 43 bottom, 91 left, 107 left, 110.

C. J. Barnard, Esq.: p.51 top, 62 top, 77, 119.

D. H. Stuart, Esq.: p.84 top left.

J. H. Court, Esq.: p.100.

P. B. Whitehouse, Esq.: p.131.

P. J. Garland, Esq.: p.59 left.

F. R. Hebron, Esq.: p.129 bottom.

P. J. T. Reed, Esq.: p.51 bottom.

R. J. Purves, Esq.: p.48 top.

O. S. Nock, Esq.: p.37, 49, 122 top right, 130.

Acknowledgement is also made of photographs in the author's collection of the following photographs taken by the late F. E. Mackay: p.24 top, 43 middle, 54, 84 bottom, 94 bottom, 95 left, 96, 104 left.

: by the late W. H. Whitworth: p.51 centre, 128 and 132 top.

: by the late E. Little: p.57.

For the remainder of the photographs, 50 in all, indebtedness is acknowledged to British Railways, and also for original drawings from which the majority of the diagrams have been made. The drawings of the Dendy-Marshall arrangement of cylinders on the 4—6—0 engine No. 1361 *Prospero* are reproduced by courtesy of the Institution of Locomotive Engineers.

The coloured frontispiece is from a water colour painting by V. Welch.

INDEX

www.ingramcontent.com/pod-product-compliance
Lightning Source LLC
Chambersburg PA
CBHW081329090426
42737CB00017B/3070